The Family Manager's
Everyday
Survival Guide

BY KATHY PEEL
Published by Ballantine Books

THE FAMILY MANAGER'S
GUIDE FOR WORKING MOMS

THE FAMILY MANAGER'S
EVERYDAY SURVIVAL GUIDE

THE
Family Manager's Everyday Survival Guide

KATHY PEEL

BALLANTINE BOOKS • NEW YORK

A Ballantine Book
Published by The Ballantine Publishing Group

Copyright © 1998 by Family Manager, Inc.

All rights reserved under International and Pan-American Copyright Conventions.
Published in the United States by The Ballantine Publishing Group,
a division of Random House, Inc., New York, and simultaneously in
Canada by Random House of Canada Limited, Toronto.

Family Manager is a registered trademark of Kathy Peel.

http://www.randomhouse.com/BB/

Library of Congress Cataloging-in-Publication Data
Peel, Kathy, 1951–
The family manager's everyday survival guide/Kathy Peel.—1st ed.
p. cm.
ISBN 0-345-41985-5 (alk. paper)
1. Women—Time management. 2. Homemakers—Time management.
3. Family—Time management. 4. Home economics.   I. Title.
HQ1221.P367   1998
640—dc21   98-22166
                                                                            CIP

Text design by Ann Gold
Cover design by Cathy Colbert
Cover photo by Matthew Barnes

Manufactured in the United States of America

First Edition: October 1998

10 9 8 7 6 5 4 3

To the Family Managers
I've met in my travels
and to those I haven't met

Contents

ACKNOWLEDGMENTS

"We, rather than I."—Charles Garfield

That statement is never more true than when one is writing a book. From cover to cover, this is a team project. My thanks to:

My husband, Bill, and our three sons, John, Joel, and James, for twenty-seven years of patience, support, and cheerfully attempting new ideas. They've been through the trenches with me—and for me. They've taught me most of the principles in this book.

Jan Johnson. All authors should be so blessed as to have Jan for their book editor. Jan's lightning bolt of a mind brings my books to life. (I'll share with you my ideas on Family Management, but you can't have her phone number.)

Holly Halverson, my home-team editor who cleans and polishes my books until they shine—even when it takes industrial-strength elbow grease. She is a veritable magician and indispensable to me.

Jodi Bodenhamer Thomas, my bright, perceptive, good-natured personal assistant. She's got it all—and does it all. (No, you can't have her phone number, either.)

Kitty Moon, the dedicated-to-excellence chief executive officer of Family Manager, Inc. She brings brilliant organizational skills to every task and has the rare ability to ask the right questions.

Phil Pfeffer, Linda Grey, Judith Curr, Ellen Archer, Susan Randol, and Rachel Tarlow Gul, my friends and colleagues on the Random House/Ballantine team who believe in my vision enough to invest their time, money, ideas, and energy in my projects.

Marcy Posner, Betsy Berg, and Brian Dubin, my "I believe in you" team at William Morris Agency.

THE FAMILY MANAGER'S CREED

I oversee an organization—
Where hundreds of decisions are made daily,
Where property and resources are managed,
Where health and nutritional needs are determined,
Where finances and futures are discussed and debated,
Where projects are planned and events are arranged,
Where transportation and scheduling are critical,
Where team-building is a priority,
Where careers begin and end.
I oversee an organization—
I am a Family Manager.

Introduction
Beyond Chaos

"If a home doesn't make sense, nothing does." —Henrietta Ripperger

Picture, if you will, a bona fide Family *Mis*management expert: domestically challenged, overwhelmingly disorganized, and regularly discouraged. Note the unpaid bills, the library books under the bed, and the kitchen floor that needs to be raked before it can be mopped. Her sons can't find their soccer uniforms or clean socks. Her husband looks hungry. See the unhappy woman in the middle of it all. You're looking at me—once upon a time. I found myself trying to be a good mother to three boys, keep up my end of a marriage, manage myriad tasks in our home, tackle another career with never-ending deadlines . . . and more. It was when *more* got tacked onto my already overextended schedule that I wanted to jump from the nearest tall building.

Since then, I've learned that I wasn't alone in crisis mode. The past ten years, as I've traveled the country talking with women about their jobs as Family Managers, I've heard countless variations on the same theme: "I don't have time to get organized, and not being organized takes up all my time."

Almost any business consultant who's worked with start-up companies will identify time and organization—two sides of the same coin—as

> "If we don't change the direction we're going, we're likely to end up where we're headed."
>
> —Chinese proverb

the places those enterprises flounder. In the beginning, with a hot new product or service, everything goes fine. People are committed to success, and they'll work twenty-five hours a day to ensure it. Then, as the customer base and product line grow, things get complicated. Twenty-five hours a day aren't enough anymore. Customer complaints go unheard. Vendors go unpaid. Time for long-range thinking and careful planning is consumed putting out everyday fires. Employees burn out. Things fall apart. All for the want of a little organization applied in a timely fashion.

Family Management applies good business principles to the work of making home a warm and welcoming, healthy, happy, and productive place for you and your family to grow and be. But families aren't start-up companies. We can't resign from our job as Family Manager and go find a new one. So what's the alternative?

Getting organized. It's fun. It's easy. It's profitable. And as soon as I discover how to get totally organized and stay that way in the midst of the growing and changing needs and demands of daily family life, I expect to win the Nobel Prizes for Peace, Science, and Literature—all in the same year. The literature prize will be for fiction, because as we all know, any system of organization can organize some of the people all of the time, and all of the people some of the time, but it's a myth that you can organize all of the people all of the time.

The truth is, a few appropriate, well-used organizational ideas and plans can make life much simpler, more rewarding, and a lot more fun. The ideas in this book are meant to supplement and seed your own ideas and Family Management style. The point is not to turn you into a control freak or a domestic diva. It's to help you fulfill your role as Family Manager more efficiently, which for some will mean being able to find your kids' immunization records in less than two hours and for others, knowing on most nights what you're cooking for dinner and having the ingredients to fix it. For other Family Managers it will mean never again holding your breath, waiting to see if your credit-card purchase will be approved because you're not sure if you paid last month's bill.

The strategies in this book are twenty-seven years, one husband, three children, two apartments, and six houses in the making. A

> Organization has more benefits than just efficiency. Knowing your life is in some order reduces stress, lessens black-mood outbursts, and increases confidence. In short, establishing your own survival method for domestic chaos means that you, the Family Manager, have a more enjoyable job. And everyone feels the effects of that.

few months ago a friend from college came to visit me. We laughed as we reminisced about how when I would walk into her dorm room, it was always neat as a pin, everything from paper clips to hair spray in its place. She'd visit me—that is, if she could get into my room—and shake her head. Piles everywhere. I tossed, strewed, littered, and lost.

When I was first married, I had grand intentions. I vowed I'd make a home where Miss Manners's white gloves would stay white no matter what she touched, where the flat surfaces didn't look like an archeological dig in process, and where the closets could pass a surprise inspection by the toughest Marine sergeant. The reality, needless to say, was a rude awakening. I had no idea how fast dirty socks could get lost under last week's newspapers. By the time I had two toddlers, my house made my dorm room look clean by comparison. Experience may be a hard teacher, but it *is* a teacher. Finally, bit by bit, I began to clean up my act.

Now, thirty years later, after being in my home for three days, my college friend put her hands up. "I'm a believer," she said. "If the Family Manager system can work for you, it can work for anyone!"

I developed these ideas in the

> "Experience gives us the tests first and the lessons later."
> —Naomi Judd

> "I not only use all the brains I have, but all I can borrow."
> —Woodrow Wilson

(literally) messy laboratory of everyday experience. And I didn't develop them alone, either. A successful businessman once told me that a key to his success was believing he could learn something from every person, whether gardener, banker, doctor, or plumber. I took his message to heart. I learned from my husband, Bill, from our boys, and from hundreds of others.

We can all gain from each other's successes and failures. I've picked brains wherever they were available, made notes, exchanged ideas with young and old Family Managers, men and women, people who excelled in different areas. Some were excellent organizers. Others good in the kitchen. Some stretched dollars and others stretched minutes. Everyone has strengths, and we are each other's best teachers.

Welcome to the Idea Zone

In the "Seven Days a Week" section of this book, you'll find ideas for daily organization—from morning till night. In the "House Works" section, you'll find dozens of ways to make and maintain your home as a place in which people like to live.

Anticipation is half the battle: knowing what's coming up in the months ahead and having a plan to do what you need to do. Who among us hasn't had the experience of forgetting to service the car, the furnace, or the air-conditioning until it's too late? In "Twelve Months a Year" you'll find ideas for planning ahead that add sanity to tomorrow—and today. Every Family Manager deals with dramatic changes: having a baby, sending a child off to college, moving, changing jobs. You'll find ideas and plans for these and more in the "Big Life Changes" part of the book. The tips in the "Special Occasions" section will help you plan and pull off memory-making moments—big and small—throughout the year.

Finally, in the "Holiday Bonus" section at the end, you'll find a number of ways to make memories and begin family traditions for holidays throughout the year, plus a sane way of coping with The Big Season: Thanksgiving through New Year's.

When you're at your wits' end, wouldn't it be nice to have someone hand you a plan to get your house clean in a weekend? To have at your fingertips fifty ways to entertain bored kids, none of which is planting them in front of TV cartoons? Throughout the book, look for Emergency Measures to solve these and other problems, which, I continue to learn, are just opportunities in disguise. They are opportunities—for personal success and satisfaction, for discovering new ways to approach and solve problems, and for learning how to live and work together as a happy family through the ups and downs of life.

There are a number of ways to use this book. If you're just starting out as a Family Manager—or if you are about to experience meltdown—you may want to read it from front to back. As I've said before in my other books (and will say again), no Family Manager is equally proficient in all the departments she oversees. So if you're an experienced Family Manager who has most things under control most of the time, you may want to use the Contents or the Index to look for ideas to supplement your weaker areas. If you've read my other Family Manager books and are already running your home via the seven departments, and your team members (a.k.a. family members) are functioning pretty well by the ground rules you set up in family meetings, you may wish to skim part 1 and then skip to part 2. Whoever you are, and however you operate as a Family Manager, this book can help. Take the ideas you like and adapt them to your family and your life.

You can start today: June seventeenth, January first, April fourth, October twentieth, or November eleventh. You don't have to wait for a new year, a new month, or the perfect time, because, to be perfectly frank, there is no perfect time to get organized—other than now.

The Big Three Principles (Times Two)

Organization is an ongoing art, a process, not an end product. It's something to practice, to experiment and live with. Beyond chaos, beyond holding on for dear life by the tips of our breaking fingernails, there is survival, and there is life.

THE FIRST BIG THREE PRINCIPLES: NO, NO, NO

1. There is *no* such thing as perfection. I am not perfect. You are not perfect. We're all human beings dealing with other human beings. When we give up trying to be perfect, we can get on with a rewarding life.

2. There are *no* standards but your own and your family's. You get to decide how clean is clean enough; how fast is fast enough; how much work, time, money, and energy to devote to what. Don't fall into the Mother (or Sister or Best Friend) Knows Best trap, or the What Will the Neighbors Think trap. Your standards are *your* standards, and they're the ones you're striving to meet.

3. *No*, it won't ever all be done. Bathrooms, once clean, have a way of getting dirty. Home is a place, as the saying goes, where they *have* to take you in. I prefer a more positive outlook: home is meant to be lived in, in the fullest, most potential-fulfilling way for everyone in it. That means that some things just won't be important enough to spend time on.

THE SECOND BIG THREE PRINCIPLES; YES, YES, YES

1. *Yes*, creating a home that's a good place for you and your family to be is a worthy goal.

2. *Yes*, you can manage your home according to your family's style, goals, and standards.

3. *Yes*, you can allow yourself to count your accomplishments, not your shortcomings. Doing that can only lead to more accomplish-

ments, according to your standards, and to feeling satisfied rather than overwhelmed.

Ten Reasons to Get Organized

1. You won't have to keep inventing grown-up versions of "the dog ate my homework" excuses.
2. If your child appears at school wearing two different-colored socks, it will be her personal artistic expression, not the result of sock diving in the laundry hamper.
3. When it's time to pay the piper—or the mortgage or the utility bills—you'll be able to find your checkbook.
4. When your grown-up child is invited to the White House for dinner, he'll know what to do with his napkin and his forks.
5. You won't need to check into the Halfway House for the Terminally Tired and Bewildered.
6. Your grown-up children will remember family dinners as the place they learned to carry on interesting conversations, not as basic training for World War III.
7. Your toddler won't think a dust bunny is a cute pet.
8. Your husband will recognize the woman he married (and vice versa).
9. Your children will grow into can-do adults who solve problems and generally keep things under control, because they'll have seen that modeled at home.
10. You (probably) won't be half an hour late for an important meeting because the car keys are in the microwave, there's no coffee to get you going, and the washing machine ate your son's lunch ticket.

But, life being life . . .

Ten Reasons You'll Never Get Organized and Stay That Way Forever

1. Toddlers are the closest things to perpetual motion machines we'll ever see on this planet.
2. The pasta will boil over.
3. The dog will make a mess in the entrance hall right before a realtor and prospective buyer come to see your house.
4. Dropping everything to console a sad child is a lot more important than cleaning out the basement.
5. The best-laid plans are often led astray by sick children, a beautiful day that's better spent in the park, or any one of an almost infinite number of possibilities that can throw you off track.
6. The cat will hide someplace mysterious when it's time to go to the vet.
7. The fuses will blow right before your holiday party.
8. You'll know where your checkbook is, but there won't be enough money in the account to cover expenses.
9. Life *is* change, on a daily basis.
10. Change and children are unpredictable.

Use this book as a planner, a reminder, and a good friend with good ideas. And especially, see it as an affirmation of your desire to be the best you can at all you do.

"Challenges make you discover things about yourself that you never really knew. They're what make the instrument stretch— what make you go beyond the norm."   —Cicely Tyson

ONE

Mission Possible

"What we need is more people who specialize in the impossible."
—Theodore Roethke

Mostly we Peels think of home as a fun and reasonably clean place for us to be. For us that means the dog hair is mostly where it belongs—on the dog or in the vacuum cleaner. It means I know for the most part what we're having for dinner for the next few nights, who's in charge of fixing it, and nothing's currently growing in the refrigerator. Does that seem like an impossible mission? I'll admit there have been times in my life when it seemed like an unreachable goal. But I've learned that there's one surefire way to move from "I can't do this" to "I might be able to do this": *knowledge*.

As any business manager knows, to perform efficiently takes thought and preparation. It starts with a solid understanding of your job description, the tasks you are expected to accomplish, the qualities each of your team members brings to the table, and the goal of the company. In Family Management terms, these would be a thorough knowledge of all that is in your care, what skills and interests your family members offer to the family as a whole, and what you're working toward together—like a reasonably clean and organized home that's a fun place to be.

Know Your Job

The job of Family Manager is much like that of a CEO of a corporation, someone who oversees various departments. (*Oversees* is the operative word here. No CEO or manager worth his or her salt is going to do everything him- or herself.) Although most Family Managers don't have a corner office with a view, their job is just as demanding and valuable. Our job description looks something like this:

- *Home and Property.* We oversee the maintenance and care of all tangible assets, including personal belongings, the house, and its surroundings.
- *Food.* We efficiently, economically, and creatively meet the daily food and nutrition needs of the family.
- *Special Projects.* We coordinate large and small projects—holidays, birthdays, vacations—that fall outside the normal family routine.
- *Family and Friends.* We deal with family life and relationships and act as teacher, nurse, counselor, mediator, and social chairman as required.
- *Finances.* We budget, manage money and pay bills, and handle a host of other money issues.
- *Time and Scheduling.* We manage the master family calendar so the household runs smoothly.
- *Personal Growth.* We see to the needs of our own body, mind, emotions, and soul.

It's possible, even with this impressive job description, that some of you consider Family Management nothing more than regularly swabbing toilets, mopping spit-up, and slapping meals on the table—not exactly a high-level position. Yet you show me a woman who has a dozen meals up her sleeve she can produce in twenty minutes, or a woman who knows that club soda is her best friend when it comes to getting spots out of a

555

carpet, and I'll show you a knowledge worker.

Like any knowledge worker, no matter how long you've been Family Managing, you won't know everything about everything—but

> "Knowledge is of two kinds: we know a subject ourselves, or we know where we can find information upon it."
> —Samuel Johnson

you'll know where to get help. This book will help you figure out what your specific tasks are in each of the seven Family Manager departments throughout the year, then how to accomplish those tasks efficiently and effectively.

BE SENSITIVE TO YOUR OWN MANAGEMENT STYLE

Everyone does things differently, and that's okay. No one system will work for everyone. All CEOs have some way of managing, keeping track of the countless details of their position, that is unique to their personalities and strengths. Are you a write-it-all-down person? Or a keep-it-in-your-head person? I'm the former. So not only do I have a daily list of to-dos, I also have tickler files that remind me of things that need to be done on a periodic basis. I have lists of ideas that worked in the past, so I don't have to reinvent the wheel every time I have a dinner party, Christmas rolls around, or we decide to have a garage sale.

Each Family Manager must discover her unique—I repeat, *unique*—style of management. To do this, you need to know where your current picture of a good Family Manager came from. Do

> It's important to know yourself. A lack of self-knowledge can spell defeat for any Family Manager. Knowing yourself means knowing what you're good at, what you're not good at, and what kind of help to ask for. If you're better at cleaning than baking cookies, then buy some cookies from a bakery for your child's school party. If you're better at gardening than you are at bookkeeping, enlist your team members' help in figuring out a way to get both done to everyone's satisfaction.

you do things a certain way because your mother, grandmother, or Aunt Sue did it that way? Though you may feel pressured to conform, you know Mother's style doesn't fit you. Looking to people we respect can be a good way to bring new ideas into our lives. But blindly following someone else's style or path, unaware of our own strengths and weaknesses when we're deciding what to adopt, leads to a dead end. When we cooperate with who we are and our unique style, it makes our job as Family Manager a lot easier and more fulfilling.

Know Your Mission

When I visit the various companies I work with, it doesn't take long for me to get a sense of the corporate culture, the personality of the company: whether it's a good place to work, and whether the employees are glad to be working there. As Family Managers we have a lot of influence on the "corporate culture" of the organization we oversee—our home—and what the "staff"—family members—at our headquarters say about living there. Being user-friendly—that is to say, the house is there for the people who live in it—is key to a smoothly functioning home.

Does your home serve the needs of your family? Is it a good place to work, play, and live? Do the rooms reflect how you live in them? Does your home say "Come in!" or "Abandon hope, all ye who enter here"?

A Place to Start

TOP TEN WANT-TOS

As I talk with Family Managers across the country about their job, these ten desires come up over and over again. They're in no particular order, but I think we all recognize ourselves and our families in at least some of them. We all want to:

1. Get everyone up and out of the house each morning on time and on a positive note.

These tasks *can* be accomplished—but not perfectly, and not all at once.

2. Clean our house from top to bottom, so all we have to do is a once-over each week.

3. Open a closet and find what we're looking for, and get rid of closets full of stuff we never use.

4. Develop a workable system to deal with laundry and household chores.

5. Find a way to get the whole family to help more with housework.

6. Keep track of messages and schedules.

7. Create a bill-paying and filing system that doesn't create more work; get papers under control; organize a desk or work space so we don't spend half an hour in search of a postage stamp.

8. Eat family dinners together, avoid the six o'clock witching hour, and have all the ingredients actually on hand for a meal that takes thirty minutes to prepare.

9. Really enjoy vacations, holidays, and special occasions instead of feeling like we're the one who has to do all the work.

10. Find time to take care of ourselves.

All of this can be done, although I'm less sure of item 2 than any of them. We can do seasonal cleaning (see Seasonal Cleaning Plan, page 127), but I'm still waiting for the invention of a self-cleaning house. So even if we start with absolutely clean, periodically it's going to take more than a quick weekly once-over.

Which of Top Ten Want-tos are highest on your list? Where do you need help? What makes you feel like running, screaming, into the night? Take a minute to stop and think about your home and family.

"Action is the antidote to despair." —Joan Baez

Reorder the list from one to ten, starting with the thing you most want to change. You'll have a place to begin.

Then use the following list to create an honest and accurate description of your home's user-friendly quotient. Check all the words that apply. Use the blanks at the end of the list to add others that come to mind.

☑ warm	❑ tidy	☑ calm
☑ welcoming	❑ shiny	❑ soothing
❑ stressful	❑ sloppy	❑ confusing
❑ drab	☑ orderly	❑ rigid
❑ uncomfortable	❑ attractive	❑ unsanitary
❑ light	❑ formal	❑ disheveled
❑ dark	❑ dusty	❑ grand
❑ dirty	❑ smelly	❑ creative
❑ messy	❑ beautiful	❑ tacky
❑ cluttered	❑ sunny	❑ intense
❑ unpleasant	❑ spacious	❑ imaginative
☑ happy	❑ cold	❑ fragrant
☑ user-friendly	❑ expensive	❑ purposeful
❑ perfect	☑ relaxed	☑ simple
❑ coordinated	❑ eclectic	❑ appropriate
☑ cozy	❑ energizing	❑ immaculate
❑ different	❑ homey	❑ functional
❑ unique	☑ convenient	❑ fresh
❑ spirited	☑ joyful	❑ _____
☑ balanced	❑ charming	❑ _____
❑ bright	❑ positive	❑ _____
☑ neat	☑ well arranged	❑ _____
❑ noisy	❑ tense	❑ _____
❑ chaotic	❑ quiet	❑ _____
❑ unorganized	❑ fun	❑ _____

Were you surprised at the words you checked? Is your home what you'd always hoped it would be? Go back through your choices and, using these words and words of your own, complete the sentence, "I want our home to be . . ." If you chose *immaculate*, is that appropriate for your family at this stage of life? Or would introducing a bit of informality and maybe even some controlled clutter—say, in the art-projects corner of a child's bedroom—be a good idea?

One Family Manager's idea of *functional* may be another's nightmare. If you're the kind of person who likes to have everything in plain sight, you might prefer open shelves for games, puzzles, and books in the family room. But if you like everything to look simple and uncluttered, you might be better off putting some doors on those same shelves.

No matter what your current situation, if the description of your home is less positive than you want it to be, you as the Family Manager can make changes that will benefit everyone. First and foremost, don't forget that your mission is to organize and enhance your home for you and your family—the people who live there twenty-four hours a day, seven days a week, 365 days a year—not for occasional guests, a magazine editor, or your mother.

Building Your Team

An important part of successful Family Management is understanding that the very strategies that help companies run smoother can also help your family run smoother. One of those strategies is team building. A good manager delegates tasks to others, assuming responsibility for initiating projects and providing needed assistance toward completion. A good Family Manager is always learning how to better get her family to work as a team. Even the smallest children can begin to learn to pick up

We're doing our kids a favor when we involve them in family maintenance. We're teaching them skills they are going to need in life, such as running the washing machine. But we're also teaching them cooperation and collaboration skills that will serve them in any walk of life. Delegating also helps balance responsibilities and workloads between marriage partners. And it builds on the idea that home belongs to everyone; therefore, everyone contributes to its care.

their own toys, to help fold laundry by matching socks, and to set the table.

There are a number of ways to involve your family in the process of becoming a one-for-all-and-all-for-one team. The principles company managers use to motivate employees, improve productivity, and boost morale work for Family Managers as well.

EIGHT STEPS TO A WELL-BUILT TEAM

1. Help team members buy into the cause. It's a concept multimillionaire Sam Walton put into practice early on when he arranged for employees to be stockholders. Because they felt ownership of the profits, they gave their all—and the results made history. Family members won't buy into the idea of organization just because Mom says so or the Joneses do it that way. If a family understands how and why a new system will better their lives, they will be more likely to try to follow it. For example:

- If the house is cleaner, you can have friends over.
- If we all pitch in, it will get done sooner and we'll have more time for fun.
- Mom will be in a better mood. (This has great value.)
- If your husband helps put the kids to bed you'll have more energy for him afterward.

"I was so busy doing things I should have delegated, I didn't have time to manage."
—Charles Percy

2. Seize the high ground. No one will jump at the chance to be on your team if you're negative: "I'm sick and tired of living in a pigpen." Or critical: "If you ever did anything around here . . ." Or playing chief nag: "I've told you that a thousand times." Or neutral: "Who cares if we eat dinner together?" A team has to be inspired, and that means aiming for improvement with a positive attitude.

Again, it's important to translate your vision for being a family team into actions that are valuable to them. Someone once said that the key to willpower is *wantpower*. People who want something badly enough can usually find the willpower to achieve it.

3. Come up with a *family* definition of "clean and organized" so kids will know when the kitchen is well ordered or your husband will know what a picked-up family room looks like. What seems clean and orderly to one person may seem filthy and disorganized to another. Everyone has a different tolerance level for dirt and disorder. Bear in mind that you will more than likely have to compromise sometimes. If your spouse doesn't see the need to declutter his work space or closet, maybe you need to re-think your own standards or at least consider leaving his space alone.

4. Assign tasks specifically and set realistic goals. "Just do your best" instructions can lead to frustrating results because you haven't set a mea-surable goal. Let each assignee know what the end result should look like. After assigning chores, let team members who are old enough develop their own ways—which work in accordance with their skills and talents— to accomplish them. Older kids will appreciate your trust in letting them take personal responsibility for developing the strategies to get jobs done.

(Note: See also Ten Tips for Successful Family Meetings, page 23.)

Brass Tacks—and Who Picks Them Up

Here's a sample list of household tasks you will need to discuss and assign:

Plan meals.	Assist with homework.
Shop for food.	Participate in school activities.
Prepare meals.	Shop for clothing.
Clean up after meals.	Pay the bills.
Pick up the house.	Take clothes to the dry cleaners.
Vacuum and mop.	Maintain the car.
Make the beds.	Get gas.
Do the laundry.	Take care of the yard.
Clean bathrooms.	Do household repairs and maintenance.
Take out the trash.	Contact repair services.
Arrange for child care.	Water the plants.
Chauffeur children to their activities.	Feed the pets.

5. Be supportive and express confidence in your team's ability to achieve goals. Your positive expectations often set the stage for higher performance and create a more positive relationship between you and your team members. Thank your husband and children for every task they do, even if it's something you expect of them.

6. Offer fair rewards for big tasks. "When the garage is cleaned out—trash hauled away and extras given to charity—we as a family will . . . [a mutually agreed upon treat]." "When Kevin has raked the lawn, we'll go out for ice cream." "Once the family room is decluttered, we'll rent a video and make popcorn."

7. Be flexible. Unexpected events can interrupt the best routines. Bend with the interruption instead of standing against it. Your investment in your discouraged daughter will pay far higher dividends than a vacuumed house. Attending your son's basketball game in another city as a family speaks volumes to him about his worth in your family. And making a snowman together might do more for family morale than a day spent wielding dust rags and cleaning musty closets.

8. Solicit input from family members and listen, listen, listen. Let each person talk openly and honestly about what makes him or her not feel like a valued team member. Talk about what would have to happen for those feelings to change.

> Here's the bottom line: a home is where human beings develop. The choices we make about our home involve a lot more than carpet color, window treatments, and number of closets. Home isn't just a place to hang a hat; it's a place to restore souls, find shelter from outside pressures, grow support for talents, receive inspiration, comfort, and aid. It is a place where family members learn to love and be loved.

Make sure your team knows you're committed to each family member's best interest. You're not trying to make them miserable or burden them with extra responsibilities; you're simply trying to make everyone's life a little easier by spreading out the work more evenly.

A WORD ABOUT RELUCTANT TEAM MEMBERS

Countless mothers have told me their kids won't help around the house. If your child is one of them, consider the following questions: Does your son or daughter talk on the phone? Does he or she watch TV? Play video or computer games? Does he or she like to borrow the car and go out with friends?

Those activities, and others like them, are *privileges*, not rights. We do our kids a favor when we have a policy that says: until you fulfill your responsibilities, you do not get your privileges. Granted, kids won't like this, but they'll bow to it. Properly motivated, kids will do anything.

Even more important than the child's cooperation is the lesson he or she learns about real life. After all, that's the way the adult world operates. If you don't fulfill your responsibilities on your job, you won't have the privilege of getting a paycheck or maybe even having a job at all.

Don't be afraid to trade permission for contribution. Your child deserves to learn this at home, where the stakes are small, rather than in the cold, cruel world, where the stakes are enormous.

WE'RE IN THIS TOGETHER

But are you and your spouse in the same place? States of mind are important and often different. What do we do when we see a perfect day to clean out the garage and our husband sees his only opportunity to play golf for the next three weeks because he'll be taking several business trips? When we see a disaster zone in the basement and he sees a project in progress? When we see the perfect used piano for the family room and he sees the price, the size, and the problem of getting it down a narrow flight of stairs? When we see a to-do list with twenty-five items on it (many with his initials behind them) and he sees a piece of fiction? What do we do when we see a sloppily cleaned kitchen, with pots and pans in the sink, and he sees a job satisfactorily accomplished?

We stop, sit down, and describe the place we're in. That's what we do. If your spouse is reluctant to buy into the role you've cast him in on your Family Management team, you need to talk—about your roles, your goals, and your standards.

Remember:

1. Mutual standards mean exactly that. Have you really taken his point of view into account? Where can you compromise?

2. Men and women look at the same room or situation and often see things in a different light. Use this to your mutual advantage. There's more than one piece of furniture I might have bought if I hadn't looked at it through Bill's eyes as well as my own. If you want to rearrange furniture, paint your bedroom, or institute a new policy for kitchen cleanup, ask your spouse what he sees.

3. If we use guilt to try to accomplish our goals, what we usually get is a cranky spouse and an undone task. Guilt has a way of growing and making both of us ugly.

4. Barking orders is for Marine platoons and packs of dogs. Asking goes a lot farther than telling. And asking is a two-way street: Would you do . . . ? Would you like me to . . . ?

5. Spouses are people, and people who feel like you're on their team are a lot more likely to play by your game plan when you demonstrate a willingness to play by theirs.

6. How to create conversation with a reluctant or uncooperative spouse; do it

- at a time when the kids are in bed or have been farmed out for the evening.
- over a leisurely meal and after you've both unwound from the day.
- in a way that asks what both of you see and explores solutions without jumping to conclusions or unrealistic plans and expectations.
- with an open mind and a listening attitude. A heart-to-heart talk in which you do all the talking isn't going to get you anywhere. Ask his opinion with open-ended questions. "What's your best-case scenario for getting the garage cleaned out?" Not, "Don't you want to help me keep this place up?"

Clearing the Air: Stress Relief

We all carry stress from the outside world into our homes. A first grader who isn't picked until the last round for kickball feels stressed out and re-jected just like Mom and Dad do when their proposal is scrapped at the office. Ideally, we want our home to be a place where we put away stress and embrace peace. While there is no perfect home because there are no perfect people, there are some simple ways to reduce the stress level.

First, you need to identify the recurring pressure points in your home. Some of these seem like little things. But when you confront them day after day, or when you're faced with a pile of them all at once, they can wear you down. Dealing with recurring stressors requires a lot of emotional energy.

Family Manager's Sample Pressure Points

Do you feel frustrated when you walk through your house and . . .

- your teenager's empty soda can is on the end table—again?
- your third grader's science-fair project is scattered all over the game table?
- there's cat hair in every corner and spiderwebs festoon the ceiling?
- the leaky faucet your husband promised to fix still drips?
- your eyes hurt because there's not enough light to read by?
- your dog tracked mud across the floor and no one cleaned it up?
- you have to tell your teenager every day to get his feet off the coffee table?
- your mother-in-law hints that you're a bad housekeeper because there are toys everywhere?
- your kids constantly argue over whose turn it is to play a video game?

Other Family Members' Sample Pressure Points

Do the people in your family feel stress when . . .
- they feel nagged to do chores they didn't agree to do?
- they feel they don't get a say about when and how chores should be done?
- they can't bring friends home because the place is too messy? Or too clean?
- they don't have anyplace they can call their own to work on hobbies or just be?
- they can't find the remote control?
- they can't count on finding food in the refrigerator?
- they don't know where their clean laundry is?
- they don't know what happened to the latest issue of their favorite magazine?

All of us cope differently with mess, bickering children, and pet refuse. But the way I see it, no matter what your toleration level is, if you can do away with some of the stress, your home will be a better place to be for you and your family. And that, after all, is your mission.

There's no time like the present to take some time to talk with your family members about how to relieve stress around your house. One way to do this is a family meeting.

TEN TIPS FOR SUCCESSFUL FAMILY MEETINGS

1. A few days before, post the time for the meeting on the refrigerator or somewhere everyone will see it often. Unless you have an unusual family, don't expect them to jump for joy over the fact that you're having a family meeting. Just make sure everyone knows attendance is not an option. Fix their

"To be happy at home is the ultimate result of all ambition."
—Samuel Johnson

favorite snack or dessert. Good food has a way of fostering goodwill and cooperation.

2. Before the meeting, discuss the agenda with your spouse. Keep it simple. Begin the meeting with a statement of purpose and the agenda. You might explain that you want your home to be less stressful, more organized, and a good place to be for all of you. You don't have to cover all the issues in one meeting. In fact, you can't. If you try, your kids might still be sitting in their chairs, but they won't be participating. They'll be envisioning their future as Cinderella: scrubbing floors, missing balls, and palling around with birds and mice.

3. Appoint one person to record all the ideas everyone has on a large sheet of paper or an erasable board.

4. Ask each family member what would make home a good place to be for him or her. Ask them to be as specific as possible. Note: This may instill fear in your own heart because you're afraid of their answers. Fear not, because (a) they haven't thought about this so they don't have a long mental laundry list of what they'd like to change, and (b) they don't want this to be a long meeting.

5. At this brainstorming stage, no idea is out of bounds. Trust me on this. The requests your family make will be very doable. And it's going to mean a lot to them that you're willing to be flexible on some of your standards and that you care about what they think makes home a better place.

6. Once everyone's had his or her say, review the list and decide which of the suggestions are most important and most doable. What can you all agree on? What are bottom-liners for Mom and Dad?

7. Make plans to implement some of your ideas and strategies by discussing who will be responsible for each item. Give people a chance to volunteer. (The teenager who wants a well-stocked refrigerator may be willing to make weekly trips to the grocery store to get it.)

8. Make a brief list of what you decide and post it where it can remind everyone. (Remember, change doesn't happen overnight. Reminders are good for everyone.)

9. Use this time to affirm each member's efforts in fulfilling the mission of making home a place everyone can use and enjoy. Thank each member for his/her specific contribution.

10. Schedule a follow-up meeting for a week or a month down the road. Let everyone know that meeting will be for checking in to see how things are going.

Some families swear by family meetings. Others, particularly those with very small children, might find they're not so useful. It helps if you get in the habit of having them on a semiregular basis. We have them for everything from planning who will take care of the five new puppies to creating family vacations. Chances are, you might already have some sort of family meeting system going in your house, even if you don't call it that.

SETTING GROUND RULES
Another good way to relieve everyday stresses is to set ground rules. People who know the rules, buy into them, and follow them feel more comfortable. Some Family Managers prefer to articulate the rules after hearing input from all interested parties, sort of like a judge. For some, a more collaborative system of setting them in family meetings might work. Whatever your preferred style, setting the rules is important, but it's only the first step. Make sure there's a built-in reward-and-debit or -consequences system that applies to everyone. (For instance, if nobody eats in the living room, *nobody* eats in the living room, including Mom and Dad. This is not a "Do as I say, not as I do" proposition.)

Also, understand that setting ground rules is not a onetime deal. As your family grows and changes, you edit, adjust, and add to them. In our case, Bill and I made our first ground rules when the boys were preschoolers. They were too young to help create them, so we taught them the rules we decided would make all our lives saner. As they grew older, we adapted the rules to fit the new needs of our family.

Realistic ground rules create cleaner air space so everyone is less stressed and more comfortable.

SAMPLE GROUND RULES

Following are some of the Peel Family Ground Rules. These are positive and easily understood rules that help our family create the kind of environment we need. Pick and choose which ones might work for your family. Or use these as inspiration to develop your own.

- No outside voices inside, unless there's an emergency.
- Put away what you take out.
- Use good manners with family as well as guests. (See "Tips for Teaching Kids Common Table Manners" on page 217.)
- Respect each other's belongings. Ask if you want to borrow something.
- Do your assigned chores.
- Treat others as you would want to be treated. No name-calling. Phrase requests nicely. Learn to use "Please" and "Thank you."
- Knock before opening a closed door.
- If you fix a snack in the kitchen, clean up after yourself. Rinse your dirty dishes and put them in the dishwasher.
- Everyone is responsible for his or her own laundry.
- Everyone participates in a once-a-week cabin cleanup of common areas. As well, each person is responsible for keeping his or her private space (bedroom, work area) clean according to mutually agreed-upon standards.
- No leaving wet towels or dirty clothes on the bathroom floor. Clean up the tub or shower after yourself.
- Let others know in advance if you need to watch (or record) a certain TV program for work or school. Check with others before you play loud music. If you need to leave a project out overnight in a common area, get approval before you begin.

• Take thorough phone messages for each other.

• In every room: make sure your trash is in the trash can. (No matter how much we love our kids, picking up their used tissues, scraps of paper, food, and garbage is disgusting.)

FAMILY MANAGER SIMPLE STRESS RELIEF PLAN

• Schedule some time for yourself. Maybe it's five minutes to sit by the window contemplating the grass growing. Maybe it's an hour at the gym. Whatever it is, make a commitment and keep it. Repeat daily. (See also Daily Joy Breaks, page 100.)

> Remember, any team, at home or at the office, will accept change better if they are involved in the process; asked to contribute their feelings, opinions, and suggestions; told the reasons for and advantages of a given change; respected for their feelings, even though they may oppose the change; and given appropriate and deserved recognition for their contribution in implementing the change.

• Work at not feeling guilty. This might be hard to do when you're taking a much-deserved bubble bath and your ten-year-old is standing outside the bathroom door asking you to help her with her school report, your mother's voice is on the answering machine wondering if you've moved to Australia (it's been so long since she's seen you), the dog is barking like he hasn't been on a walk for six months, and the meter reader is ringing the doorbell. See how many opportunities to feel guilty you can ignore in any given day.

• Let yourself stretch and grow. Take a walk. Start an exercise program. Read a book. Take five to meditate. Take another five to talk with a friend about a new idea.

• Indulge yourself periodically with a new CD or book, some bath salts, a colorful scarf.

• Use your tools and your team to reduce your stress level. Microwaves were invented for nights we don't have time to cook. If your daughter wants you to take her shopping on Saturday, share with her what else needs to be done. Work together on things you might have done alone and have time to enjoy shopping and maybe even lunch out.

• Count your blessings, not your problems.

Five Ways a Kitchen Timer Can Save Your Sanity

1. Kids arguing over who's played the video game the longest? Set the kitchen timer for eleven minutes (or whatever length of time you decide) and when the timer dings, the player automatically knows his turn is up.
2. Put a kitchen timer in the bathroom and time showers in the morning.
3. Set the kitchen timer in the mornings for ten minutes before walk-out-the-door time to give family members a warning.
4. When you ask your child to do a chore and he nicely asks if he can do it in five minutes, fine. Set the timer so he'll know when five minutes is up.
5. If you've got ten thousand things on your mind, as usual, and you don't want to forget to pick up your daughter from ballet, set the timer to help you remember when to leave.

"Start by doing what's necessary, then what's possible, and suddenly you are doing the impossible."
—Saint Francis of Assisi

TWO

House Works

"If the environment that people live in is good, so be it. But if it is poor, so is the quality of life within it."   —Ellen Swallow Richards

Whoever we are, our house works as a home when we work at making our house a place we want to be. That means making wise choices about how we furnish and decorate. That means providing space for who we are and what we do. Since adding on a new room every time an old one gets full of stuff—plastic toy parts, last year's magazines, outgrown clothes that fit someone (but no one in our family), catalogs we ordered birthday presents from three years ago, shoes the dog ruined when we left them out overnight, parts to a vacuum cleaner we had when we were first married, books our high school senior learned to read from, and paper of all sorts that makes like rabbits and multiplies—is not an option for most of us, we have to find another way to provide the breathing space we need to make our house work as a home. No matter how different our circumstances or routines, we all have to start with the same issue: clutter.

Clutter Control

CLUTTER: AN EQUAL OPPORTUNITY WASTER

In a word, clutter is a thief.

1. Clutter takes up far more than space. It raises the stress level of the whole family.
2. Clutter wastes time. We've all spent valuable minutes and hours searching for something we need right now.
3. Clutter wastes money. One Family Manager told me she found five cartons of brown sugar when she recently cleaned out her pantry cupboard. When any item is buried in an abyss you may find yourself buying a duplicate, even though you suspect you already own one.
4. Clutter wastes energy. You'll have to clean it, work around it, or move it to get behind or under it.
5. Clutter is unsightly. Visual clutter causes stress and anxiety. Walking into a cluttered house after a long day on the job invites a bad mood.
6. Clutter is dangerous. It can cause household accidents.

Defeating clutter in your home or in your life is not done in a day. In fact, it's *never* really done. Controlling clutter is an ongoing process. I try to think of it as akin to breathing, and do it all the time.

Getting rid of what we don't need, taking care of what we do—that's what clutter control is all about.

> Order begins with restoring out-of-place items to their places; only then can deep cleaning and organization take place.

ELIMINATE AND CONCENTRATE

That's all you have to remember. But these two words can change your life. They're the key to reducing chaos, relieving frustration, and turning a Danger Zone into a Safety Zone. *Eliminate* what you don't want, need, or use. *Concentrate* on what you use, need, and care about. Do you really need that "See Rock City" ashtray your cousin Irma brought you from her vacation? Can you get by with fewer than fifteen back issues of *TV Guide*? Do you really need check stubs from twenty-five years ago?

When I was getting out the Christmas decorations this year, I came across a tired silk flower arrangement I hadn't seen since last January when I shoved it to the back of the shelf. "What," I asked myself, "should I do with *this*?" I put into use a quick test I apply to every underused item in our house. I asked the Clutter Control Inventory Questions:

- When is the last time it was used? Worn? Played with?
- Does it deserve space in our home? If it wasn't here, what would be here instead?
- Are there memories attached to it?
- What will I do with it? Fix it, sell it, store it, toss it, or donate it?
P.S. I threw away the flowers.

BIG BAD EXCUSES FOR CLUTTER COP-OUT

- *Everyone has one, so I must need one, too.* Or the opposite: *It's unique, so I've got to have (or keep) it.* I once knew a family who nearly broke up over a suit of armor. She wanted to buy it from a restaurant that was going out of business. He wanted to know where she was going to put it, since they didn't live in a castle and he rarely went out to slay dragons.
- *It may come in handy some-day.* Like that down coat a friend of mine held on to for ten years after she moved from Minnesota to Florida.

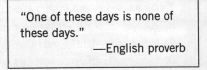

"One of these days is none of these days."
—English proverb

- *I'll keep it until I find someone to give it to.* And when you finally meet that person, how are you going to find it?
- *I don't have time to sort through my stuff.* How much stuff could you accumulate in the next twenty-five or fifty years? And how do you feel about leaving your by-then grown-up children the monumental task of sorting through it all once you're gone?
- *If I get rid of things, I'm throwing money away.* Maybe it's time to apply the time-and-energy equation. How much time and energy do you think you spend taking care of things you don't use? Cleaning up around them? Looking for things you really need amidst the clutter? Maybe you can't afford *not* to get rid of some stuff. Plus it's a well-known fact that one person's castoffs are another person's treasure. Have a garage sale. (See Garage Sales: Turning Trash into Cash, page 137.) Or take your stuff to a consignment store.
- *I don't know where to start.* Take five to read Take Five on page 35. Then just do one thing. See how you feel. Be careful: decluttering can be habit-forming.

In with the New . . .

Whenever you're thinking of acquiring something new, no matter what it is, ask yourself these ten questions before surrendering more space:

1. Do I/we really need it?
2. Can I/we make do with what I have?
3. How often will I/we use it?
4. How much space will it take up?
5. How much care does it require?
6. Is it durable?
7. Do its design and quality meet my standards?
8. Is there information available to help me make my decision?
9. Is the price right? Could I/we find it at a secondhand store?
10. How much difference will its addition to our home really make?

POINTS TO PONDER

- Buy things because they are useful, not because a Madison Avenue ad executive says they'll make you prettier, smarter, in the know, or in the flow.

> Rest stops are great when you're on the highway . . . but not in your home. Whenever possible, don't take things halfway to their destination. Put them away right when you're finished.

- Refuse to be propagandized by the purveyors of modern gadgetry.
- Look with a healthy skepticism at all "buy now, pay later" schemes.
- Develop a habit of giving things away.
- Learn to enjoy things without owning them.

A little bit of barter is a better way of buying—especially when kids are little, growing through outfits in less than a month, graduating from infant to toddler car seats, and getting bored with last week's favorite book. One of the ways you can declutter your home is to share with another family such interchangeable items as tools and kids' clothing and toys. Start small. Offer to exchange something you no longer use with a friend who has children both younger and older than yours. Or talk with your babysitting cooperative (if you have one) and see if you might set up a clothing, toy, and equipment exchange.

Barter works for other things as well. Clean out your closet. What's hanging in there that might look better on your sister or best friend? Offer to make an exchange. You can reduce the clutter in your closet and extend your wardrobe without spending a cent. (See The Friend Connection on page 97 for more ideas about bartering.)

DECLUTTER CAMPAIGN:
STRATEGIC BATTLE PLAN

1. If possible, arrange your schedule to do clutter battle

> "Out of clutter, find simplicity."
> —Albert Einstein

during one large block of time, like a Saturday. This way you save on start-up/knock-down time, you'll be more serious and do a better job, and the results become visible more quickly—which will give you more momentum.

2. Dress so you can put all your energy into the job. Wear comfortable clothes and tennis shoes.

3. You'll need three boxes—labeled Give Away, Garage Sale, and Store—and a garbage bag for every room. You may want to add a contingency box for things you're not sure about. But give yourself a deadline as to when you're going to decide where the items will end up. Designate an older child to be in charge of sorting through and folding the clothing items that will be stored or given away. Unusable clothing can be cut up for rags, and the buttons can be cut off for crafts.

4. Start with one room. Begin each room by clearing a spot where you can see some measurable results soon, so you'll feel good about making progress. Work your way around the room, removing clutter from shelves, bookcases, drawers, tabletops, floors, and walls.

5. Don't allow nonemergencies to interrupt your clutter-clearing time. Eliminate all distractions. Turn on your answering machine, turn off the TV, and put on some peppy music. When you find the umbrella your friend left months ago, don't call her now to tell her you found it.

6. Toss or give away as much as possible. Be ruthless with things like gift boxes, grocery sacks, old magazines and catalogs, and craft materials you saved to use but haven't.

7. Remember that you have a bigger purpose than just getting rid of clutter. Order will help you and your family live more efficiently and peacefully.

TAKE FIVE

When clutter has moved in like a boarder who never pays the rent, it's easy to feel stuck. Feeling like a guilty or weak landlord doesn't help. Nor does fantasizing how you'll get rid of the clutter

> "Inanimate objects are classified scientifically into three major categories—those that don't work, those that break down, and those that get lost."   —Russell Baker

when . . . the kids are grown-up, spring comes, or you have seven hours free. For most of us, the large blocks of time are few and far between. If your schedule allows for a family clutter-clearing day, have at it. For those who can't see a free Saturday in the next five years, try getting into the five-minute mind-set. You'd be surprised how much you can accomplish in five minutes, and how many five-minute blocks of time you can grab here and there. No, you won't finish tasks like unloading the basement of years' worth of magazines you've saved for those articles on how to get organized, but you'll make progress (which will make you feel better about yourself) a little bit at a time and you'll eventually finish the chore.

Here are some ideas:

• Take five minutes to make a list of clutter hot spots in your house. Post the list to remind yourself to spend five minutes decluttering on a regular basis.

• Purge your pantry of food you never use but have somehow acquired. Give it to a shelter. Do one shelf at a time in five-minute segments.

• Sort through a junk drawer. Just toss items you don't need or use. You can organize it later.

• Clean out odds and ends from your refrigerator and freezer.

• Remove duplicates from kitchen drawers—again, one drawer at a time. How many cheese slicers do you really need? Even the messiest of drawers probably won't take more than ten minutes.

• Reorganize your dish cupboards one shelf at a time. Remember to apply the Clutter Control Inventory Questions to that pan you find in the back corner of the bottom shelf. Be honest: You're not sure *what* it's for, let alone the last time you used it.

• Clean out your medicine cabinet a couple of shelves at a time. Toss old, outdated items.

• Cull children's clothing one drawer or shelf at a time. Save outgrown clothing for younger siblings in labeled boxes, or trade for clothes your kids can use now. Or give them to charity or someone you know who can use them. Go through your children's clothing this way three times a year. (I do this before school starts in the fall, after Christmas, and before summer.) Involve your kids in the process, and by the time they're teenagers they'll be able to do it on their own. Go through your own clothing and accessories twice a year, one shelf or drawer at a time.

• Declutter your linen closet one shelf at a time. Count the beds in your house and keep two sets of linens for each bed. Give away the leftovers or turn them into rags.

• Put a bookshelf or basket in every room of the house—including your children's rooms—where you read or collect books, papers, or magazines. Make a daily practice of putting the books, magazines, or papers on the shelf or in the basket instead of on the floor, on the dining room table, or wherever such clutter accumulates. When the shelf or the basket is full, cull, cull, cull. (Again, you can do this one shelf or basket at a time, probably in five minutes or less.)

• Make it a game. Walk through your house with a plastic garbage bag and see how much clutter you can throw away in five minutes.

Declutter Your Desk

Put a large trash container beside your desk and throw away the following items:

Business cards you don't need

Last season's catalogs

Magazines and journals more than two months old

Junk mail

Pens that don't write and pencils with bad erasers

Children's school papers that you don't need

Expired coupons

Old sticky notes you've already taken care of

Articles you clipped and copied but don't have time to read

Recipes you don't have time to try

Emergency Measures:
Quick Decluttering Scheme

I can't count the times an unexpected guest calls to say he or she is coming by just when the kids are practicing their multiplication tables in the dust on the coffee table. Or when there's a day's worth of dirty dishes in the sink even the houseflies won't touch. When I'm caught off guard, I refuse to let the situation get the best of me. I throw myself into high gear and launch the Quick Decluttering Scheme.

Ready, set, go:

- Grab a laundry basket and pick up as much clutter as you can in a minute. Hide the basket in a closet. (After company leaves, take the opportunity life has given you to put the things in the basket in their proper places.)

- Stack all the mail, magazines, and newspapers in a neat pile or in an attractive basket.

- Fluff sofa and chair cushions. Fold the throws.
- Close all cabinets and drawers.
- Run into the bathroom and put away counter clutter. Grab the all-purpose glass cleaner and a rag that you keep underneath the sink (right?) for regular cleaning and such occasions as this, and wipe off the mirror and fixtures. Put out a decorative hand towel and a small bar of guest soap in a pretty dish next to the sink. (If you're like me, you'll have a nice towel and soap tucked away at the back of the linen closet, out of the kids' sight.)
- Load the dishwasher, or fill your sink with water and bubbles for dishes to soak. Quickly wipe down the kitchen sink, fixtures, and countertops.
- Sweep up crumbs, dog hair, etc. If you don't have time to damp-mop, dab the big spots with a damp paper towel.
- Focus on ambiance. Turn down the lights. Close the doors to rooms you haven't picked up. Put on some soothing background music. Light a scented candle.
- Catch your breath. Smile and welcome your guests.

A DOZEN WAYS KIDS CAN CONTROL CLUTTER

1. When your children get a new game or toy, help them decide where to store it. Involving them in the "where it goes" decision also helps remind them to put it there when they're not using it.

2. Limit the number of toys that can be out at one time.

3. Have designated toy-pickup and put-away times.

> Never walk through your house empty-handed. Train your family members to do the same. When you leave a room, look around. What needs to be put away in the direction you're headed? There's always something.

4. Put a laundry basket in each child's closet.

5. Mount hooks at child level so they can hang hats, jackets, pajamas, etc.

6. Buy assorted sizes of clear plastic boxes for kids to categorize and store their belongings.

7. Avoid toy boxes and trunks. Small items sift to the bottom and you have to empty the whole box or trunk to find them.

8. Paint young children's shelves different colors to encourage sorting things like puzzles, games, books. Label drawers and storage containers; paste on appropriate pictures for small children.

9. Keep a clean plastic dustpan in your child's room to scoop up multipiece toys.

10. Establish specific food and nonfood places in your house. (For example, eating in the kitchen, family room, and TV room is okay; eating in the bedrooms is not.)

11. Create an after-school unloading routine. Designate where coats, mittens, hats, and backpacks should be put.

12. Encourage the regular weeding out of toys your kids have outgrown. Let your kids go with you to take them to a mission or shelter so they can see how their contributions help other people.

Whether clutter is a big or a little problem for you, you'll notice when it's gone. Maybe the best measure of clutter's uselessness is how much easier your life is when you don't have it—and how it clogs your life when you do. Believe me, every step you take toward clutter control in your home will be more than worthwhile, and you'll be able to tell from your increased efficiency and better mood right away.

> "Children are a house's enemy. They don't mean to be—they just can't help it. It's their enthusiasm, their energy, their naturally destructive tendencies." —Delia Ephron

Go Directly to Jail

Train family members to pick up their things by creating Clutter Jail. If
something is left out, it goes into the Clutter Jail (a box or laundry basket
will do) and can't be reclaimed until Sunday night, when the family member can post bail.

Sane Storage

I believe that some of the best contemporary fiction is written by organizational "experts." If only they would write realistically with clutter-
impaired women like me in mind, organization could be a reachable goal.
The picture-perfect storage areas—closets, basement, garage—in magazines never look like mine. I doubt that any one of these writers ever
needed a mini "jaws of life" machine to extricate a small child from the
back of the cupboard where she sent him on an expedition for loaf pans.

Over time and through experience, I've concluded that having picture-
perfect closets, drawers, cupboards, and other storage spaces is not important. Being able to find what we need when we need it, and being able
to get to it without a cherry picker, is.

There are times when I've been so desperate to find a place for everything that I've tried some pretty outlandish systems. But not all organizational gurus are created equal, and in my continuing search, I have
discovered some common themes from most of them that make sense.

HOW TO BEAT THE "I CAN'T FIND IT TILL I TRIP OVER IT WHEN I DON'T NEED IT" BLUES

1. *Store like items together.* Think in categories. Gather all items used
for the same kind of project and put them in one spot convenient to the

user. Use inexpensive drawer organizers to keep small items from getting jumbled together. Clear plastic boxes (they come in all sizes) are good for medium-sized items. Use fifty-five-gallon plastic trash cans for big things like sports equipment or garden tools.

A–Z CHECKLIST OF LIKE ITEMS TO BE STORED TOGETHER

Use this list to help you start thinking about your belongings and which ones should be stored together:

Arts and crafts supplies
Auto-care items
Baby clothes (outgrown and to-be-grown-into, sentimental)
Books (general reading, reference, special interest, children's)
Boots and rain gear
Business documents
Camera
Camping items
CDs and cassette tapes
Children's school papers and art
China, crystal, and candles
Cleaning supplies
Cosmetics
Documents—marriage and birth certificates, social security cards, passports
Extra foodstuffs—canned goods, pasta, rice
Extra paper products—towels, napkins, lunch bags
Family memorabilia
Financial records
First-aid necessities
Flashlights and batteries
Gardening equipment

Games
Greeting cards/stationery
Hobby supplies
Holiday decorations
Household tools
Keys
Kitchen items
Kitchen items that are seldom used
Linens
Luggage and travel kits
Magazines
Maternity clothes
Medications
Office supplies
Pet supplies
Picnic supplies
Road kit (1) toys, maps, wipes, snack packages, and bottled water
Road kit (2) for extreme winter climates—extra clothing and blankets, hand-warmers, shovel, ice scraper, cat litter (for helping with traction on snowy road shoulders)
Party supplies
Photos and albums, negatives
Seasonal clothing
Sewing supplies
Silver—flatware and serving pieces
Sports equipment
Tax returns and canceled checks
Toys
Trophies
Vacuum accessories
Vases and flower-arranging supplies

Videotapes
Warranties
Wrapping paper

They're Not Just for Sandwiches Anymore

I'm not sure how I organized things before someone invented self-sealing plastic bags. If you think their use is limited to lunch items and frozen foods, think again. I've used them to corral and store marbles, kids' action figures, small video-game cartridges, coins, makeup, travel-size toiletries, loose batteries, small hardware like cup hooks and picture hangers, and much more.

---

2. *Store items as close as possible to the place they are used most often.* That's pretty simple for something like the coffeemaker. You want it close to the sink or water dispenser. Other things might seem to have no clearly defined category or place. Don't simply store them in the first handy or seemingly logical space. It will defeat your purpose of getting organized. Think about how you're going to use the object. If you do floor exercises in front of the TV in the family room, then store your mat nearby.

Some things might fall into more than one category. On paper it might make sense to store binoculars and flashlights with camping equipment in the basement because you use them when you're camping. But you might also use your binoculars to spot birds on day outings to a reservoir, or to be able to see better at a sports event or concert. Which instance occurs more frequently? If you go camping annually and rarely use them for anything else, by all means, put them with the camping equipment.

On the other hand, flashlights are another item you need for camping. But most of us need them for other things as well. It only makes sense to have one flashlight and maybe candles and matches in an easily accessible central spot for when fuses blow and the lights go out.

3. *Allocate your most accessible space to the things you use most often.* Shelves between eye and waist level are prime storage areas in the kitchen. Don't store the deep-fat fryer you use once a year there. And don't store your bundt pan, which you use infrequently, in front of your saucepans, which you use daily.

4. *Make finding as easy as storing.* Use see-through containers whenever possible; when you can't, label the containers. Especially when you stash something in a hurry—and we all do—nonlabeled containers make it that much harder to find it later.

5. *Give every possession a "home."* Whenever you acquire a new possession, from a pasta maker to a pair of skates, decide where it's going to be stored as soon as you bring it into the house. Actually, for bigger items, it's probably a good idea to figure that out before you even think of bringing it home. Can you really get that antique rolltop desk up the stairs into your daughter's bedroom? No matter how useful, attractive, and cheap that corner cupboard is, it's not going to work in your breakfast nook if it's too wide for the space between the wall and the door. You may think buying twenty-four marked-down wineglasses for your big spring party is a great idea. But where are you going to put them after the party? (And how frequently are you going to use them? Could you rent them for even less than you can buy them?)

STORAGE SURVEY

This can be a great exercise if you've recently moved. Or if you're redecorating or just rearranging furniture. Or if you're undertaking a major decluttering campaign. Pick a time when you have an uninterrupted half hour. With a notebook and pen in hand, walk slowly around your house. Jot down all the storage spaces you see. Be sure to look for the unusual spots you may have overlooked.

At the same time, in a separate column or on another page, make a note of things that don't have a proper storage space or aren't close to where they're used. (A friend told me that for years she kept games in a storage space in her basement, which didn't make much sense because her kids always played them upstairs in the family room.)

When you're finished, you might want to ask your spouse to repeat the exercise, pointing out spots you missed. A teenager could be very useful in this exercise as well. A kid who can find her favorite music store on the Internet might well know more about organization than she's letting on.

Once the survey is done, you can begin to match up items with places to put them. Then declare a stow-it family workday, especially if you're undertaking bigger tasks such as building storage units or hanging Peg-Board. And/or begin to create and use new spaces using the Take Five method.

"SECRET" STORAGE SPACES

• Move a chest of drawers into your closet. You'll free up space in the bedroom and make use of the space under the hanging rods that hold shirts and jackets that don't go all the way to the floor.

• Garages and basements aren't the only places Peg-Board is useful. Use it to organize a child's room. Lots of different toys can be hung from hooks on it. Use it in a pantry cupboard or on a utility room wall to hang utensils on.

• Put stacking vegetable bins under your kitchen sink to get the most use out of this area.

• Screw hooks into the ceilings of your cabinets and hang coffee mugs by their handles.

• Put another shelf inside a tall cabinet to elevate some items and create space underneath for others.

• Hang bath-towel racks on the backs of closet doors to hold scarves and belts. Hang a rack on the back of your linen-closet door to hold tablecloths.

• Mount shallow magazine racks on the insides of closet doors to hold children's books, tapes, or CDs.

• Use large clips or a clipboard on the back of a cabinet door to hang paper bags and place mats.

• Attach small containers or racks to the inside of cabinet doors for envelope mixes and other small, hard-to-store items.

• Think "up high." Hang bicycles and other sports equipment from the garage ceiling. Put boards across the rafters in your garage to make a ministorage loft over part of the garage. This is a particularly good place to store things you need only seasonally—outdoor Christmas decorations or lawn furniture. Build a high-border shelf around the perimeter of a room to store/display decorative items such as baskets, decorative dishes, old dolls, and stuffed animals.

• Think "down low." I know one Family Manager who lives in a small home in a city. She keeps two folding cots under her children's bunk beds and sets them up in the living room for overnight guests.

• Small rolling carts that fit underneath desks or in closets work nicely for storing and easily accessing art supplies or sewing machines and materials.

• Hang a three-tier wire basket from your kitchen ceiling to hold potatoes, onions, peppers, and fruit.

• Store baskets you use only occasionally in the space between your cupboard tops and the ceiling.

• Add a to-the-floor dust ruffle to the bottom of a baby crib for hidden floor storage.

• Put a mattress on a platform with built-in drawers, or attach casters to plastic storage boxes and slide them under beds.

• Store your dining-room table leaves behind the china closet or breakfront. A folding game table might fit behind the couch in the family room. A fold-up easel may hang on the wall behind a child's closet door. "Behind" places are often overlooked.

- Nest luggage or use seldom-used pieces to store things like ski clothes.
- Have a carpenter build a window seat with drawers underneath.
- Build shelves under stairwells.
- Protect out-of-season clothes by covering the walls of a small closet with cedar-chip particleboard.
- Restore an antique trunk to double as a coffee table and storage place.
- Hang speakers on a wall to free up floor space.
- Convert an old armoire into a cabinet for your TV and electronic equipment.

MAXIMIZE YOUR ATTIC
You can convert even the smallest attic into a great storage area. Install a plywood floor and light if it doesn't have them already.

1. Categorize like items into "departments" so you won't have to dig through everything when you need an item. (Your departments might be seasonal decorations, baby furniture, luggage, memorabilia, a place for next year's garage-sale stuff, technical equipment and/or the boxes they came in.)

2. Use a footlocker for each child to store clothes, artwork, and other items they will treasure when they're older. Label each in bold letters so you can identify them easily.

3. Use inexpensive shelving and large plastic garbage cans with lids to store seasonal items.

User-Friendly Rooms

When our kids were small, Bill and I decided to make our family motto "Life's too short not to have a good time." We wanted this principle to

Photo equipment should be stored in an interior closet at room temperature. Extreme temperature change can cause condensation that will damage equipment.

> "Make every room a living room." —Alexandra Stoddard

influence every aspect of our life— how we spent our time, how we spent our money, how we communicated with one another . . . and how we decorated and managed our home.

We believed then (and still do) that kids don't grow up and remember whether they could eat off the kitchen floor or if the towels were folded in perfect squares in the linen closet, but they do remember if home was a good place to be. We decided that we didn't want to fill our home with expensive furniture and appointments that would put us on edge every time a child or one of his friends walked into the room. (Not that we could afford them anyway, but we decided if we ever could afford to do this, we wouldn't.) We wanted to order and decorate our home in an attractive way that expressed who we are as a family and encouraged spending time together doing things we enjoy. Now, more than twenty-five years later, I'm glad we made that decision. And so are our kids, judging by the number of friends they bring by and the fact that our out-of-the-nest sons want to come home every chance they get.

MENU DRIVEN: OPTIONS THAT WORK FOR YOU

Menu-driven software programs allow people to easily pick and choose what suits them. The term has come to mean user-friendly, because the user gets to choose. Just as with software, you get to choose for your home what you need to suit your family's personalities and activities. And every family is different. One family's definition of a user-friendly home environment might be another's museum atmosphere. One family's sense of order and design might be another's idea of a condemned zone. Remember, this is your family's home. I've said it before and I'll say it again: your standards and taste are what is important.

TWO FUNDAMENTAL QUESTIONS FOR EVERY ROOM IN THE HOUSE

1. What do we use it for?

2. Is the current setup conducive to that use?

A third question might be, Are we satisfied with the use we currently make of the space? If because of changing family circumstances—e.g., a new baby and the need for a nursery—there won't be room for a separate office or sewing room, you may be forced to rethink the first question. What changes might you make to create room for these activities somewhere else?

Time also enters into the equation. For instance, if you have a family room set up mostly for watching television, but your family doesn't watch much TV, you might consider putting the set on a rolling cart that can be stashed in a closet, leaving room for a table for games, homework, or hobbies.

Setting up or decorating rooms so they're conducive to what we use them for involves several considerations. Is there enough light? Space? Are the things we need in that room stored so they're accessible? Are the furnishings and decor in line with both your family's style and the way you use the room?

Creating user-friendly rooms doesn't mean you have to go out and spend hundreds or thousands of dollars so you can drastically change each room in the house. Some small changes can make a big difference.

THE STATE OF THE ESTATE

At least once a year, it's a good idea to do a walk through your home, looking at all the rooms, and make decisions about whether you're using the room to optimal value for your current needs. Ask yourself the two basic questions. If you don't like the answers, make plans to make changes.

Start a home journal. Keep a notebook with a page or several pages devoted to every room of your house. A simple five-subject notebook with

> "My kitchen has never made the cover of *Good Housekeeping*. Although it's been the feature story in *Health Department Monthly* twice.
> —Martha Bolton

dividers and folder pockets is ideal. Jot down problems and possible solutions. "Shop" magazines or catalogs for solution ideas. Clip them and put them in the notebook so when you're ready to make changes you'll have a variety of solutions to choose from. Keep paint chips and fabric swatches in the folder pockets. As you complete projects, note the salient details in your notebook. Enter the names of painters, plumbers, and other resource people in the notes for the rooms you had them work in.

USER-FRIENDLY ROOMS MAKE A USER-FRIENDLY HOUSE

What room is getting you down? Where do the most family fights happen? Where do you, your spouse, or your children feel most frustrated because you can't find what you need when you need it? Whatever room that is—bathroom to garage, master bedroom to kitchen—it's probably the place to start.

A cautionary note: reorganizing all the rooms in your house in one day, weekend, or week is probably impossible and likely to increase rather than decrease stress. Nobody can handle that much (even positive) change at once. As you tackle each room you want to make more user-friendly, refer back to Sane Storage, pages 40 to 47, for more helpful ideas.

Kitchen

Times have changed. The kitchen's no longer just Mom's territory. It's the hub of the home. A lot of traffic flows through this little room—parents, kids, grandparents, neighbors, guests, and caretakers—so organization is essential. If your kitchen is really out of control, you'll need to take some time to rethink and reorganize. This investment will pay off and save you time in the long run. Enlist your family to help. If they help you get it in order, they'll be more likely to help keep it that way.

QUESTIONS TO CONSIDER

1. If you have small children, do you have a lower cabinet dedicated to plastic dishes for them? Do you have safety catches so they can't get into dangerous things? Are there items that need to be stored out of children's reach?

2. Are things you use every day stored where you can get at them? How high can you comfortably reach? Do you have a safe kitchen ladder or step stool to extend your reach?

3. Who cooks at your house and how often?

4. Are you right- or left-handed? Particularly short or tall? Do you or other family members have other physical needs or limitations? How might you rearrange your work areas, countertops, and storage spaces to accommodate your family's needs? (This could be something as simple as reversing the side of the sink the dish drainer is on.)

5. Do you like to stand or sit when you're working in the kitchen? If you're a sitter in a kitchen designed for a stander, you might consider something like a folding stool that you can get out easily. A more long-term alternative might be to build a work island at a sitter's level.

6. Do your kids do their homework in the kitchen? Can you devote a drawer or part of a shelf to storing paper, pencils, and the other supplies they regularly use? Or use TV trays for temporary workstations?

7. Do you shop in bulk and need a lot of storage space? Or do you buy a lot of fresh foods, in which case you need a lot of refrigerator space?

8. Can you reach cooking utensils without moving from the stove?

9. Are food cabinets well organized so items are as easy to find as possible—like when you're in the middle of a recipe and you need the vanilla?

10. Are table accessories—napkins, dinnerware, place mats, salt and pepper shakers—easily accessible to the dinner table?

If you are near your wit's end because you nearly always spend extra time looking for what you need in the kitchen, you might find it easier to apply the Take Five method (see page 35) to getting your kitchen into user-friendly, tip-top shape. If you have only a few minutes every day, or if you have toddlers or young children around who could get into big trouble if you tore the whole kitchen apart to reorganize it, this method works particularly well.

One cupboard at a time, one shelf at a time—begin with the one closest to the sink and work your way methodically around the kitchen. Take everything out of each cupboard. Clean the shelves. Replace only the items that you usually use from that cupboard, with the most frequently used at the front. (Either set the rest aside to be placed in another cupboard during another Take Five organization break or place them in a giveaway box.)

KITCHEN STORAGE TIPS

- Keep only the glasses you use regularly in prime storage space. Store glassware and cups upside down to prevent dust and discourage insects. Line them up in neat rows according to type or stack them if possible. Let younger kids organize their own lower cabinet for plastic cups and dishes.

- Store extraneous pots and pans, bowls, casseroles, and dishes in a high, seldom-used cabinet. Keep only items used at least weekly in prime storage.

- Store all pot lids in one place. Designate a deep drawer to stand them on their sides in order of size. Or get a pot-lid organizer, available in houseware and organizing stores.

- Install vertical dividers in a lower cabinet close to the oven to store cookie sheets and pizza pans.

- Use only clear glass or plastic containers for storing food in your refrigerator so you always know what you're saving.
- Hang kitchenware used daily on a high-tech wall grid in your favorite color. Store oversize utensils in a crock by the stove.
- Install wire or plastic sliding shelves, or use plastic vegetable bins to store items in the usually dead space under the sink. (Position shelves or bins so that you can get to the shutoff valve easily.) Hang a towel rack on the inside of the cabinet door for wet dishrags and gloves.
- Use lazy Susans on deep shelves or in corner cabinets.
- Hang a foil, wrap, and bag organizer inside a cabinet or pantry door.
- Use wall space for wall-mountable dispensers and portable appliances. Some coffeemakers, microwaves, and radios can be mounted underneath high cabinets.
- Install slide-out plastic drawers to simplify the retrieval of items at the back of deep base cabinets.
- Give away space-taking cookbooks you never use. Cut out favorite recipes and file them in inexpensive photo albums.
- Place a decorative hook on the wall above the kitchen sink so you can hang your watch on it when washing dishes.
- Store canned goods by category and with labels facing forward so you can see what's on hand at a glance.
- Keep regularly used seasonings and spices near the stove. Store others in a cool, dark place.

Smart Moves

- Bag your own groceries so you can put items together the way they go in your kitchen.
- Most foods store best in cool, dry places in a temperature of 40 to 60 degrees. Do not store food near heating ducts, furnaces, hot-water pipes, or other heat sources.
- Rotate food and supplies. Place new items behind old ones. If you buy in bulk, be sure to label all containers. Indicate the contents and date of purchase.
- Discard all bulged or leaking cans—without tasting the product.
- If you have partially used containers of the same items, check to see that they have approximately the same expiration dates, and then combine them.

KITCHEN CHAOS-REDUCTION IDEAS

- Save only five grocery bags at a time. They seem to multiply between the counter and refrigerator.
- So dishes won't be exposed to dust and grease, try to store them in cabinets with doors instead of on shelves.
- Keep silverware within arm's length of the dishwasher.
- Save search time by labeling the shelves in your freezer. Mine are labeled Breads and Quick Meals, Vegetables, Desserts and Beverages, and Meat.
- Number lids and bottoms of plastic storage tubs with a permanent marker so they're easy to match up.
- Keep all coffee-brewing supplies near the coffeemaker.
- Keep a measuring cup in the flour and sugar and a measuring spoon in the coffee.
- Use the inside of kitchen cabinet doors to post information such as kitchen measurements and favorite recipes.

- If you're going to make a big mess cooking, spread inexpensive butcher's paper over the counters. (This paper is also good to have around for kids' crafts.) Just wad it up and throw it away when you're finished.
- When a new appliance comes with extra packaged parts, write on the package what the parts belong to and store them in a parts box in the garage.
- Set your table straight from the dishwasher. When you keep it set, it's always ready.
- Designate a drawer for healthful snacks so kids can help themselves when hungry.

FIVE KITCHEN DECORATING DON'TS

1. Unless you like to clean constantly, don't have mirrored surfaces in your kitchen. Ditto glass-topped tables.

2. Don't choose grass cloth or flocked wallpapers for kitchen walls. They absorb grease, and they're extremely hard to clean.

3. Don't upholster kitchen chairs in light fabric. Choose washable, soil-hiding prints or vinyl. (Spray all fabrics with a protector like Scotchgard.)

4. Don't choose a light-colored floor that shows every bit of dirt.

5. Avoid tile floors on which glass breaks more easily, especially if you have younger children.

Bathroom

Maybe you always wanted to be in movies, but starring in *Murder by Mildew* is not what you had in mind. People who like to clean and maintain bathrooms are few and far between, and none of them live at my house. Therefore I am always looking for better ways to organize it and easier ways to clean it. Here are my best bathroom tips.

STORAGE

• Don't waste time searching for small scissors, tweezers, and clippers. Attach a long, straight magnet to the back of your medicine cabinet to hold these and other small metal objects.

• Use small plastic crates to store each person's personal bathroom items.

• Store bath toys in dishpans under the vanity, or put them in a mesh bag that hangs from the shower nozzle or the shower wall so they can drip-dry in the tub.

• Install hooks on the back of the door for hanging bathrobes and damp towels.

• Mount vinyl-coated wire racks on the inside of cabinet doors to hold bathroom items.

• Keep bathroom drawers neat with divided plastic silverware trays.

• Consider buying a wall-mounted hair dryer for easy access and storage.

• Store prescription medicines and over-the-counter remedies on higher shelves, in clearly labeled containers, out of the reach of small children. Go through them twice a year and discard expired items. I store mine in small plastic crates according to category: topical and skin medications; cold and flu medications; stomach and intestinal medications; and pain relievers.

USAGE

• Coordinate towels and washcloths; assign a color to each family member. This way everyone knows who left the wet one in the middle of the floor, and how many each person is using at one time.

• Install a paper-cup dispenser.

• Take bubble baths or use water softeners instead of bath oil, which leaves a ring. Encourage kids to swish their hands and feet around the water line to loosen bathtub ring before they let the water out.

- Install a handheld showerhead so you can rinse the tub when you're finished.
- Turn on the exhaust fan when taking a shower to draw out excess moisture. You'll have less mildew.

CLEANING

- When cleaning shower walls, run the shower water at the hottest temperature before you start. The steam will loosen dirt before you scrub it off.
- Clean soapy film from shower doors with a soft cloth dipped in baby oil.
- Keep the shower curtain closed so it won't grow mold in its folds.
- Clean vinyl shower curtains in your washing machine. Use warm, soapy water and three bath towels. Take the shower curtain out before the spin cycle.
- Keep a toilet brush in a caddy next to the toilet. Train family members to give it a frequent swish.
- Quick-clean your toilet by dropping in several denture-cleaner tablets. When they've finished bubbling, swish with a toilet brush and flush. Or treat your toilet weekly to an overnight soaking with white vinegar.
- Spray your soap dish with vegetable cooking spray. Soap gunk will come off easier. Better still, use liquid soap in a pump dispenser for hand-washing and showers—no soap slime to clean.
- Keep a sponge on a vented soap dish next to the sink.

> When using heavy-duty cleaners in the bathroom, be sure to open a window or turn on the exhaust fan.

> Rubbing alcohol is a good mirror cleaner and removes hair-spray residue especially well. Dilute with water, one part alcohol to three parts water.

> "When friends enter a home, they sense its personality and character, the family's style of living—these elements make a house come alive with a sense of identity, a sense of energy, enthusiasm, and warmth, declaring, this is who we are; this is how we live."
>
> —Ralph Lauren

Ask family members to wipe the sink after using.

• Keep a box of disposable rubber gloves underneath the bathroom sink for unpleasant cleaning tasks.

Living Area

Family room, living room, den— these are the rooms that set the tone for your family life. Not only for who you are together in your leisure time, but also for how you welcome people into your home.

After assessing your personal taste and style, the ages of your children, and the condition of your family budget, you can arrange living areas that suit your family and make your home a good place to be.

Peruse the following list of tips and facts with your own living areas in mind.

• For most of the people most of the time, considering use and budget, one fundamental principle applies: less is more. Less cluttered rooms seem larger and invite people into them.

• When considering furniture arrangement, start with the focal point of your room—like a fireplace or tall piece of furniture—and plan seating from that point.

• When choosing upholstered furniture, stay away from solid dark and solid light colors. Dark colors show every speck of lint, dust, and pet hair; light colors show spills and dirt. If you prefer solid-color fabrics, choose nubby textures that hide soil. It's a good idea to have furniture sprayed with a professional protective coating that repels spills.

• For durability, choose upholstery fabrics with a tight weave. If the fabric has a pattern, make sure it is woven in rather than printed on the surface of the fabric. It will last longer.

- One of the most important pieces of furniture is a sofa. Shop around and sit on a lot of them before you buy.

- For each chair and sofa, there should be a table or surface where you can put down a book or drink.

- Arrange lighting so you can read in all seating areas in your family room. Use three-way bulbs and install dimmer switches for flexible lighting.

- If you have a coffee table in front of your sofa, place it about thirteen inches in front of the sofa and allow approximately nineteen inches at either end so people can move easily around it. If you have small children, avoid a glass coffee table or one with sharp corners.

- End tables don't have to match, but they should be about the same height—from twenty-six to thirty inches. A one-inch difference is okay.

- Paint is usually better than wallpaper for a family room. You can hang paintings, photographs, and quilts without a distracting background.

- Behind a bookcase store a folded table you can easily pull out and set up for board games, cards, or jigsaw puzzles.

- Use Velcro tape to attach the remote to the side of the TV.

- If you have small children, keep handy an attractive basket with a lid to hold a few favorite toys in this area. (Note: This should be a room that you, your spouse, and your children can claim as a personal retreat—where you can catch a quiet moment, nap, read, play games, as well as watch TV. If toys are strewn everywhere, it's not inviting. Use the basket and set some limits on how many toys can be out at one time.)

- For children, teens, and adults who like to sit or lie on the floor, provide several twenty-four-inch square pillows covered with colorful, durable fabric. They can be spread in front of the TV or fireplace. They provide great extra

> To find out how intense a color will look in a room, look at the inside of the paint can. The shadows inside the can will give an idea of the hue's effect on a room.

seating for spryer guests in a crowded room. And when they're not in use they can be stacked in an otherwise unused corner.

• Group two chairs around a table with a shelf under it (to hold books in process) and a good, bright reading lamp on top of it. A designated reading area won't make people read, but they're more likely to if they have a comfortable spot to do it in. (Note: This area could be near your pillow corner. Some kids love to sprawl to read.) Consider designating a reading time, maybe not every day, but on a regular basis, when the family gathers in this corner, each to read his or her own book.

Bedrooms

Our bedrooms are more than the places where we are unconscious for six to eight hours a day. They are also our personal sanctuaries, where we feel and contemplate the joys and sorrows of life. Whether you're married or single, you deserve a bedroom that encourages rest on every level: physical, emotional, mental, and spiritual. In short, this should be one of the most user-friendly rooms in the house.

How friendly is your bedroom currently? What do you see when you first wake up? Is it a pile of clothes awaiting cleaning or ironing? Stacks of books that belong in a bookcase? A closet that looks like it exploded? And how restful is the room, not just the bed, as a whole? Do you get stressed looking in the closet for an outfit? Have you slept well because it's a quiet room, or were you bothered all night by a flapping shutter? Is the room tastefully decorated, or is it stress-inducing "unfinished until further notice"?

Don't neglect the nest of the home.

FEATHERING THE NEST: THINK INTIMATE. When we hear the word *intimacy*, we usually think of two things—physical closeness and emotional openness. Intimacy, however, involves more than those. It encompasses our entire being—mind, emotions, body, and spirit. So as you make your master bedroom a friendly place to be, think in those terms. Maybe that means a small bookcase for favorite books and magazines, or a comfortable chair and ottoman, with a good reading light on a table nearby. Or if you don't have room

> If you or your husband likes to watch TV in bed, but the other wants to go to sleep, keep earphones that work with your television in the bedroom.

for a chair and table, perhaps two bolster pillows to prop up against in bed and wall-mounted lights. Maybe each of you needs a corner devoted to reading or writing. For instant romantic atmosphere, install a dimmer switch to the overhead light. To ensure occasional privacy, attach a working lock on your bedroom door.

Work with your emotions instead of against them by considering what colors soothe you. Pastels work well for bedroom walls. Are there any eyesores that bother you every time you walk into the room? Do something about them. The bedroom is an ideal place for favorite family photographs and other sentimental decor.

Soothe your body by getting the most comfort from your sheets. One hundred percent cotton, 300-thread-count sheets are an investment, but in my mind, they're worth it. The bargain sheets might not cost as much money, but they'll cost you sleep because they're scratchy. Plus, sheets with high thread count last longer. (We had one set last for fifteen years.) Your choice of mattress and pillows deserves the same amount of thought. After all, we spend a third of our lives in bed.

Making Your Closet Work for You

- Hang work clothes, play clothes, and dressy clothes in their respective category, giving prime placement to the kind of clothes you wear most often. Group the same types of clothing within each category: shirts with shirts, skirts with skirts, and so on.
- If you have trouble remembering what goes with what, post a list of possible outfits, including accessories, on the inside of your closet door.
- Good lighting is important when selecting clothes. Make your closet as bright as possible.
- Don't keep wrong-size, -color or -style clothes—or items with permanent stains or irreparable tears—in your closet or in your house. Give or throw them away. (See Eliminate and Concentrate, page 30.)
- Keep clothes to be mended in a designated place.
- Remove all wire hangers and donate them to the dry cleaners. Replace with plastic tubular hangers. They don't misshape clothes or create rust marks, and they space garments nicely.
- Store off-season clothes in another closet or trunk, or put a sheet around them and hang in the back of your closet.
- Store shoes in transparent boxes on a shelf above the clothing rod. Roll up magazines and put them in boots to store in an upright position.
- Use a clear shoe-organizer hanger to store socks, hosiery, shoulder pads, small purses, gloves, etc.
- Have one clear plastic box or a basket for unmatched socks you still have hope for. Keep another box for hose with runs that you can still wear under pants. (Avoid frustration by keeping them separate from good hose.)
- Hang a mesh laundry bag with a tie for dirty hose and delicate lingerie. Toss it into the washer with other clothes.
- Use plastic shower-curtain hooks to hang belts.
- Install a men's tie or belt rack to hang leotards and lingerie.
- Keep a laundry bag in your closet for clothes to go to the dry cleaners.

The Kids' Part of the Castle

Kids' bedrooms are their very own worlds, in which they wind up, wind down, play, learn, dream, create, and express who they are. Kids value their space and their stuff. They want to feel "at home" in their room when they're there, which means they don't want expensive bedspreads and furniture they can't play and hang out on. And they want to be proud of their room when their friends visit.

- Use rolling plastic containers to store toys under the bed or in a closet.
- Buy a chest or use a footlocker to store odd-sized toys. These items do double duty when it's time to pack your child's things for camp or college.
- Remember that children don't care if their room has expensive appointments. A wall covered in butcher paper and some colorful markers will mean more than walls covered in fancy wallpaper.
- Don't put a crib on an exterior wall, since it is the coldest wall in the room.
- Frame your child's artwork in inexpensive, clear plastic frames to hang on the walls.
- Consider installing ceiling track lights that can be targeted at study and play zones.
- If your kids share a closet, paint each half of the rod a different color to prevent bickering.
- Since cleaning does not come naturally to many children, make it as easy as possible by creating storage areas that they can reach.
- Keep fragile toys and old books on a top shelf so they are on display but won't be damaged.
- Hang a mirror at your child's eye level.
- Use comforters instead of bedspreads on the beds. They'll be easier to make up.
- Sheets—especially those with favorite characters—can be a big

deal to a child. Let your child pick them out, even if they cost a little more money.

• Put glow-in-the-dark stars on the ceiling of your child's room for a wonderful effect when the lights are out.

• Make sure your children's books are easily accessible. Help them arrange their books by topic or author so they'll have a sense of pride and ownership in a growing library.

• Provide some low shelves for your child to display personal treasures.

• Be sure to cover electrical outlets with outlet covers or plugs so your child cannot poke anything into the sockets.

• Position light switches so your child can reach them easily. Use paint pens to personalize the cover plate with your child's name.

• Make sure furniture is stable and there is no possibility of pulling over tall dressers, shelves, or stacked items.

• Tape pictures on a preschooler's dresser drawers of whatever is in it—underwear, shorts, socks, jeans, and shirts. This way your child won't have to go through drawers, throwing clothes on the floor, in search of an item to put on.

• Paint a small table and chairs in primary colors. Paint your child's name on the top of the table or the seats of the chairs. (Use only non-toxic paint.)

• Designate a place in the room where your child can keep a creative (and oftentimes messy) project going.

• Don't allow television in your children's bedrooms. This promotes isolation from family activities.

Home Office

Increasingly, businesspeople are finding ways to work from home. If you're one of the fortunate folks for whom this ideal is possible, consider these issues to make this space user-friendly.

• Do you want to look out a window? Do you want to look out into the room or can you work with your back to the door?

• Where will you put the telephone? Will you need to reach the file cabinet or bookcase while you're on the phone?

• Will you have an answering machine, fax, and modem on separate phone lines from your residential one?

• Do you have enough electrical outlets? Does your office equipment require a dedicated outlet?

• Do you have enough space to comfortably house all the equipment you'll need? (It's easy to overlook all the machines you're accustomed to using at the office.)

• If you hire employees, is there space for them?

Here's a list of equipment to make your home office user-friendly:

EQUIPMENT	SUPPLIES	FURNITURE
Computer with modem	Envelopes, letter and legal size	Desk with drawers
Laser printer	Stationery	Desk lamp
Copier	Large manila envelopes	Filing cabinet
Answering machine	Stamps	Chair
Fax machine	Paper: printer paper, fax paper, and notepads	Good lighting
Telephone		Bookshelves
Calculator		
Tickler file holder	Sticky notes	
Bulletin board	Pens and pencils	
Wastebasket	Correction fluid	
Clock	Eraser	
Dictionary and synonym finder	Transparent tape	
	Felt-tip pens	

EQUIPMENT	SUPPLIES
Pencil sharpener	Highlighter pens
Rolodex	Paper clips, large
Stapler and staples	and small
Staple remover	Colored file folders
Scissors	Hanging file folders
Stackable trays	
Letter opener	

Garage

On a sunny day, take everything out of your garage. If you have time, paint the walls a light color. If your floor is badly soiled, saturate grease and oil spots with paint thinner. Then cover the soiled areas with cat litter or sawdust. Sweep it away the next day, then paint it with porch paint. This makes a concrete floor easier to clean. Then put things back in the garage in a manner that makes sense to you. Use these tips to help you organize.

• Install utility shelves on one wall for storing things like gardening supplies, paint, and auto-maintenance supplies. (Be sure to put poisonous products on a high shelf.) Assign a shelf to each family member for boots and equipment.

• Install Peg-Board for hanging hand tools. Outline the silhouettes of tools on the Peg-Board with a permanent marker so they'll be easy to replace after use. Paint a bright-colored stripe on the handles of your tools so when they're borrowed it's easy for the borrower to remember they're yours.

• Install plenty of hooks on walls for shovels, rakes, and other tools. Screw some towel racks into walls to hold long poles, lumber, and other tall items that might topple.

• Use an old golf bag and pull cart to haul tools when doing yard work. The pockets are ideal for holding small tools and gloves. The golf bag can also double as a storage place.

• String a hammock along a wall to hold sports equipment and light-weight items.

• Store nails, screws, and bolts in jars or plastic tubs, and label the containers.

• Keep similar-size nuts and washers on large key rings or shower-curtain rings with latches that are easy to open and close.

• Store rarely used items such as long ladders and snow shovels on rafters.

• Store paintbrushes in coffee cans, brush side up.

• Clip loose sheets of sandpaper to a clipboard and hang it from a wall hook.

• Store single-edged razor blades in a block of Styrofoam. (Keep up high if you have small children.)

• Attach a secondhand school locker to a post in your garage for extra storage.

• Provide sturdy storage for all kinds of tools and supplies with old four-drawer metal file cabinets.

• Attach the spine from a three-ring notebook horizontally on the garage wall. You'll have three hooks for extra keys.

• Keep a wastebasket on the driver's side of the garage so car debris can easily be thrown away.

• Paint parking spaces for bikes, wagons, scooters, and mowers. (Let your kids take turns being Garage Police and collecting fines when equipment is not parked correctly.)

• Use larger hooks to hang bicycles from the rafters.

• Use large plastic tubs or trash cans with lids for potting soils, compost materials, fertilizers, etc.

GARAGE SAFETY INSPECTION

1. Is the circuit-breaker box well marked?
2. Are electrical outlets covered?
3. Are cabinets containing toxic chemicals locked?
4. Is the fire extinguisher easily accessible?
5. Are windows and doors secured against break-ins?
6. Are there signs of rodent activity?
7. Are lawn mowers and other cutting machines in good repair with necessary guards?
8. Are products that have safety packaging properly closed?
9. Is gasoline stored in approved, clearly labeled containers?
10. Is scrap wood, sawdust, or other waste lying around on the garage floor?
11. Are solvents and paints in sealed and labeled metal containers and stored away from heat sources, such as your furnace or water heater?
12. Do any electrical power tools have frayed cords or bad plugs?
13. Are electrical power tools unplugged and stored when not in use?
14. Is there adequate ventilation so you can rid the area of harmful vapors or dust that might form during a project?

Control Central

Every Family Manager deals with countless daily details and responsibilities in each department. The fundamental key to making and implementing those decisions well is having a home management base or Control Central. By setting up your own Control Central, you'll better manage your time and schedule, which in turn will help you manage your home and family more efficiently. Here's how.

• Choose a smart location. It should be central, with a place where messages can be posted. Many families run their homes from the front of the refrigerator. If you don't have room in the kitchen, you can use a corner of the family room or a bedroom, a hallway, or the space under a staircase. One Family Manager turned a centrally located closet into her Control Central. She had a phone jack installed, created a desk from an old door and two filing cabinets, and made a big bulletin board out of foam board to hang on the wall above the desk.

• Hang a family calendar, a place from which to plan your daily activities. At my Control Central, I keep a big calendar on which everyone writes his activities, appointments, and important dates, plus pads of paper for my daily to-do lists. I also have a smaller pad for phone messages.

• Store commercial phone books and your Family Yellow Pages here.

Family Yellow Pages

Buy a one-inch three-ring binder, a package of alphabetical tabbed dividers, and some notebook paper to put behind each divider. Write the names, addresses, phone and fax numbers, and other pertinent information for each person or company vital to your family on the appropriate page. Keep the page containing emergency numbers in front. Use this list to help you decide which numbers would be helpful in your family's personal yellow pages.

Accountant	Cleaners
Air-Conditioning Service	Decorator
Alarm Company	Delicatessen
Appliance Repair	Dentist
Attorney	Dressmaker/Tailor
Auto Repair	Electrician
Babysitters	Exercise Class
Bakery	Exterminator
Banks	Electric Company
Cable Company	Firewood
Carpenter	Florist
Carpet Cleaning Service	Furnace Maintenance and Repair

Church
Gas Company
Golf Club
Grocery Store
Hairdresser
Handyman
Hardware Store
Health Club
Hospitals
Housekeeper
Kennel
Landscape Contractor
Lawn Maintenance
Library
Movers
Neighbors
Newspaper Delivery
Nursery (child care)
Painter
Party Supplies and Rentals
Photographer
Physicians

Furniture Refinishing and Repair
Piano Tuner
Plumber
Police
Post Office
Printer
Real Estate Agent
Restaurants (for reservations and
   home delivery)
Service Stations
Shoe Repair
Stockbroker
Swimming Pool Service
Synagogue
Telephone Company
Television Repair
Tennis Courts
Travel Agent
Upholsterer
Vacuum Cleaner Repair
Veterinarian
Wallpaper Hanger

Every time you look up a number in the phone book that you think you might call again, add it to your Family Yellow Pages.

- Stock a desk or a countertop where you can work. If you work on the countertop, use a plastic shoebox to hold pens, pencils, notepads, and other desk supplies. Store it in a kitchen cupboard when not in use.
- Establish a "safe place" for those pieces of paper everybody needs and everybody loses (for example, permission slips for kids' school field trips). When my kids were younger, I had three different-color file fold-

ers that stood in a tickler file holder on the counter. That's where each boy knew to put important papers and permission slips. Years later, with two of them out of the nest, I still keep three files, one for each of them, to organize any correspondence or information.

Control Central won't help you make decisions and keep track of details on a daily basis if you don't use it on a daily basis. Once you've set up your space to suit your needs, the next step is to work with your family so Control Central works for all of you.

Family members need to understand, first and foremost, that everyone, not just Mom, has responsibility for managing the family. You can use a family meeting to introduce your Control Central to your team members. (See Ten Tips for Successful Family Meetings, page 23.) Or you can take your team members on a "tour" of the new Control Central. Explain where they're supposed to put phone messages. If you need to, reiterate what constitutes a good message: the person's name, the time and reason for the call, whether or not the message needs a call back, and if so, what are some convenient times to reach that person.

A chore list is part of my Control Central, since I'm firmly committed to everyone in the family being part of the team that helps run our home. I strongly recommend this. A central chore list has the advantage of being a reminder to everybody, potentially minimizing the "nag factor." Chore lists can be weekly to-do lists, with space for unusual or periodic chores at the bottom. They can include a place for the designated team member to check off or initial once the chore is done.

Once you've instituted Control Central, don't give up just because there are one or two glitches. All new systems take time to learn and implement. Besides, nobody's perfect. That's why we need Control Central.

Ways and Means

Adapt these guidelines for Control Central to meet your family's needs:

- *Write* your commitments on the big family calendar—parties, appointments, etc.
- *Contact* Mom or Dad about details—if you need a ride, if you need to take a gift, if you need to pick up anyone else—by writing a note, if you're old enough.
- *Tack* all phone messages on the bulletin board at Control Central. Don't throw them on top of the desk.
- *Post* invitations and other pertinent items on the bulletin board.
- *File* your important papers in your special folder (assign one to each child) so Mom knows where to find them.
- *Leave* supplies in this area.
- *Alert* your Family Manager (a.k.a. Mom) if you see you're running low on anything you need—toiletries, school supplies, groceries, whatever. Write it down on Mom's to-buy list.
- *Check* with Control Central and a parent before committing anyone's time for anything.
- *Communicate,* especially about conflicts in schedules or preferences in activities. Do not make Control Central what it is not: a substitute for talking to each other.
- *Commit* as a family to keeping Control Central as neat as possible.

File Systems

Set up a filing system. Using the seven Family Manager departments is an easy way to categorize the information you need to track.

Home and Property
  Decorating ideas
  Appliance warranties
  Gardening information

Auto info
Dream house: pictures and plans
Household inventory list
Appraisals
Costs and receipts of all major home improvements, additions, and
  repairs
(These documents can help you reduce your taxes if you sell the
house at a profit in the future.)

Food
Recipes
Party menus
Nutritional information
Takeout menus
Substitution ideas

Family and Friends
(Each person in your family should have his or her own current file and
to-be-saved file.)
Birth certificates
Immunization records
Résumés
School history
Hobbies
Prescriptions for eyeglasses and contacts
Pet records

Finances
Banking: checking and savings
Loans
Mortgage or rental papers
Insurance
Receipts
Tax information
Investments

Organizations to which you pay annual dues
Retirement information

Special Projects
Vacation information
Maps and tourist info
Travel
Birthday parties
Holiday ideas
Garage-sale research; what did and didn't work at the last one
you held

Time and Scheduling
Last year's calendar pages (in case you need to look something up)
Time-management information

Personal
Beauty and wardrobe information
Weight loss
Personal interests
Personal medical records

USER-FRIENDLY WORK CENTERS MAKE WORK EASIER

Because work centers collect all the necessary items for a task in one place, we eliminate hunting and become superefficient. Work centers also help abolish clutter, make sensible storage, and keep you working smarter, not harder. Here are some ideas for work centers to create at your home:

• Designate a drawer or cabinet for a Gift/Wrapping Center. Store everything you need for wrapping. Keep a few generic gifts for adults and children there, too. Stock with blank cards and cards for birthdays, anniversaries, holidays, graduations, engagements, weddings, babies, confirmations, bar/bat mitzvahs, deaths, and retirements.

• Create a Sewing Center with a sewing chair and a basket for family members to put to-be-mended clothes in. Keep quick-fix mending supplies on hand—iron-on matches, fusible bonding, and fabric glue. Help buttons stay on longer by coating the center of each one with clear nail polish.

• Set up a Bill-Paying Center where you keep pens, stamps, envelopes, return-address labels, a calculator, and a basket for bills.

THAT'S WHAT PAPER IS FOR
Don't try to keep records in your head. You've got too much to remember already! Write down appointments on your family calendar. Keep notepads and pens in convenient locations, like by each phone and on your nightstand. But don't let your record- and information-keeping become paper clutter. Post it on a bulletin board near your Control Central, then act on it, file it, or toss it ASAP.

• Set up a Mail Center—a place to sort your mail every day. Keep a trash can close by so you can toss junk mail as you sort. Buy cardboard magazine storage boxes at an office-supply store. Write each family member's name on a box and label one for bills, another for magazines and catalogs. Especially in smaller homes, the Mail Center and Bill-Paying Center might be in one place, maybe even sharing a desk with Control Central.

• Create Kitchen Work Centers where you perform specific tasks like cleaning, chopping, cooking, and making lunches. Each center revolves around a major appliance, some storage space, and a work surface. Think of how you can store equipment and food near the center where they'll be used—pots and pans near the stove, baking goods and utensils near the mixer, dishes near the dishwasher.

• Create a Laundry Center. Have everything you need in one place:

detergent, bleach, stain remover, presoak, fabric softener, soap for hand-washables, starch, zipper mesh bag for delicates, measuring cup, old toothbrush for stubborn stains, hangers, laundry baskets, and ironing supplies.

Laundry Tips

- Keep a stain-removal stick in the bathroom so family members can rub it on stains before putting clothes in the hamper.
- Wash all parts of an outfit at the same time. If they're going to fade, at least they'll fade evenly.
- Write down and post directions near your washing machine on how to wash different types of clothing so family members will know.
- Don't use fabric softener every time you wash towels. They'll lose their absorbency.
- Cut down on ironing time by using fabric softener and not overloading permanent-press clothes in the dryer. Start ironing garments that require lowest heat and work up to the ones that require a hot iron. It takes less time for an iron to heat up than it does for it to cool down.

On an average, a family of four does two tons of laundry each year. In my mind, that's reason enough for family members to be responsible for their own laundry as soon as they can reach the dials.

"I'm working to improve my methods, and every hour I save is an hour added to my life."
—Ayn Rand

THREE

Seven Days
a Week

"The forty-hour week has no charm for me. I'm looking for a forty-hour day."
                                          —Nicholas Murray Butler

Unlike other "businesses," the family never shuts down. As the Family Manager, you know that much of what goes on in your home—productivity, morale, organization—depends upon you. The plain truth is, you set the tone for the family. Is it chaotic? Relaxed? Uninspiring? Fun? What are mornings like at your house? What goes on at night? What about afternoons and weekends?

Our pace and routines are not always the same, but how we manage each of those seven days makes all the difference in what kind of attitude reigns at our house. Creating morning, afternoon, and evening routines—plans for daily housework and weekly maintenance tasks, laundry, meals, saving money, communication between family members, family fitness, taking care of ourselves (even God rested on the seventh day)—are critical to our family's peace of mind and evenness of spirit.

> When we see the job of running our home and family from the perspective of a true manager, life gets immeasurably better, and easier—for everyone.

> The key: deciding what the truly important things are. But remember, organization is a daily business.

Organization Is a Daily Word

Before I ran my home and family like a manager with seven departments to oversee, I regularly felt overwhelmed. I'd wake up in the morning thinking, *I've got so much to do, I don't know where to start.* Lots of days, going back to bed sounded like my best option, but with preschoolers tugging on my arm, a dog barking for its breakfast, and a husband searching for his other navy sock, I knew I had to find a way to get a handle on my life. At that point life seemed like a knotty ball of yarn, an end sticking out here, a snarl there. I couldn't follow any of it through to completion.

But when I began to see my tasks and responsibilities through the eyes of a manager, I was no longer tempted to ignore the alarm clock and bury my head under a pillow. I had a plan. I got up every morning with a clearer view of what needed to be accomplished. While the number of tasks can still produce anxiety at times, I now always have a strategy for getting the most important things done.

DAILY HIT LIST

Every day of my life I make a to-do list. I call it my Hit List. In fact, I made daily lists before I began looking at myself as a Family Manager. Some of them were pages long. In that respect, and given the fact that I rarely accomplished all that I set out to do, they were more like outlines for a novel than anything else. At the end of almost any day, what I wanted was a list with items crossed off and a sense of completion, accomplishment, and even progress; what I had was frustration.

Now I divide my daily to-dos into departments. The simple act of organizing what needs to be

> "Seize the day." —Horace

Daily Hit List

Date:
6-10

Home and Property
vacuum
call plumber
pick up dry cleaning
buy a shower
curtain for
boys' bath

Food
Dinner: Bill—Grill burgers
Joel to wholesale club—make a list

Time and Scheduling
Make dental appt. for James
Pick up tennis carpool at 5:30
Ask Bill what day he's leaving town

Finances
Pay bills
Call about water bill—why so high?

Friends and Family
James—get camp physical after
     school
Bathe dogs
Send birthday card
to Patti

Special Projects
Research beach options for vacation
Reserve room for Mom & Dad's 50th
     anniversary party

Personal
Work out
Hair appointment—8:30
Call Cynthia—set a date for girls' trip

Notes & Messages

Joel—David
called
James—Richard
called

James—please
bathe dogs

Groceries:
Milk
Plastic wrap
cereal
vanilla

If you are regularly tempted to be a daily member of the Let's-Bag-It-and-Go-Back-to-Bed Club, I suggest you try sorting your jobs by department and asking yourself three little questions every morning:

WHAT SHOULD I . . .
 do?
 delegate?
 delete?

done by category allows me to weigh the importance of various tasks and establish priorities. For example, if I know no one's coming to visit, I might decide vacuuming the living room is a lower priority than doing my weekly shopping because if I don't, I know that we're going to be out of milk, cereal, and coffee. (The latter makes breakfast conversation more like the reading of a criminal indictment than a pleasant interlude.) In fact, over a period of time, I've learned to balance my daily to-dos so that a big task like the weekly cleanup and the grocery shopping do not appear on the same day.

The Three Ds: An Integral Part of Every Family Manager's Daily Hit List

DO: Every day, I think about and list everything that needs to be done—for starters, putting food on the table, gas in the car, and money in the bank. On most days it's a pretty substantial list.

DELEGATE: Then I ask myself, "What can I delegate?" If it's laundry day, whose turn is it to fold the clothes as they come out of the dryer? Can I get my teenager to drop off the bank deposit on his way to baseball practice? Is there an able-bodied person around who can run the vacuum cleaner?

Post delegated chores so everyone knows who is responsible for what. When our kids were young we used a chore chart. As they got older, each had his own list of responsibilities. On family cleanup day we had a big list of jobs with the responsible person's name beside each job.

Remember to delegate according to age, skills, and availability, not according to gender. "Women's work" went out with cotton house dresses with matching aprons. At our house, the men can cook, sew, and clean just as well as I can (sometimes better). And I can mow the yard, wash my car, and use a screwdriver. It's vital to realize that when you delegate chores to kids, you aren't just getting some help, you're helping the children grow into responsible, capable human beings.

DELETE: Once I've delegated everything I can, I look at what's left. Are there some items on my list that really don't need doing? Do I really have to make muffins from scratch? Can I help my neighbor choose fabric for curtains next weekend instead of today? Even the busiest of us— *especially* the busiest of us—need to look for things we're doing that simply don't need to be done as frequently as we're doing them.

Might you have a saner day if you let some truly unnecessary things go? Managing the daily affairs of your home and family is a matter of priorities—deciding what really matters to you and your family based on the quality of life you desire and the values you want your children to embrace. Knowing your priorities means knowing what you want to give time, emphasis, and care to in your life.

> "Selectivity—the determination to choose what we will attempt to get done and what we won't—is the only way out of the panic that excessive demands on our time can create."   —Andrew S. Grove

---

Really Bad Reasons Why
We Don't Delegate and Delete

- We don't like to admit we can't do it all.
- We know how to do what needs to be done.
- We see a potential crisis on the horizon we think we can forestall.
- We don't like to ask for help.
- We don't like to let people down.
- We like to be known as someone who knows how to get a job done, and get it done well.
- We care about the person, project, or goal that is making demands on our time, even though the request doesn't fit with our priorities.

Try It, I Think You'll Like It

Commit to a week's worth of organizing your to-do list by department. Use the list as a "best-case-scenario" tool—that is, write down everything you think needs to be done to ensure the overall smooth functioning of your home. Don't be surprised if the list seems impossibly long. Don't panic. Remember, Superwoman doesn't live at your house.

Give it your best shot: apply the Three Ds, and see what happens.

All of us have numerous responsibilities, some fun and meaningful, some mundane and monotonous. The priorities you select—the goals that are really important to you and your family—and the way you choose to view time—as a commodity you use, not just spend—will help you make decisions. Learning what tasks to do, to delegate, and to delete will revolutionize your life.

> "Learn to use ten minutes intelligently. It will pay you huge dividends."
> —William A. Irwin

Your Time Is Valuable

We can learn a lesson from attorneys. We have many lawyer friends and we've heard lots of jokes about their billable hours. Whatever your attitude about lawyers, the way they see their time, tasks, and expertise—as very valuable—is the way we should look at our own time, tasks, and expertise. When you view your time as a commodity, like money, you can look at your days and discern whether you spent too much in one area.

Did you lose an hour at the grocery store because you went at a high-traffic time of day? Did you talk too long on the phone with that friend who bends your ear about her problems when you really needed to spend time with your child? If you have trouble deciding what to delegate, ask yourself, "What difference will it make if I do this—or don't do that? Whose life will it affect? Will doing this meet a priority?"

Time adds up, 24 hours, 1,440 minutes, 84,600 seconds a day, whether we use it or not. A little action now can add up to a big result at the end of the day. Take advantage of a lull to make a phone call, to outline a project, to plan ahead. First we make the little decisions, then we take the little actions, and then things add up to make our homes a better place to be.

Prescription for Procrastinators

At times we all need a jump-start to get us going or to keep us going. Try one or two of these ideas to help you accomplish a task you've been dreading.

1. Gear up the night before. If you plan to tackle a project one morning, set out the supplies or tools you'll need and the clothes you'll wear.

2. Go to bed a little earlier than usual so you'll wake up refreshed and ready to go.

3. Speed up your metabolism. Before starting the task, take a brisk, twenty-minute walk.

4. Put on some peppy music that makes you want to move.

5. Buy a little something to make the task more pleasant. If you dread spending a day in the kitchen cooking and freezing a week's worth of meals, buy yourself a cheery apron or a new pot you've had your eye on.

6. Ask a friend or family member to monitor your progress and encourage you along the way.

7. Fix yourself a treat to keep you going. On attic clean-out day, put a plate of enticing fruit on a counter or table near the door leading outside to your garbage cans. When you travel to and from the attic, you can grab a bite.

8. Post inspirational quotes in your work area. Read them when your motivation starts to wane.

9. Decide beforehand how you will reward yourself when you complete the job.

10. Give yourself the freedom to stop and rest if you need to.

11. Stop and pat yourself on the back when you finish a segment of the task. If you have six drawers to clean out, congratulate yourself each time you conquer one.

12. Ask someone you enjoy to help you out with the job.

13. Listen to a motivational tape.

14. Start a fifteen-minute rule. Spend fifteen minutes every day on something you've been procrastinating about. Before you know it, you'll have the dreaded task licked.

15. Visualize how you will benefit from finishing.

> "Nothing is so fatiguing as the hanging on of an uncompleted task."   —William James

Top Ten Time Wasters

1. Whining about how little time you have
2. Dwelling on failures you can't do anything about
3. Nervous snacking
4. Perfectionism
5. Procrastination
6. Not having a plan
7. Answering phone calls you don't want to take
8. Nagging family members
9. Not delegating something that could be delegated
10. Television

DOZENS OF WAYS TO MANAGE SMARTER AND FASTER: SAVE TIME AND ENERGY IN EVERY DEPARTMENT

All businesses, even those that aren't open seven days a week, twenty-four hours a day, have to figure out how to conduct their daily business in an efficient, sensible way. Below are some tried-and-true ways to make family management more efficient and enjoyable on a daily basis.

Read through this list of actions and ideas with a pencil in hand. Make check marks by the ones that might work for you and your family. As you read, keep in mind the areas of stress in your family's daily schedule.

TIME AND SCHEDULING

1. Turn on your answering machine fifteen minutes before you need to be out the door. That way, if any last-minute calls come in while you're getting ready, you won't be delayed.

2. Read magazines with scissors in hand to clip articles. Put them in a to-read plastic pocket folder and keep it in your car. Designate your in-car waiting time as time to catch up on reading.

3. Keep a map of your city in the glove box of your car. No need to waste time being lost.

4. Create forms instead of writing the same information over and over. Make standard procedure forms for babysitters, medical emergency releases, lists for the grocery store (make the list according to the way things are arranged in your store), the discount store, the drugstore, the office-supply store, and the health-food store.

Add Time by Spending Less . . . on the Phone

We can't live without the telephone, nor would we want to. But if we're not careful, the telephone can rob us of a lot of precious time we can ill afford to lose. Here are simple ways to use telephone time wisely.

- Call service businesses on Thursdays or Fridays. You'll get faster service. Their busiest days are usually Monday and Tuesday.
- Call during slower times. The busiest phone time for service businesses are from 10 A.M. to 2 P.M. and from 5:30 to 7:30 P.M.
- Before you make a call, ask yourself: "How much time is this worth?" Set a limit before you dial, and keep a watch, clock, or timer handy.
- Eliminate phone tag. If you must leave a message, make it detailed. Give not only your name and number but why you called and when you can be reached.
- If you can't hold when you're asked to, say so.
- Keep a project by the phone so you can work while talking.
- Break the "I have to answer the phone" habit. Let your answering machine or voice-mail service answer it. Then return the call when it's convenient for you.
- Cut solicitation calls short. Say, "Thank you for calling, but I'm not interested." Ask them to take your name off their list.
- Gently guide nonstop talkers to the point. Whether it's your sister, a friend, or a business associate, you can make conversations shorter by:
  a. Saying, "I really want to give you my full attention, but right now is not a good time for me. Let's schedule a time when I can call you back."

b. Setting limits right away. "Mom, I have only five minutes to talk."

c. Asking questions. Direct and specific questions will get direct answers and can steer the conversation your way.

d. Nicely interrupting. Use the person's name and ask a question, or quickly summarize what he or she has been saying. If the talker is rambling, this will usually get him or her to stop and focus.

- Call long-winded friends just before lunch or at the end of the day.
- Set aside a certain time of day to make phone calls. Save time by looking up all numbers at once and writing them on a list.
- Highlight all numbers you look up in the phone book. It will be easier to find if you have to redial. Add the numbers you think you might call again to your Family Yellow Pages (see page 69).
- Keep a list of frequently called numbers by each telephone in your home.
- Use e-mail to communicate as much as possible. It's usually faster than a phone call.
- When you need to call someone back at a later date, put his or her name and phone number on the calendar on the date you're supposed to call so you don't have to look up the number again.
- Keep a box of stickers, activity books, and small toys near the phone to distract a small child when you have to make an important call.
- Call and reserve a babysitter at the same time you RSVP to a party or wedding invitation.
- Let your phone assist you. When you're away from home, if there's something you must remember to do and you don't have paper or pen to write it down, call and leave yourself a message on your answering machine. Get into the habit of checking it right when you walk in the door.

5. When running an errand, think of other errands you can accomplish at the same time. For example, when mailing a package at the post office, stock up on stamps. In general, consolidate errands and do them on certain days, avoiding Saturdays as much as you can.

6. Avoid the bank or post office from noon to two or on Friday afternoon. If you can't avoid the trip, take something to do or read while you're waiting.

7. Save time making trips to the post office by purchasing a postal scale and keeping various types of stamps on hand.

8. Don't waste time looking at mail you don't want. Whenever you get a catalog or mailing that doesn't interest you, call or write the company and ask to be taken off their mailing list.

9. Take your calendar notebook with you everywhere you go.

10. Post your goals and priorities someplace where you can see them regularly. I keep mine in the front of my calendar notebook. They help me make decisions about how to spend my time.

11. Every time you begin a task, have an idea of how much time you want to spend on it. Try to do it in that amount of time. If you can't, evaluate whether it's really worth doing at the level you're doing it. Is there a simpler, quicker way?

12. Don't schedule energy-draining tasks on days when you're tight on time or tired.

13. Call before you make a trip to a store to see if they have a certain item, to see if a plane is leaving or arriving on time, to see if a friend is home before you drop by, to see if your hairdresser is on schedule, or before a doctor's appointment to see if the doctor is running behind.

14. Learn to skim rather than read. The first and last paragraph, and the first sentence of each paragraph, can tell you quickly if the material is something you want to read.

15. Look in the Yellow Pages or ask friends for references for businesses that offer delivery—pizza parlors, other restaurants, drugstores, grocery stores, dry cleaners. Be careful about cost comparisons, but depending on your schedule, the savings in time and sanity may make up for a few extra dollars.

16. Always carry an extra key to your car and house. Calling a locksmith is time-consuming and costly.

17. Hire a responsible teenager to do errand running, grocery shopping, drop-offs and pickups of your children from after-school activities.

> "There is time for everything."
> —Thomas A. Edison

FOOD

18. Avoid long lines at the grocery store by shopping when others don't. One friend shops at seven on Saturday morning. I shop at six on a midweek morning.

19. Keep an ongoing grocery list at Control Central so family members can record needs. When you open the last bottle or package of any item, add it to the grocery list.

20. Get home milk delivery if it is available; this costs a little more, but it is a real time-saver.

21. Develop a repertoire of five meals you can prepare in less than thirty minutes. Always keep the ingredients on hand. For example, keep a jar of prepared spaghetti sauce in the pantry and 1 pound of Italian sausage in the freezer for a quick dinner. Sauté 1-inch slices of sausage, add the jar of sauce, and simmer for 10 minutes. Tastes like homemade! Serve over pasta.

22. Whenever possible, cook a double portion of dinner for the freezer. Date and label all leftovers to be frozen.

23. Set up a dinner preparation routine. Alert your family ten minutes before dinner is ready so they can wash hands and do preassigned tasks: set the table, prepare beverages, and put food on the table.

24. When cooking, return used ingredients immediately where they belong and toss all wrappers and scraps. This saves time and keeps you from forgetting whether or not you added that pinch of baking soda.

25. Always fill your sink with warm water and soap. As you mix and measure, put utensils and bowls in the water. Instead of grabbing for a clean bowl or utensil, just rinse and reuse the ones you've already worked with.

26. For easier cleanup, pour salt on oven spills while they're still hot and spray pans and bakeware with nonstick spray, whether the recipe calls for it or not. You can also spray measuring cups before measuring ingredients such as honey, shortening, or peanut butter.

27. Soak pots, pans, and utensils in warm soapy water while you eat dinner for easier cleanup later.

28. Keep disposable aluminum pans on hand for times when you won't have much time to clean up.

29. After dinner, don't stack dishes on top of each other—food sticks on the bottom and makes more work.

30. Make it a family policy to not leave dishes in the sink when you go to bed.

31. Cut down on search time by assigning specific foods to certain refrigerator shelves. Include one for leftovers.

HOME AND PROPERTY

32. Keep a cordless hand vacuum in kitchen for quick cleanup of crumbs.

33. Next time you take out the garbage, store a few extra plastic trash bags under the bag in present use. When it's full, another is standing by.

34. Always keep your car keys in the same place. (We keep ours on hooks by the exit door.)

35. Have a central location for extra keys, like the back of a cupboard door. Use cup hooks or tiny nails to hang them. Buy colored plastic key covers so you can identify the key you need at a glance.

36. Make a master list of tasks family members can do when they have an extra five minutes.

- Take out the garbage.
- Unload the dishwasher.
- Wipe off kitchen counters.
- Sweep the kitchen floor.
- Organize one pantry shelf.

- Clean off one refrigerator shelf.
- Start a load of laundry.
- Sweep the front porch.
- Clean the bathroom countertop and mirror.
- Collect and throw away old newspapers.
- Get the mail and sort it at the Mail Center.
- Fluff sofa and easy-chair cushions.
- Vacuum one room.
- Wipe off all telephone receivers with rubbing alcohol.
- Change the cat litter.
- Pick up toys.
- Make a bed.
- Give the toilets a quick once-over; spray on bowl cleaner and give a good swish with bowl brush.
- Add your own!

37. Have a rubber stamp made with each child's name. This makes it easy to put names on belongings.

38. Don't call a repairperson immediately when electronic equipment or an appliance breaks. Many companies have toll-free numbers and can answer repair questions by phone. Call the 800 directory (1-800-555-1212) for numbers.

FINANCES

39. Set aside a special time each week to do home-office work. Treat this time as you would any important appointment.

40. If you don't do it every time you write a check, set a time each week to sit down with a calculator and keep your check register current.

41. Pay bills just twice a month. Store them this way: put the bill in its mailing envelope, stamp it, and write the due date on the outside.

42. Arrange to pay regular monthly bills—insurance, health club, utilities, loans—by automatic deduction from your account.

43. To avoid late fees and interest charges, pay bills on time and pay as much of the balance on your charge accounts as you can afford each month.

44. Let your teenager help you pay your monthly bills. This eye-opening experience encourages frugality.

45. Keep exact records of tax-deductible expenses, particularly if you are self-employed or make money from a hobby. Checking with an experienced tax person can increase your deductions.

46. Consider using one low-interest credit card for all purchases and dealing with one monthly bill.

47. Use automated phone banking to check on balances and transfer money between accounts.

48. Start a family routine of collecting change from pockets and purses at the end of each day. (On average, Americans carry $1.28 in change. If you save $1.28 each day for 365 days, you'll have $467.20!)

49. Keep a money bag of change and small bills for kids' lunch money and unexpected activities.

50. Have an easy-access box or file to keep all credit-card and cash receipts in case you need to return something.

51. To track your finances more accurately, consider buying a home-budget software system for your computer.

52. Remember that banks and credit-card companies make mistakes. Check your bills carefully.

FRIENDS AND FAMILY

53. Carry a list of family members' clothing sizes in your organizer notebook or purse. When you discover something that you like, you'll have the information you need. But don't buy anything just because it's on sale.

54. Get to know a salesperson at your favorite gift shop. Keep your personalized gift enclosure cards on file, so you can simply call and have a gift wrapped and mailed when you're short on time.

55. Have one of your kids keep track of all family members' birthdays and send cards as they roll around. (See Gift/Wrapping Center, page 74.)

56. Send a pretty postcard with a short note instead of writing a long letter to a friend.

57. Schedule family members' dentist and doctor appointments back-to-back.

58. Put your pharmacist's telephone number next to your doctor's so you can call in prescriptions quickly.

59. Make a list of symptoms and questions to ask before visiting the doctor. Take notes when the doctor explains the diagnosis and treatment.

SPECIAL PROJECTS

60. Plan backward. If you want to have a garage sale September 15, write down the target date. Give yourself plenty of time and intermittent goals, such as: clean out the attic on August 30, work on closets September 2–3, drawers and cupboards September 7–8.

61. Start a special-projects reference notebook. Whenever you finish a project, jot down important information like the guest list and the amount of food and utensils needed to host a party for twenty, or the number of bags the family packed for a vacation. Record what worked and what didn't at Thanksgiving, a birthday party, or a family reunion. These lists will help you cut down on the time it takes to plan future projects and prevent you from making the same mistakes twice.

62. If you travel often, keep a prepacked overnight bag and toiletries ready at all times.

DOZENS OF WAYS TO SAVE MONEY IN EVERY DEPARTMENT

1. Fix sack lunches for you and your kids. You'll save hundreds of dollars a year.

2. Avoid late charges. Rewind rented videotapes immediately after watching and place in an easy-to-see location near the door.

3. Before buying new books, check to see if they're available at the library.

4. Avoid paying fines for overdue library books by writing the due dates on your calendar.

5. Buy bargain tires marked "blems" for your car. They usually have only minor cosmetic blemishes on the sidewalls.

6. Bury a piece of rusty metal under a plant instead of buying plant food.

7. Save money by learning to do things yourself. Check out how-to videos from the library.

8. Fresh flowers will last longer if you drop two or three pennies in the vase.

9. Check out local consignment shops before buying furniture or seldom-worn clothing such as ski clothes, formal wear, and boys' blazers.

10. Ask your insurance agent about ways to decrease your premiums. Some offer discounts for things such as installing smoke alarms, taking a defensive driving course, and having a student driver with a good report card.

11. If you use credit cards, use as few as possible. Fewer bills to pay and fewer stamps to lick also mean more time saved.

12. Go to the matinee movies rather than the prime-time, full-price ones.

13. Nurture low-cost hobbies and activities, such as gardening, card games, walking and hiking, creating inexpensive crafts, taking picnics and exploring parks.

14. Instead of buying a new couch, consider having your old one reupholstered. Check to see if there is an upholstery school in your area. Students take a little longer but charge a fraction of the cost.

15. Save money by having your hair cut at a beauty school.

16. Enjoy low-cost family fun. Get up early, watch the sun rise, and cook breakfast out at a park. Go on a bike-hike as a family, ride to a favorite eating spot, then ride back. Call your local parks and recreation department and ask about inexpensive programs and activities that your family might enjoy.

17. Take your own rafts, life jackets, and snorkeling gear to water parks or the beach. Renting these items can be expensive.

18. Drink water when you eat out at restaurants. This can add up to big savings if you have a big family.

19. Beware of buying or receiving anything that requires you to call a 900 number.

20. Take your family's used clothing, books, toys, etc., to a consignment shop. Some will give you more dollars' worth in trade than in cash.

21. If you can't afford to buy tickets to a special concert or play, find out if you can attend a rehearsal.

22. When shopping for large appliances, ask to buy floor models at a reduced price.

23. Look into joining your local YMCA or community center instead of a fancy health club; they often provide the same services for a lot less.

24. When you're having a party, don't choose oversize invitations that will require additional postage.

25. Ask your local electric and water company to send a customer representative to your home to give you energy- and water-saving suggestions. Most will do this free of charge.

26. Store candles in the refrigerator. They'll last longer.

27. If your kids want something badly, let them earn the money to pay for half of it, and you pay the other half. They'll appreciate it more and take better care of it.

28. Don't get caught in the trap of spending money on your children to ease the guilt of not spending enough time with them. Adjust your schedule and give of your time.

If you are under financial stress month after month because of accumulated debt, consider consulting a financial planner or talking to your banker about creative options for paying off your debt. Or shop around for a lower-interest credit card and consolidate your debts so you'll have only one payment each month.

Stretch Your Food Budget

There are four ways to cut back your food bills: planning, shopping, preparation, and avoiding waste. Use these tips to help you get more bang for your grocery buck.

29. Find out if your store gives the best value. Compare prices at your usual supermarket and at least one other store. Prices can vary as much as 20 percent.

30. Use coupons wisely. Coupons don't save money if they're for products you don't need or that are more expensive than similar products. And if the coupon is for a large-size portion, you might waste most of the food.

31. Buying a more expensive lean cut of meat may be more economical than buying one that requires you to throw away excessive bone, gristle, or fat.

32. Rethink meals so they don't always contain a "meat and three." Incorporate more beans and grains instead of meat.

> "I can account for every dime I spend. It's those twenties and fifties where things start getting a little foggy."
> —Martha Bolton

33. Eat more ethnic meals. Often Italian and Spanish recipes make creative use of beans and pasta, and it's amazing how little chicken breast you actually need to make vegetable-packed Chinese stir-fry.

34. Keep in mind what fruits and vegetables are in season—they'll be less expensive.

35. Compare cost per ounce or other unit of measure on different items. Single-serving containers are usually the most costly; buy the brand that sells for the least amount per unit, unless you can't store a large amount. Carry a calculator if necessary.

36. Beware of foods displayed as "featured" or "new." These may simply be promotions of regularly priced items. And don't be lured into buying something just because a sign reads "Limit Four Per Customer"; consumers tend to buy more when the stores impose a limit. When possible, use manufacturers' coupons to purchase store specials to get larger savings—they'll be greater if double coupons apply.

37. Try no-frills and store brands. Compare label ingredients: the expensive and generic brands may be identical. If you like them, your small "investment" will pay a high rate of return.

38. Know the price of everything you put into your cart. Some supermarkets give you an item free if the cash register scans it at a higher price than is marked on the shelf.

39. Buy less of the foods you throw out each week.

40. Don't shop when you're hungry or tired. You won't make the best decisions.

41. Buy bread and baked goods in bulk at day-old bread stores or bakery outlets and freeze.

42. Supermarkets usually place the most expensive items at eye level. Look at the entire group of products before making your decision.

The Friend Connection

Friendship gleans many gifts beyond great conversation; try these tips to discover the way friends benefit your bank account.

43. Ask a neighbor to split the cost of renting a carpet-cleaning machine for a day.

44. Share magazine subscriptions with a friend. Order different magazines that you both enjoy, then swap.

45. Trade books, CDs, or movies with friends. You not only save the cost of buying, but you experience the joy of getting to share and discuss your mutual tastes.

46. Start a toy-swapping club with other mothers. Trade toys your kids don't mind living without for a couple of weeks. The kids will love having different toys often, and you'll save money not buying new ones.

47. Invite eleven other families to join a fruit- and vegetable-buying co-op; items can be purchased cheaper in large quantities. Each family takes a specific month to take care of shopping at a farmers' market, dividing and distributing items, and collecting money.

48. On Monday and Wednesday nights, cook doubles. Enlist coworkers to cook doubles of their dinner on those same nights. Bring a Styrofoam carrier to work and trade the double portions of last night's dinner. This will save you from cooking on Tuesday and Thursday nights.

49. Instead of paying to board pets while you're out of town, ask a friend to come to your home to feed, water, and exercise them. (Cats like this system much better anyway.) Return the favor, and you both save money.

50. Start an errand co-op with neighbors or coworkers. One person goes to the post office, another to the toy store, a third to the beauty-supply store.

51. Rather than spending money going away on a romantic retreat with your spouse, trade babysitting weekends with a friend and have your weekend at home.

52. Start a gourmet club. Take turns preparing fancy dinners rather than eating out at restaurants.

53. Trade chores with a friend with abilities and gifts different from yours. If you enjoy working in the yard, you can do the gardening for both homes. If she enjoys housecleaning, let her do the interior chores.

54. Host a swap party. Decide on a theme—videos, costume jewelry, tools, children's or women's clothing, kitchen utensils.

55. Form a dinner co-op. You cook one night a week and deliver to three other families. They will deliver dinner to you the other three nights. This is a great way to cover meals Monday through Thursday.

56. Hang a bulletin board at work for employees to post services or skills they are willing to barter or to list used items they'd like to sell.

Family Fitness Day by Day

Medical evidence shows that tendencies to gain weight, along with other qualities that detract from lifelong fitness, are genetic. We can do our kids the favor of passing along good habits along with our less-than-perfect genes. Make a habit of doing one thing per day to encourage family fitness. Try to incorporate some of the following into your life:

• Stress healthy eating habits. Introduce new vegetables and other healthy foods with a "try it, maybe you'll like it" injunction. They don't have to eat things they hate. They do have to take a taste.

• Serve at least two vegetables with each meal. For young children, these can be the same thing over and over—carrot sticks and green beans.

• Enlist older children in menu planning.

• Make sure your kids take advantage of the organized sports activities they're interested in.

• Ask your favorite fast-food restaurants for calorie and food-content information. Make up a multiple-choice quiz about the calorie count of different favorite items. Our kids couldn't believe that fries, a chocolate shake, and large cheeseburger contain 1,310 calories.

• Schedule a weekly family sports night. Try out different sports such as basketball, rowing, racquetball, skating, or tennis.

• Your local intermediate or high school track is a great place to take the family running or walking in the evening.

• Read a newspaper or magazine article about nutrition together at the dinner table.

• Hold a family push-ups or crunches contest. Record how many each family member can do at the beginning of the summer. Do sit-ups or crunches three times a week, then at the end of vacation hold another contest to see how much each person has improved.

• Go on a long bike ride. Map your route before you leave, choosing new and interesting destinations every week.

• Incorporate calisthenics into family cleanup time. Do fast-paced walking, squats, and stretches while completing regular household duties.

• Enroll in a family summer recreational program at your local YMCA or parks and recreation department. High schools sometimes offer swimming programs.

• Develop a family workout schedule. Here is a sample plan: Do twenty minutes of calisthenics or other strength-building exercises on Mondays. Do thirty minutes of aerobic activities like running, swimming, or walking on Wednesdays. Do fun recreational sports such as biking, hiking, or skating for one hour on Fridays.

Daily Joy Breaks

While getting your household under control, don't forget the importance of living a balanced life—mixing work with play. Without play and leisure time, you risk the chance of burnout and even loss of your health. Give yourself permission to play and have fun regularly. Do something fun every day—alone, with members of your family, or with a friend—even if it's for a short period of time. It's good for your health, your productivity, and your personality.

Make a list of activities that are fun and refreshing to you. Everybody has time for something. Use these ideas to get your fun ideas jelling.

> "People need joy quite as much as they need clothing. Some of them need it far more."
> —Margaret Collier Graham

TWO- TO FIVE-MINUTE IDEAS

Look at travel brochures; plan a dream vacation.

Glance through a favorite magazine and mark articles you'd like to read later.

Keep a bottle of bubble solution in your desk drawer. When you're feeling stressed, take a short break to go outside and blow some bubbles.

Work on a crossword puzzle.

Tell your child a joke or funny story. Or have her tell you one.

Read a story aloud to your child.

Exchange a quick neck or back rub with a friend.

Call a friend and make a date.

Play a hand of solitaire.

Look at photographs of favorite memories.

Make yourself a nonfat chocolate soda—half diet chocolate soda pop and half skim milk. Or have some other good-for-you food treat.

Listen to a favorite song.

Put music on and take a short dance break with whoever is home or by yourself.

Buy a book with your favorite cartoons. Read at least one a day.

FIVE- TO THIRTY-MINUTE IDEAS

Read some of those magazine articles that you've been saving.

Work on a needlework project.

Go to a local park and read from a book of your favorite poetry.

Give yourself a manicure or facial.

Curl up in a chair and read part of a good book you're working on.

Order a present for a friend or yourself from a catalog.

Work on a large jigsaw puzzle together with a child.

Take turns reading a chapter a night in a book with a grade-schooler.

Play a musical instrument.

Update a photo album.

Get out old LPs and enjoy music from days gone by.

Sketch in your sketchbook.

Surf the Internet; if you don't know how, ask a family member or friend to teach you.

HALF-A-DAY-OR-MORE IDEAS

Take a sack lunch to the zoo or a museum with your kids.

Get old games—Monopoly, Parcheesi, Clue, or Risk. Have an ongoing tournament.

Attend a lecture with a friend or an older child on a subject that interests you both.

Take a picnic lunch and go kite flying.

Go to an art exhibit.

Play tourist for a day. Drop by your local chamber of commerce and pick up a visitor's guide.

Take the whole family, or just your spouse, on a drive in the country.

Go antiquing with your spouse or a friend.

Take a nature hike and do some bird-watching along the way.

Mornings and Evenings:
The Best Parts of the Day

Mornings and evenings are important times, and not just because they're the main interaction periods we have with our families during the

workweek. They're also important
because choices we make about
how we handle these precious
hours can help determine whether

> "Day's sweetest moments are at dawn." —Ella Wheeler Wilcox

our home is a peaceful, pleasant place to be or just an extension of the chaos we face in the outside world. As family members go out into the world, we don't have as much control over the quality or quantity of time they spend, but we can have control over mornings and evenings.

MORNING BLUES OR MORNING BLESSING?

What would need to happen at your house for mornings to run smoothly? My personal goal for my family every morning is that we experience a peaceful, positive environment that prepares us to take on the pressures of the day ahead; that we leave the house with everything—school papers, lunch money, briefcases, umbrellas, gym clothes—except pandemonium; that we see morning as a good start to a great day.

Sounds wonderful, I know. And actually, it's quite simple. Not easy, but possible. Here are some tips for making those few hours a lot more pleasant.

• Set your alarm for the exact time you want to get up. I always set two alarms (one is battery powered) and keep them in the bathroom so I have to get out of bed to turn them off.

• Get up earlier than everyone else to get your head screwed on straight, and spend some quiet time thinking or meditating. Give yourself some quality time so you're under control before other feet hit the floor.

• Attach a timer to your coffeepot so your coffee will be ready when you are.

• Know what you are wearing. The biggest time waster in the morning is choosing what you're going to wear, only to find there's a spot on your blouse or a button is missing. Instead, choose your outfit the night before. Examine it for spots and missing buttons. Make sure there are no runs in your hose. Pick your accessories.

• Put a clock in every room so everyone is always aware of what time it is.

• Figure out what time everyone has to be out the door and work backward from there. How long does it typically take each person to get ready? Set a wake-up time that gives each child enough time to wash, dress, eat, do chores, and get out the door, and then add ten minutes for schedule snags so they won't miss the bus or car pool. Missing rides is the surest way to waste your morning. It makes you frazzled and the kids scrambled, and worst of all, you'll all be late for school and work.

• Have teenagers get up fifteen minutes earlier than younger siblings since they need extra time in the bathroom. Put a mirror in teenagers' bedrooms.

• Make a rotating schedule for the bathroom and assign each child a time.

• Make sure your kids know what they are wearing. Ask kids to decide and set clothes out the night before. (Pack away all clothing that doesn't fit and put away out-of-season items to simplify choices.) For children who like to decide in the morning, make decisions easier by hanging all their school clothes in one area of the closet, and build your kids' wardrobe on bottoms in basic colors that will coordinate with a wide variety of tops. For example, my thirteen-year-old's wardrobe is built around khaki and navy pants and shorts. All of his shirts coordinate with these.

• Buy socks all of one kind and color for each child. This saves searching for mates.

• Buy clothing with elastic waists and shoes with Velcro fasteners so young children can dress faster.

• Prepare a "no cooking, no special requests" breakfast. It's important for children to begin their day right with a healthy breakfast. Create a healthy morning breakfast with "no cooking" foods like cereal (offer only two choices), or a bagel, fruit, and juice. Save pancakes and eggs for the weekend. Sit down at the table together, even if it's only for four or five minutes, and talk about your children's day. Ask about tests and activities, and inquire if there's anything you need to pick up for them at the store. This is an easy way to show them you care about what's going on in their world.

• Set the table for breakfast and dinner the night before. By placing the cereal bowl on top of the dinner plate you can avoid setting the table for dinner. Make sure each child clears and rinses his or her bowl.

• Create a morning chore chart kids can follow. Post it at child level on the refrigerator or on a kitchen bulletin board. Have each child check off tasks as he completes them. This way kids won't argue over whose turn it is to feed the dog or take out the garbage.

• Have one person be in charge of giving family members a ten-minute warning—ten minutes before it's time to walk out the door.

• If you have a baby, restock your diaper bag for day care the night before.

• Keep all shoes, knapsacks, and coats in a closet near the back door. This will prevent the kids from scrambling around in the morning looking for missing items. When homework is done the night before, it goes in the backpack and the backpack goes on a hook by the door, along with shoes, mittens, rain gear, and gym clothes.

• Grown-ups abide by the "back door rule," too. Keep keys, errands (like dry cleaning), purse, and briefcase in a designated basket or on a shelf by the door.

THE KEY TO GETTING SLOW MOVERS
INTO HIGH GEAR: INCENTIVE

Tired of playing chief nag with children who operate in slow motion each morning? Try positive motivation instead of nagging or yelling, which leads only to frustration for the parent and the child. Children respond in different ways to various types of positive motivation—tangible rewards,

Many Family Managers have told me that they saw a large improvement with slow-moving kids in the morning when they implemented the use of the "Sunshine Jar" that I've suggested in my previous books. This is where a quarter (or whatever amount you set) is dropped into the Sunshine Jar when your child gets up quickly and with a smile on his or her face. The child can then buy him- or herself a treat with the money accumulated in the jar.

checklists, verbal praise, games, and challenges. Be a student of your children to learn what types of incentives spur them on. If one method fails, try another. The important thing is to be patient and keep trying. The end result—responsible, self-disciplined children—is worth the effort.

• Be sincere and specific with your praise. Notice the times your kids cooperate and thank them for it.

• Try to focus more on things a child does right than on things he or she does wrong. Otherwise you can fall into a negative-attention cycle, where a child does not cooperate because that's a way to get Mom's or Dad's attention.

• Release a child from an onerous task as a reward for following a morning schedule.

• Put a kitchen timer in the room of a child who likes a challenge. Break the morning routine into five-minute tasks and let him try to beat the clock.

• Eliminate distractions. Don't turn on the TV unless a child needs to watch a news report for a class.

• Make a work-before-play rule, and stick by it. Play is a natural reward after doing something you're required to do. Purchase a special game or toy to be played with only if your child is ready to leave for school earlier than necessary.

EVENINGS: CHAOS OR CALM?

When your kids arrive home from school or you arrive home after work, don't underestimate the importance of transition time. Everyone needs to relax and acclimate before beginning end-of-the-day activities. Change into comfortable clothes, turn on music, and don't take any phone calls. Talk to your kids about their day.

The following are some helpful tips that can make evenings into a peaceful end to your day.

• Share dinner responsibilities. One parent can cook while the other spends time with the kids. Let the older kids take turns helping in the kitchen. Simplify dinner preparations. Schedule certain dinners for certain nights, like hamburgers on Tuesdays, build-your-own baked potatoes on Wednesdays, and pizza on Friday. Double a recipe you cook over the weekend and have "planned-overs" (a.k.a. leftovers) on Monday nights.

• After dinner, share kitchen cleanup chores. Load lunch boxes with nonperishables. Make sandwiches and store them in the refrigerator. (Add lettuce to sandwiches in the morning to retain crispness.) You can even make nonsoggy peanut butter and jelly sandwiches the night before. Simply spread peanut butter on both sides of the bread (it acts like a sealant), then put the jelly in the middle.

• Place frozen juice in refrigerator to thaw for breakfast.

• Create a homework-friendly environment. Mom and Dad do "homework" as well. Sort the mail, read, or work on a project. Don't turn on the TV, and keep other distractions to a minimum. Be available to help with kids' homework when needed.

• Prepare for tomorrow morning. Make a checklist for yourself, noting appointments for the next day and items to take—library books, bank deposits, videos.

• Crying, overtired children will not get up or cooperate without the right amount of sleep. Set a specific, reasonable time for them to bathe, brush their teeth, and go to bed. Although they may stay up later on the weekends, don't alter the schedule greatly if you want the school-day routine to be easy to maintain. Kids learn a daily rhythm.

• Enforce bedtime and "lights out" policy for younger children by installing a timer on their light. If they are not yet ready for sleep when you put them to bed, turn on the timer for twenty minutes. Tell them they can stay up and read or look at books, or listen to books on tape, until the light goes out.

• Pick your arguments carefully, especially on weeknights, when time is short.

• Have a family ritual of saying good night in a special way every night. At our house we tuck each child into bed every night; even when they become teenagers we still go into their bedrooms, remind them that we love them, and say good night.

Helping Kids Learn to Manage Time

• Teach your children to multitask—accomplishing two things at once— while watching TV. They could polish shoes, brush the dog, sort coins. (Refer to the list on page 90 earlier in this section for more ideas.)
• Buy your children their own alarm clocks so they can be responsible for getting themselves up in the morning.
• Teach kids to make lists of what they need to accomplish. Help them understand the importance of doing advance work, such as making sure their baseball uniform is clean and getting all equipment together in plenty of time before the game.
• Many times having to suffer the consequences is the best teacher. If they're constantly running late for school, don't "save" them. One trip to the principal's office might be all it takes to make them prompt.
• Model the behavior you want them to embrace. If they see you procrastinating or constantly running late, don't expect them to behave differently. Talk about how you can learn together to be better managers of time.
• Encourage kids to keep their own calendar notebook where they can record important facts and dates. Make sure they know to transfer important dates to Control Central.
• Help them break a big task—writing a book report or cleaning out their drawers—into small segments.

A TIP FOR TEACHING PRESCHOOLERS
Start teaching them the concept of time when they're in the car. Bring a roll of dimes or quarters. Give each child a plastic butter tub with a slit in the top. Every ten minutes give each one a coin to drop in the tub. They'll start getting an idea of how much time ten minutes is. They can look forward to buying a treat with the money when you stop for gas.

SICK-DAY COMFORT PLAN

It never fails. The day your to-do list seems endless will be the day a child gets sick. Use this sick-day plan to help keep your frustration to a minimum.

1. Be prepared. Have numbers handy for your doctor and pharmacy. When you call your doctor, be prepared with this information:
   - Child's temperature
   - Symptoms—headaches, pulling at ears, sore throat, vomiting, diarrhea, stomachache, rash, unusual sleep patterns
   - Medication you've given so far

2. Keep your medicine cabinet well stocked with necessary over-the-counter medications and medical supplies.

3. Create a special box that you keep on a high closet shelf and get down only on sick days. Keep it filled with activity and coloring books, crayons, stickers, a pad of paper, watercolors, glue, construction paper, pieces of ribbon and yarn, magazines with lots of pictures for cutting up. Younger children will enjoy a play doctor's kit to nurse their stuffed animals; older kids might enjoy a model or craft project to work on.

4. Provide a CD or cassette player so your child can listen to stories on tape and music.

5. Designate a special shelf for "sick foods" such as chicken noodle soup, clear soda pop, flavored gelatin, and soda crackers. Tell family members these items are for sick days only.

6. Be sensitive to what your child prefers when he or she is sick: to be left alone in bed or in the middle of things on the family room sofa.

7. Create a fresh atmosphere for a child with a lengthy illness. Put on clean pillowcases daily, and keep a fresh-cut flower by the bed. Clear broth is nicer to drink when served in a special cup or bowl.

8. For a prolonged illness, send your child a small gift each day through the mail—new markers, a pack of gum, a package of flower seeds, a small book. Watching for the mail carrier will be something fun to do every day.

9. Buy or make a large-size bib with the words "I Feel Better" painted or monogrammed on it. This is a big help when the sick one is attempting to sip broth or eat a meal on a bed tray.

10. Flavored gelatin is more fun for kids when it's prepared in a nine-by-twelve-inch cake pan. Use cookie cutters to cut fun figures for your patient to eat. Dry toast also tastes better when it's cut into shapes.

11. Brighten your sick child's room with colored crepe paper and a cheery poster taped to the ceiling.

12. Encourage family members to slip get-well cards under the patient's door or put them on a meal tray. See if your child's class will make get-well cards if he or she will be out of school for a long period.

13. Call your child's teacher and ask if you can pick up schoolwork. Encourage getting as much done as possible while at home.

14. Play board games or work puzzles. Read new or old favorite books aloud; get out family albums and pictures to look at together. Tell your child stories about what he or she did when younger. Reminisce about the attractions and highlights of a favorite vacation.

> "We must not . . . ignore the small daily differences we can make which, over time, add up to big differences that we often cannot foresee." —
> Marian Wright Edelman

FOUR
Twelve Months
a Year

"Timing is everything. It is as important to know when as to know how."
—Arnold Glasow

Once upon a time, service-station attendants kept track of when the oil in your car needed to be changed. The furnace company called in the fall to schedule an annual checkup. And the neighborhood grocer gave away free yearly calendars that women hung on the wall. They often had a serene seasonal picture for every month and calendar grids with no more than a two-inch square to note the day's events.

Frankly, I could not keep track of one hour in a square that size, let alone all the scheduled events for each day. Not to mention noting the important jobs that need to be done less frequently to insure smoother operation of my home and family. When I invented the Family Manager concept I was on a quest to make my days chaos-free. The first scheduling device I invented was the daily Hit List (see page 78).

It was good, as far as it went. But as many of us know from our professional experience, whether as Family Managers or in the business world, daily planning is not enough. We have to think long-term. A project manager would never plan a new product launch with only daily checklists to guide her. She'd use a coordinated checklist of long- and

> "An intelligent plan is the first step to success."
> —Basil S. Walsh

short-term tasks that need to be done in a variety of departments—from accounting to manufacturing to marketing—at certain points along the way. Depending on the industry and the manager, this list might be kept by calendar year or fiscal year, quarterly, or month by month. It might be kept on a computer system that associates could access. Or it might be in a calendar notebook, with entries in the daily, weekly, monthly, and tickler sections of the book.

As Family Managers, we too need to keep long-range plans, with deadlines and reminders. And it doesn't matter whether we keep them in a computer, on sheets of paper in a file folder, or in a yearlong planning calendar notebook. What does matter is that we keep them.

A little bit of preventive maintenance can save a lot of time, money, and aggravation. I learned this the hard way on the first hot day of the year when the temperature shot up off the charts. I turned on the air conditioner and got a blast of hot air. It was not a good time to discover what can go wrong when an air conditioner is not regularly serviced.

Over the years, I've developed quarterly checklists to remind myself of tasks that need to be done at a certain time. Other chores on these checklists could be done at any time, but the point of scheduling them for specific times is (a) to spread them out over the year so they don't all pile up at once and (b) to remember to do them.

The third kind of category of tasks I put on a quarterly checklist are want-to items. These are things that are part of my goals for the year. In my other books I've written about taking myself off for a mini-retreat (often just half a day) at the beginning of every year. During that time I set goals for myself during the year. Once those goals are set, I put items in this third category on my checklists.

For instance: if I know in January that I want to redecorate the family room before my son graduates from high school in the spring, I put it on my schedule. I include things like looking for a new couch early enough that I'm not rushed and can allow for the probable twelve-week delivery period. I'd also begin early to collect paint and wallpaper swatches. Closer to the time, I'd either schedule a workday if we were doing the work ourselves or begin to get bids from professionals.

Another want-to might be to organize a family reunion next summer. If I know the second week of July is my target date, I first check with my family members and other extended family to see if that time works for them. I ask two or three relatives (ones I know are good at organizing and getting things done) to be on the steering committee—even if they're a long distance away. We can hold meetings via e-mail, phone, and fax. After we come up with a timeline and list of topics to research and do, I make a note on my calendar of the deadlines we set.

The point is that it's extremely helpful and stress-relieving to keep up with year-round projects by entering tasks and deadlines on a calendar, not necessarily on a certain date, but around the time they appear. I've found that checklists, like the ones following, help me remember what to do. As you've probably figured out by now, I always think by department, which helps me remember the myriad tasks that need to be done. You'll notice that some departments have more responsibilities at certain times of the year.

Use these checklists to develop your own yearlong plan for tasks that need to be done at a specific time of the year, tasks that need to be done and might otherwise be forgotten, and tasks that help you meet a specific long-term goal.

Quarterly Checklists

FIRST QUARTER—JANUARY, FEBRUARY, MARCH

- Plan any major remodeling or repair projects. Start getting bids from contractors and schedule work.
- Begin to shop for furniture you've budgeted for this calendar year.

> **A leaky toilet can waste up to 10 gallons of water an hour, 240 gallons a day. That costs an average of $36 a month, $432 a year.**

There are often preinventory sales at the beginning of the year.

• Check your plumbing system for leaks.

• Unscrew the aerator from the end of each faucet, wash carefully, then replace.

• Inspect ceramic tile grout around tub or shower. Caulk as needed.

• Clean mineral deposits from inside the dishwasher by pouring in a gallon of white vinegar and running through a wash cycle.

• Tackle indoor painting jobs.

• Use a tiny artist's brush to apply spackle to hairline cracks in walls.

• Repair or replace wallpaper as needed.

• Check the pressure-release valve on your hot-water heater. (See your owner's manual.)

• Vacuum coils beneath refrigerator. (This will increase energy efficiency by 6 percent.) Make a note to do this three more times at regular intervals this year.

• Replace heating-system filters. (Check your manual and note on your calendar how often this should be done.)

• Do an attic and basement safety check. Make sure there's no accumulation of trash or dirty rags. Look for evidence of frayed wiring. See that your circuit-breaker box is well marked. Check that no paint or flammable liquids are stored in the same area as the furnace or hot-water heater.

• Treat septic system. (If you have one, make a note on your calendar to do this once a month.)

• Clean out all closets and drawers; maybe set a goal to tackle one closet and three or four drawers a week until you're done.

• If you have the storage space, buy in bulk enough nonperishables for three months.

Smart Bulk Buys

Rushing off to the store every time you need an item wastes time, energy, and money. By purchasing nonperishable items quarterly in bulk, you will spend less unscheduled time at the store, never run out of necessities, and save money—since quantities usually cost less than single items. Smart bulk buys include: paper products, diapers, toiletries, cleaning supplies, pet food, school supplies, batteries, videotapes, and lightbulbs.

• Make out three weeks' worth of your family's favorite dinner menus. Recycle these menus all during the year. Supplement these with special meals when you have a little extra time to cook, eating out, ordering in now and again, and meals your family members like to cook themselves. This will give you a good basis for a menu to use all year long.

• Write birthdays you want to remember on your calendar. Make a note one week before the date to send a present or card if you need to.

• Restock your Gift/Wrapping Center with various kinds of greeting cards, gift wrap, and gifts.

• Write a gift list for next Christmas and work on Christmas bit by bit, all year long. Buy presents as you find them, and hide them away. (See Yearlong Christmas Plan, page 283.)

• Make a list of a few close friends that you don't see as often as you'd like. Call to see if they'd like to eat lunch together on the first Friday of every month or maybe once a quarter.

• Talk to your husband about scheduling a date night at least once a month. If you both know you've decided on the first Thursday night of each month, you can put it on your calendar and think in advance about what you want to do. Line up a regular babysitter for this night.

Researchers at the University of Vermont in Burlington recently found that a flagging metabolism is not an inevitable part of aging. It's due primarily to a loss of muscle mass—something you can prevent. Pound for pound, muscle burns more calories than body fat does—a pound of muscle burns about 35 calories a day at rest, a pound of fat a mere 2 calories a day. After the mid-twenties, an average adult loses half a pound of muscle every year.

THREE RULES FOR INCREASING YOUR CHANCES OF SUCCESS WITH AN EXERCISE PROGRAM

1. Be realistic—choose a program that suits your age and physical abilities. Be consistent—choose a regular time of day when you can implement the program.
2. Launch your new practice as strongly and vigorously as you can. Tell others what you are doing.
3. Be persistent. Try to maintain the regimen for twenty-one days. On the twenty-second day, you'll

• Start gathering information needed to file income tax. If you don't already have one, set up a family filing system so information for filing next year's return will be at your fingertips. (See the sidebar on File Systems on page 72.)

• Start or enhance a regular exercise program.

• Take care of dry skin. Treat yourself to a facial.

• Enroll in a continuing education class you've always wanted to take.

• Decide now which months you'll schedule checkups for family members with the physician, dentist, optometrist, etc. Make a note on that month's calendar page to call for an appointment.

• Pencil in time to get your oil changed at least once each quarter. (Check your owner's manual for recommendations. Also check how often you should have your tires rotated and schedule this.)

SECOND QUARTER—APRIL, MAY, JUNE

• Pick one weekend to spring clean as a family. (See Seasonal Cleaning Plan, page 127.)

- Have a garage sale. (See Garage Sales: Turning Trash into Cash, page 137.)
- Check your attic for roof leaks. On a rainy day, use a flashlight to locate water drips and spots. On a sunny day, stand in your yard and use binoculars. Repair or replace any broken, bent, or missing shingles or tiles.
- Watch for carpenter ants and for termites swarming. Call an exterminator if necessary.
- Hire a chimney sweep to clean soot, remove birds' nests, and inspect for cracks.
- Moth-proof and store winter clothes.
- Start planning your family vacation.
- Check into summer plans for kids—camps, lessons, volunteer opportunities. Brainstorm with them about possible summer jobs. (See Beyond Babysitting: Super Summer Jobs for Kids, page 153.)
- Plant a garden.

find it harder not to exercise than it was to get started exercising on the first day.

Twice a year, designate the day you adjust your clocks for daylight savings time and then back to standard time as Home Safety Day. Change the batteries in your smoke detectors. See that your fire extinguishers and flashlights are in working order. Make sure everyone knows what to do in case of fire, including how to get out of the house in the middle of the night. This is especially important if you have upstairs bedrooms with only one stairway, in which case you should have inexpensive rope escape ladders in every bedroom. Depending on where you live, check to see that you have necessary provisions in case of an earthquake, tornado, hurricane, or ice storm.

Outdoor Safety Tips

When working outside:
- Put on goggles when mowing the lawn.
- Wear long pants and sleeves to prevent against insect stings.
- Use sunscreen on all unprotected areas.
- Wear a sun visor or hat.
- Wear garden gloves.
- Use a plastic-covered pillow or wear old hockey or skating knee pads for weeding and planting comfort.

If you use chemical products in your yard:
- Work on a windless day.
- Wear goggles and a nose-and-mouth mask while spraying or spreading fertilizers or pesticides.
- Read labels and follow instructions carefully.
- Keep children and pets away while you're working with any chemical.

If you find poison ivy:
- Clean any tools that touch the ivy, as the oil will stay on the tools.
- Wear a long-sleeved shirt, work pants, gloves, socks, and sneakers.
- Work on a windless day.
- Never burn poison ivy, as the smoke can carry the particles.
- Remove and wash your clothes, including your sneakers. Take a shower and use plenty of soap.

- Get your hair and makeup done by a stylist. Try a new look for warmer weather.
- Clean outdoor furniture; repair as needed.
- Clean your barbecue grill with a wire brush and oven cleaner to prepare for summer cooking.

Get Outside Fast

Reorganize your kitchen and storage areas a bit for impromptu summer suppers outside.

- Store barbecue tools, charcoal and lighter, apron and hot pad in an easy-access place.
- Keep hamburger/hot dog condiments—ketchup, mustard, mayonnaise, relish—in a plastic tote in your refrigerator.
- Put paper plates, cups, napkins, plastic utensils, unbreakable salt and pepper shakers, and a tray in a cabinet near the back door for quick table-setting outside.
- Keep a bag of ice on hand in the freezer for refreshing drinks outside.
- Stock your picnic basket with disposable dishes and utensils for when you get the urge to eat at the park.
- Stash old bedspreads or quilts in a closet to lie on at night and stargaze.

- Shut off furnace pilot light for the summer.
- Change air-conditioner filters now and several other times during the cooling season.
- Service and clean lawn mower and garden tools.
- Remove wasp nests on or around your house in early morning when it's cool.
- Open foundation vents.
- Put peel-and-apply weather stripping around windows and doors to reduce air leakage and cut utility bills.

If your filter is permanent, soak it in warm, soapy water and rinse. If you have room units, vacuum the evaporator coils behind the front grille of window units. For central units, have a professional wash the condensing coils, oil the fan motor if required, and vacuum evaporator coils located in ducting.

- Check the grading of your yard and landscaping for settling or erosion. Spread new soil if necessary.
- Move surplus firewood away from the foundation of the house.
- Trim any branches near a heat pump or air-conditioner condenser so they don't obstruct air flow or tangle the fan.
- Make sure windows open smoothly. Give the garage door hardware a squirt of lightweight oil.
- Check for damage to exterior wood trim. Look for water stains, new cracks, blistering paint, warping, and soft places—which can mean dry rot. Repair as needed.
- Check fences and decks for damage and repair as needed.

THIRD QUARTER—JULY, AUGUST, SEPTEMBER
- Replace washing-machine hoses.
- Plan at least one fun family outing each week—a picnic, an educational camping trip or archeological dig, a day at the beach or a lake, a bike-hike.
- Have carpets cleaned by a professional or rent a steam cleaner and do it yourself.
- Get together with friends or relatives you haven't seen in a while.
- Clean out and organize your garage. (See User-Friendly Garages, page 66.)
- Get school supplies and clothing ready. (See Back to School, page 171.)
- Pressure-wash driveways, walkways, and house exterior.
- Caulk all joints and cracks around posts and columns, doors, and windows. Touch up any other areas that show signs of weathering.
- Drain hot-water heater to remove sediment. Check owner's manual or consult with a plumbing do-it-yourself shop.
- Trim back any branches or shrubs two feet from your roof.
- Clean your clothes-dryer exhaust vent. Check the flapper door on

the outside exhaust vent and remove any lint buildup with a vacuum. If vent is flexible, check for kinks and patch any small holes with duct tape.

FOURTH QUARTER—OCTOBER, NOVEMBER, DECEMBER

- Replace heating-system filters; have system professionally serviced if necessary.
- Store summer clothes. Replace outgrown year-round items.
- Drain outdoor plumbing; store hoses.
- Rake leaves.
- Clean gutters, downspouts, and window wells of leaves and debris.
- Clean out and organize toy and sports equipment storage places.
- Add insulation to your attic if necessary.
- Insulate any exposed water pipes.
- Cover any delicate plants before hard freezes.
- Check all Christmas lights and extension cords for broken bulbs and frayed chords.
- Can't find time to exercise during the holidays? Work it into your normal routine. Wear tennis shoes when doing chores—bend, stretch, and move briskly; buy ankle or wrist weights and wear them when puttering around the house; do isometric arm exercises in the car when you're stuck in traffic.
- Make any necessary financial transactions before the end of the year.
- Take out window air conditioners or cover outside of unit to prevent rusting. Cover a central-air-conditioning outdoor unit with a waterproof tarp.
- Close or cover foundation vents before first freeze.
- Cover attic turbine vents and outside faucets.
- Winterize your lawn mower: clean it, change the oil, and drain the gasoline.
- Have your car serviced and prepared for winter. Be sure to check the antifreeze level.

Don't reinvent the wheel. At the end of the year, enter your own checklist items onto next year's calendar. Or make a list and put them in a tickler file.

• Weather-strip leaky windows and doors or put on storm windows, if needed.

• Check electrical system. Be sure bathroom, garage, and outdoor circuits are grounded and protected by ground-fault breakers.

Emergency Measures: A Good Manager Is a Prepared Manager

• Keep a list of emergency phone numbers so you can easily call when you have problems or breaks with plumbing, electricity, heating or air-conditioning, communications, home-office equipment. (See Family Yellow Pages, page 69.)
• Know where the main shutoffs are for water, gas, and electricity. Have the right tools to turn them off. Water can get you wet and ruin a lot of stuff, but gas and electricity can kill you.

Emergency Measures: What to Do in a Crisis . . .

It happens to all of us: the unexpected. Here are ways to handle around-the-house emergencies that do come up.

1. Frozen pipes: Open the faucet and apply heat to the pipe. Never use an open flame. A hair dryer usually works. When the pipe thaws, run water for a few minutes. Leave water dripping if the temperature in the house, the garage, or outside—wherever the pipe was frozen—is still below freezing.

2. Burst pipe: Cut off the water supply immediately. Call a plumber.

3. Overflowing toilet: Turn off water supply with the shutoff valve on the wall behind the toilet. Use a plunger to unclog. Test with a bucket of water before flushing. Open valve and flush several times when finally open.

4. Clogged drain: Check to see if other drains are working. If there is more than one clogged or running slowly, the pipe will have to be cleaned out. This is usually a job for a plumber. However, "sewer snakes" are available for rent. If just one sink is stopped, use a drain opener. Follow directions carefully.

5. No heat: Remember that gas heat that has an electric thermostat or electric fan will not come on when the electricity is out. First, check the pilot light. Sometimes they blow out. Follow the directions on your furnace carefully to relight. If you can't get it to relight, call a heating/AC service.

6. No power: If the electricity is off in only one room or in specific appliances, check the breaker box to see if any breakers have been thrown. Turn off everything connected to that circuit before you flip the breaker back into position. If the power is out in the whole house, call the electric company.

7. No hot water: Check the pilot light on your hot-water heater to see if it has been blown out. Follow the directions on your unit carefully to relight. If you can't get it to relight, call the gas company—sometimes they will relight it for you. If not, call a plumber. (Sometimes you just need to hit the reset button on your water heater.)

Know When to Shop Till You Drop

CALENDAR FOR BARGAINS

If you want to buy	Good months to find a bargain are
Air conditioners	February, July, August
Appliances	January
Art supplies	January, February
Bathing suits	After July 4, August

If you want to buy	Good months to find a bargain are
Batteries and mufflers	September
Bedding	February, August
Bicycles	January, February, September, October, November
Blankets	January, May, November, December
Books	January
Building materials, lumber	June
Camping equipment	August
Carriages, strollers	January, August
Cars (new)	August, September
Cars (used)	February, November, December
Car-seat covers	February, November
Children's clothing	July, September, November, December
China	January, February, September, October
Christmas gifts	Anytime but Christmas
Clothes dryers	January, February, March, April
Clothing (spring)	End of June
Clothing (summer)	End of August
Clothing (fall)	End of November
Clothing (winter)	End of February
Coats (women's, children's)	April, August, November, December
Coats (men's)	January, August
Coats (winter)	March
Costume jewelry	January
Curtains	February
Dishes	January, February, September
Drapes and curtains	February, August

If you want to buy	Good months to find a bargain are
Dresses	January, April, June, November
Fabric	June, September, November
Fans	August
Fishing equipment	October
Frozen foods	June
Fuel oil	July
Furniture	January, February, June, August, September
Furs	January, August
Gardening equipment	August, September
Glassware	January, February, September, October
Handbags	January, May, July
Hardware	August, September
Hats (children's)	July, December
Hats (men's)	January, July
Hats (women's)	February, April, July
Home appliances	July
Home furnishings	January, February, August
Hosiery	March, October
Housecoats	April, May, June, October, November
Housewares	January, February, August, September
In-line skates	January
Infant's wear	January, March, April, July
Lamps	February, August, September
Linens	January, May
Lingerie	January, May, July
Luggage	March
Men's clothing	August, December

If you want to buy	Good months to find a bargain are
Men's shirts	January, February, July
Paints	August, September
Party items	December
Perfumes and colognes	July
Quilts	January, November, December
Radios	January, February, July
Refrigerators and freezers	January, July
Resort/cruisewear	January, February
Rugs and carpets	January, February, July, August, May, September
School clothes	August, October
School supplies	August, October
Shoes (boys' and girls')	January, March, July
Shoes (men's and women's)	January, July, November, December
Silverware	February, October
Ski equipment	March
Sportswear	January, February, May, July
Stereo equipment	January, February, July
Storm windows	January, February, March
Stoves	April, November
Suits (men's and boys')	April, November, December
Summer clothes and fabrics	June, July
Summer sports equipment	July
Tablecloths	January, May
Televisions	May, June
Tires	May, end of August
Toiletries	January, July
Tools, yard equipment	May, June
Towels	January, May, August
Toys	January, February
Washers and dryers	March

Seasonal Cleaning Plan:
Spring and Fall

Each family has its own fables and foibles when it comes to cleaning. They generally fall toward one end of a continuum or the other: it never gets done, or you can't do too much of it. Whatever yours are, it may be time to give them up because when it comes to deep cleaning, there are some universal truths that can guide us.

UNIVERSAL CLEANING TRUTH #1: We won't do a major cleaning more than once or twice a year—because it's a lot of hard work and the demands of daily life mean we probably don't have time to. This is just one of those facts of life we're going to feel better about if we accept. It's not a negative and it's not a positive. It is okay. No family ever died for want of bookcases that were emptied and dusted more than a few times a year. No Family Manager ever earned a gold crown because she washed her walls monthly.

UNIVERSAL CLEANING TRUTH #2: We can't clean until we declutter. Just like you've got to mow before you rake or cut before you sew, you've got to clear out the debris so you can find the surface you want to scrub. So before tackling a major housecleaning, declare a Declutter Campaign (see page 33). I believe it is impossible to both declutter and deep clean a house in the same weekend.

UNIVERSAL CLEANING TRUTH #3: We can't clean without a team. Well, we can, but it's both overwhelming physically and demoralizing emotionally. It's worth repeating: your home belongs to everyone who lives in it. Everyone who lives in it benefits from its use, so everyone should and can contribute to its livability. (For tips on building your teams, see page 15; on delegating appropriately, page 19; and for motivating reluctant team members, page 80.)

> "What one has to do usually can be done."
> —Eleanor Roosevelt

Don't fall for the guilt-inducing voice that suggests a great Family Manager can and should do it all—every manager knows that isn't true. Do your family the favor of having them learn how to invest in their common ground—for their mutual enjoyment.

UNIVERSAL CLEANING TRUTH #4: No cleaning day will be time-effective without preparation. Set aside the day or weekend, make sure family members are committed to participating, and have all supplies ready and out. Expect a good cleaning—depending on how many able helpers you have—to take four to five hours. If it's just you and your spouse, or you and one friend (see bartering ideas in The Friend Connection, page 97) or older child, you may need to spread out these chores over a two-day period. If your budget and priorities allow, you can cut back on your time by hiring some things out—window washing, carpet cleaning—or having a cleaning service come in and do the big jobs, so you can concentrate on details like polishing silver and brass, organizing bookcases, and so forth.

Before you begin, read this section through carefully. Then sit down with your family and a room-by-room inventory of your house that lists what needs to be done. Put initials next to who's responsible for which tasks. Set up a rough time frame; for example, you want to have the kitchen and living room done before noon. Be sure to take a short break every two hours or so. Drink plenty of water. And play some rousing music.

UNIVERSAL CLEANING TRUTH #5: Any cleaning day is more approachable if there are rewards at the end. Maybe dinner out, pizza and a movie in—something to celebrate everyone's efforts.

Spit-and-Polish Supply Checklist

Before cleaning day, make sure you have handy:
- All-purpose cleaner in spray bottles
- Heavy-duty disinfectant
- Alcohol-based glass cleaner
- Mild oil soap (for cleaning wood)
- Dishwashing soap
- Degreaser
- Oven cleaner
- Nonabrasive sink cleanser
- Squeegee with a twelve-inch rubber blade
- Brass and silver polish
- Baking soda
- Tub and tile cleaner for bathroom
- Toilet bowl cleaner and brush
- Mildew remover
- Furniture polish
- Hard-water stain cleaner
- Sponges
- Disposable, chemically treated dust cloths (they do the best job)
- Plastic buckets
- Vacuum with crevice tool (the long narrow tube with flattened tip to reach corners and the spaces around appliances); small, circular dusting brush that gets dust from blinds, baseboards, and shelves; small, handheld vacuum for staircases or wedge-shaped nozzle known as upholstery tool
- Dust mop
- Mop and bucket
- Broom and dustpan
- Scouring pads
- Scrub brushes
- Old toothbrush for cleaning grout and hard-to-get-at crevices
- Pumice stone (to rub on stubborn rust or mineral stains in toilet bowl)

- Rubber gloves
- Paper towels
- Garbage bags
- Optional: Rented carpet cleaner and floor polisher

Tips from the Pros: The Undirty Dozen

1. Move clockwise around the room; don't crisscross. You'll save steps.
2. Clean from top to bottom. Think gravity: ceilings first, then walls. Then furniture. Finally, floors.
3. Tackle one room at a time, finishing it before you move on to the next. Begin with the kitchen and the bathroom in the morning when you're fresh and have lots of energy.
4. Read labels on all cleaning products carefully. Use chemically based products sparingly; a small amount is often enough. Don't ever mix household cleaning products. Some can create poisonous fumes when combined. Keep all cleaning products out of the reach of small children.
5. Keep cleaning products and equipment in a plastic caddy or bucket for easy toting from room to room.
6. Plan your time efficiently. If the oven cleaner needs to work for an hour or so before you can scrub it out, then start that before you begin cleaning cupboards. On the other hand, if you have a self-cleaning oven and it's a warm day, you might want to set the oven to clean the last thing before you leave the kitchen. In the bathroom, spray mildew remover that needs to work for a while and toilet bowl cleaner into the toilet before you do anything else.
7. Forget feather dusters. They only scatter dust. Buy chemically treated dust cloths or make your own: mix two cups of hot water and one cup of lemon oil. Dip lintless rags into this solution, wring out thoroughly, and let air-dry. Store them in a covered metal can.

8. Unplug any appliance before cleaning it and never immerse it in water unless specified by the manufacturer.

9. When you scrub anything, always rub in all four directions—up and down and side to side.

10. For built-up grime or stubborn stains, start by loosening all the dirt you can with a brush. Next saturate the surface with cleaning solution and allow the chemicals to go to work, then remove dirt with a cloth. If this doesn't work, try a stronger cleanser and more elbow grease.

11. Wear knee pads when you get down on your knees to clean.

12. Before you vacuum, pick up any items—small pieces of toys, coins, buttons—that could clog the machine. Check your bag frequently and change it when it gets close to full. Your vacuum will work more efficiently.

DEEP-CLEANING THE KITCHEN

• Wash windows.

• Take down curtains and launder.

• Wash walls. Use two buckets—one half full with warm water and a capful of dishwashing liquid; the other half full with clean water in which to wring out and clean your dirty sponge.

• Spray on oven cleaner, using the procedure recommended on the package. Or set your oven on its self-cleaning cycle. Put exhaust vent filter in warm, soapy water or wash in dishwasher. Remove oven racks, stovetop drip pans, and stove knobs and dials, and place in warm, soapy water. While they're soaking, use an old toothbrush to clean grooves on dials and greasy spots on stovetop.

• Clean all woodwork, including fronts of drawers and cabinets. Wipe off handles and knobs.

• Vacuum refrigerator coils.

- Defrost refrigerator and/or freezer if necessary. Clean inside of both, discarding spoiled or outdated food. Wipe off outside.
- Return to oven to finish cleaning process.
- Clean all surfaces of microwave, inside and out.
- Remove everything from countertops one area at a time and clean thoroughly. Scrub backsplash.
- Wash and disinfect trash can; replace liner.
- Wipe off table and chairs.
- Wipe off small appliances and replace on counters.
- Vacuum floor and clean thoroughly, depending on type of floor covering.

TIPS FOR CLEANING WINDOWS

- Miniblinds: Take them down and clean them in the bathtub if they are really dirty, or wear a pair of cotton work gloves. Dip your hands into a solution of all-purpose cleaner and water, and wipe the slats with your fingers.
- Do not clean wood blinds or shutters with water. They may warp. Instead, wipe each slat with a cloth treated with furniture polish or use your vacuum dusting brush attachment.
- Windows: Wipe window with damp cloth to remove debris. Mix two tablespoons of rubbing alcohol into two quarts of hot water. For stubborn dirt, clean with pure white vinegar. Dip a rag or sponge into the solution and wipe over the entire window. (Old percale sheets make the best cleaning rags. Permanent press sheets will smear and streak.) Then wring out the sponge and wipe over the edges and sill. Dampen squeegee blade and place close to the top of the frame. Pull down to the bottom of the glass. Go crosswise next, wiping blade with a damp cloth between strokes. If you don't have a squeegee, wash the windows from top to bottom and dry with crumpled newspaper. (Wear rubber gloves to avoid getting ink on your hands.) Never wash the outsides of windows in the hot

sun. They dry too fast and leave streaks.

• When washing the outsides of windows and screens, use a permanent marker to write a number on the window or door frame and mark the same number on the corresponding screen. This makes it easy to put the screens back where they belong. Put each window's hardware in a bag marked with the number. Line up screens against an outside wall or fence and rinse them with a hose. If they're extra dirty, scrub with a soft-bristle brush, rinse, then shake off excess water. Allow to dry in the sun.

> A clean blackboard eraser is a great way to shine windows after you've washed them. This is a useful task to delegate to the kids.

DEEP-CLEANING THE LIVING AREAS

• Use vacuum attachment to reach cobwebs in corners of rooms. Or let kids make a cobweb pole by putting one thick cotton sock inside another and slipping them over the end of a yardstick, securing the end with a rubber band.

• Vacuum corners and crevices of room, high and low, with dusting and crevice attachments, moving furniture out from the wall as you go.

• Wash windows.

• Wash walls.

• If window coverings need cleaning, remove them. (The air-fluff cycle on your dryer is a great curtain de-duster.) Otherwise, vacuum them with the upholstery attachment.

• Clean out fireplace.

• Wipe off light fixtures, lamps, picture frames, and display items.

• Vacuum lampshades and pictures.

• Wipe off light switches with an alkaline solution like glass cleaner.

• Vacuum upholstered furniture with the upholstery attachment, removing cushions and using the crevice tool when necessary.

• Clean woodwork, paying particular attention to heavy-use areas, such as around doorknobs. For wood paneling, cabinets, and baseboards, use a sponge to clean with warm water and dishwashing liquid. Then wipe entire area with liquid oil soap. Buff dry immediately with soft cloth.

• Clean baseboards in a twosome: one person uses small brush attachment on vacuum while other moves furniture away from wall. Let your preschooler help with sock on hand.

• Vacuum floors/carpet. Or dust-mop exposed wood floors.

Floor Tricks

• Sprinkle baking soda in carpets at beginning of cleaning time and by the time you vacuum, odors will be absorbed.

• A handheld vacuum is the best tool to do stairs in half the time; start at the top and work down.

• Clean spots on carpets and rugs with club soda or a little shaving cream foam. Rub into stain, then wash with water. (Test a small area first.)

• Turn rugs around so they'll wear and soil evenly. Vacuum the rug padding and the floor beneath it.

DEEP-CLEANING THE BEDROOMS

• Vacuum corners and crevices of room, high and low, with dusting and crevice attachments, moving furniture out from the wall as you go.

• If window coverings need cleaning, remove them. Otherwise, vacuum them with upholstery attachment.

Clean a television screen with a paper towel dampened with water. Don't use a liquid cleaner or aerosol product.

- Wash walls and windows.
- Remove bedspread/dust skirt. Launder or dry clean if necessary.
- Strip bed. Launder mattress pad and pillow protectors. (Consider sending someone to the Laundromat with comforters, bedspreads, and throw rugs from all your bedrooms.)
- Check care instructions for bed pillows and clean as recommended.
- Remove mattress and vacuum box springs. Then vacuum mattress and turn; vacuum the other side.
- Vacuum upholstered furniture with upholstery attachment, removing cushions and using crevice tool when necessary.
- Vacuum lampshades and pictures.
- Wipe off light fixtures, lamps, picture frames, and display items.
- Clean woodwork, paying close attention to heavy-use areas, such as around doorknobs.
- Polish wood furniture.
- Put on fresh bedding.
- Pull anything out that's stored under the bed. Pull bed away from wall far enough to vacuum behind it. Vacuum wall and baseboard behind bed with dusting attachment, and vacuum edge of floor with crevice tool. Vacuum floor or carpeting under bed and then put bed back in place. Replace items stored under bed.
- Vacuum floors/rugs/carpeting.
- Dust exposed wood floors with dust mop.

DEEP-CLEANING THE BATHROOMS
- Open window or turn on exhaust fan. Spray shower and tub with heavy-duty cleaner designed for removing mildew and soap scum. Pour toilet cleaner into the toilet bowl. Let these cleaners work while you move on to the next step.
- Clean vinyl shower curtains in your washing machine. (For directions, see page 58.)

The one exception to my "don't declutter and clean at the same time" rule is for garages, basements, and attics. Since these are primarily storage areas, with some space devoted to certain family members' workstations or hobbies, they should be decluttered, organized, and cleaned as a team, led by the person who uses that space most, and on a different day than the deep cleaning takes place. (See User-Friendly Rooms Make a User-Friendly House, page 50, for plans for these rooms.)

- Vacuum crevices and corners, beginning high and working your way down the walls. Be sure to vacuum door and window moldings and windowsills.
- When washing walls, having two buckets works best—one half full with warm water and a capful of dishwashing liquid; the other half full with clean water in which to wring out and clean your dirty sponge.
- Clean light fixtures.
- Clean woodwork, paying close attention to areas around doorknobs and places where water or cosmetics might be splashed or sprayed.
- Clean mirror.
- Wipe off bathroom scale and any furniture.
- Remove everything from countertops. Wipe off the items and set them aside while you clean the counter, lavatory, and faucets. Replace things on countertops.
- Scrub shower and tub with a brush or scrubbing pad and rinse thoroughly. Wipe off chrome.
- Clean toilet bowl with a brush and wipe off all surfaces of bowl, tank, and seat with disinfectant cleaner.
- Vacuum floor, then scrub well with disinfectant cleaner. Allow to dry and replace throw rugs. (Launder throw rugs in the washer, but don't put in the dryer if they have rubber backing.)
- Hang clean shower curtain and liner.
- Hang fresh towels.

PLAY KEEP UP SO IT WON'T BE HARD TO CATCH UP

1. Commit to the Take Five decluttering strategies that work for you (see page 35). Employ them on at least an every-other-day basis.

2. Institute a regular cleaning routine. To avoid devoting precious weekend time to cleaning, clean one room per day every week. If you're a dual-career Family Manager, do the pickup in the morning before you leave the house and the cleaning in the evening. You could do this during your children's homework time if you're not cleaning the space they work in, or after young children go to bed. Or you and your spouse can trade off reading to younger children while the other does a half hour's worth of cleaning.

3. An alternate daily routine is to do one task per day or evening; for example, dust on Monday, vacuum on Tuesday, mop floors on Wednesday, clean bathrooms on Thursday, and pick up on Friday and Sunday.

Garage Sales:
Turning Trash into Cash

Need quick cash? Get the whole family involved and turn the results of your closet-cleaning binge into profit. Successful garage sale-ing calls for advance planning. Allow three weeks before your sale date to cull, sort, price, and tend to administrative details.

For years, annual garage sales have been Peel family projects. We all share in the work. We all go out to eat at the end of the day to celebrate. And we all share in the proceeds. You can do that by splitting the profit equally among you, keeping track of who's selling what so each gets the money from his items, or putting all the proceeds into a kitty for a special family purchase or vacation.

Depending on the climate you live in, you can have a garage sale almost any time of the year. The advantages of spring garage sales is that people who shop them tend to hit several places in one day, and there will

See Clutter Control, page 30, and Sane Storage, page 40. I highly recommend that you implement some of the ideas in those sections before you plan your garage sale. I've been surprised at how much I actually had to sell. Also, check with your children. They may have things they'd like to sell. Getting them to help on salary is one thing, but getting them to buy in as "business partners" will make them that much more valuable to you.

be more in the spring. On the other hand, if you have a lot of kids' school clothing or sports equipment that's used mostly in the fall and winter to sell, you might do better with an end-of-summer, back-to-school special sale.

COUNTDOWN TO SALE DAY
THREE WEEKS BEFORE

• Take inventory. If you don't have enough merchandise for a sale, ask friends or neighbors to join you. If they can't help the day of the sale, work out a commission and take their merchandise on consignment. Having a wider variety of merchandise to advertise and display makes your sale more interesting to shoppers and will bring more profit.

• Set the date. Avoid holiday weekends.

• Decide what time to begin and end your sale. Experienced garage-sale shoppers like to come early, before merchandise is picked over. Count on half as many shoppers in the afternoon.

• Have a contingency plan in case of rain.

• Call your local community government to check out garage-sale regulations.

• Visit a few garage sales in your area to pick up tips. From a customer's point of view, make mental notes of what makes some sales more successful than others. Take willing children with you and ask what they noticed as well.

• Begin sorting your merchandise by category.

TWO WEEKS BEFORE

- Oil tools and repair broken items. They'll bring a higher price.
- Polish wood furniture and cover scratches with scratch remover.
- Polish silver pieces; clean dishes and glassware.
- Wash and fold linens; wash, iron, and hang clothing.
- Advise neighbors about your sale. If they don't want customers to park in front of their home, have your children make a "Do Not Park" sign to put up on sale days.
- Place an ad in a community shopper handout for the week before the sale and another ad in your local newspaper to run the weekend of your event. Make ads short and to the point. Include dates, times, a sampling of your merchandise, your address, and brief directions, if needed. Don't include your phone number unless you're selling specific items potential buyers need to ask questions about. This way you won't waste time answering phone calls about trivial things.

WEEK OF THE SALE

- Price merchandise. Don't mark prices directly on articles. Some ink may not wash out. Instead, use stickers or masking tape.
- Secure display tables and racks.
- Go to the bank. Get at least fifty singles, a few fives, and twenty dollars in quarters, dimes, and nickels.
- Make sure you have an extension cord available for customers to check items that require power, a tape measure or yardstick, bags, plastic tarps to cover merchandise in case of rain, and a full-length mirror.
- Create eye-catching, legible signs using heavy cardboard or brightly colored poster board. Keep your message simple—"Garage Sale," your address, the dates, and the times. Use stakes or tacks to place signs in prominent locations two days before your sale.
- Make notices about your sale on three-by-five-inch index cards. Post them on public bulletin boards at libraries, bus depots, churches, restaurants, supermarkets, and Laundromats.

• Prepare lunches and dinners ahead of time for sale days.

• Arrange for a charitable organization to pick up leftover items after the sale.

• The day before your sale, decorate your yard with banners, tinsel, lights—anything that looks good, draws attention to your sale, and is easy to take down afterward.

• Set up as much as possible the day before the sale. If you have an enclosed garage, arrange merchandise. If the sale is in your driveway or yard, set out tables and racks.

SALE DAY

• Get up early. Dress in comfortable clothes and shoes.

• Finish displaying goods and put a sale sign in your yard. Be ready for early-bird shoppers.

• Put cash and change in a safe location.

• Place a garbage can in an easy-access location.

AFTER THE SALE

• Take down all signs.

• Pack unsold merchandise to donate or save for your next sale. If you donate, get a receipt for your tax deduction.

• Take down tables and pick up debris.

• Write down notes about what you learned—what worked and what didn't. This will make your next sale easier.

• Double-check with newspapers to make sure your ad is canceled.

• Return any unsold consignment items and pay consignor.

• Take your cash to the bank as soon as possible.

• Thank neighbors for their cooperation.

PRICING POINTERS

Experienced garage-sale shoppers know when an item is overpriced. Use these tips to price to sell.

• Base your asking price for an item on what shoppers will pay, not on what the item is worth to you. After your sale begins, if merchandise seems to be moving too quickly or too slowly, it may be priced too low or too high. Adjust prices during a lull.

• Depending on the condition and age of the items, use as a guideline 20 to 30 percent of the current retail value as listed in a discount store catalog.

• Mark used adult clothing at 10 percent of its replacement value. Children's clothes in good condition will bring slightly more.

• For easier money handling, price everything in increments of 25¢.

• Price items high enough so you don't mind coming down when someone makes a reasonable offer. People love to bargain.

• Have one box of 50¢ items, a box of 25¢ items, and a grab box labeled "Free" filled with odd items you probably can't sell. Customers appreciate this.

• Be honest and don't misrepresent your merchandise. Mark items that are damaged or not in working order "As Is." Some people buy items just for the parts.

• If you need to keep sale money separate for family members or friends, use color-coded or initialed tags on the items for sale. Have a designated cashier keep a journal of the names of sellers and amounts collected for their items. This way you'll know how to split the money at the end of the day.

• Create signs to put on your belongings that are not for sale, such as the family lawn mower and patio chairs. Otherwise you'll have a steady stream of shoppers wanting to know prices for these things.

• Post "Please Be Careful" or "Please Do Not Touch" signs near expensive or fragile merchandise you don't want manhandled. Customers who want to make serious inquiries will ask for your assistance.

SETTING UP SHOP

These ideas will help you make your sale as appealing to the eye as to the pocketbook.

1. Provide as much light as possible in the sale area.

2. Keep articles off the ground if possible. They look better on a table and are less likely to get dirty or broken. Use any spare tables from your house or yard—card tables, folding TV tables, or patio tables. Borrow or rent extra card tables or folding banquet tables, if needed. Make tables from plywood and sawhorses. When setting up tables, leave plenty of room for customers to browse around. Remember that all tables need to be sturdy enough to hold merchandise and to be leaned on and bumped into by customers.

3. If possible, arrange displays so they look attractive from the street. This will bring more lookers to your sale.

4. Ask a local appliance store for free washing-machine or large TV boxes. Turn them upside down and use the bottom for a tabletop. When your sale is over, clean up quickly by loading leftover merchandise into the boxes to store for your next sale or to give away.

5. Make clothing racks from pipes, long dowel rods, or broom handles suspended from garage rafters with rope. Or secure an extension ladder, a long chain or rope, or a long, narrow board between garage-door tracks to create a hanging rack.

6. Use straight pins to hang necklaces and display other jewelry on a bulletin board with a dark background. They will show up better. Or make your own jewelry-display board by covering a large piece of heavy cardboard or plywood with scrap fabric.

7. Smaller, more expensive items like jewelry should be kept in a closed case or box and constantly monitored.

8. Organize your merchandise by department—household items in one area, exercise equipment in another, and toys in another. People will find things more easily.

9. Invite an older child to set up a coffee and doughnut table at your sale. Early-bird shoppers will welcome the refreshments and your child can earn some extra cash.

10. Have an outgoing child greet shoppers at the "entrance," giving a brief summary of what's available. Think of fancy department stores that have "helpers" posted at main entrances to direct people to the department of their choice. If things are moving slowly, you might decide to declare a 20 percent markdown on all women's clothes or dishes. The greeter can announce that to new arrivals. Or he or she can tell about particularly attractive items they'll find, like the wonderful selection of jigsaw puzzles on the bookshelf next to the toy table.

HOW TO HAGGLE

Keep a sense of fun in your sale! Bargaining is some people's favorite part of garage sale-ing. Here's how to do it properly.

• Lower your prices thoughtfully. If you jump at an offer too quickly, the bargainer might offer even less.

• If an item is priced at twenty dollars and a customer offers ten, this is usually a request to meet in the middle and split the difference. You must decide how badly you want to sell the item.

• Be wary of shoppers who haggle at checkout for a large number of items. If they learn you're easy to bargain with, they might offer you a lower lump sum to take all the items they're interested in off your hands. You won't make as much money as you would selling the items individually.

• Haggle discreetly. If other shoppers hear you bargaining, this might give them the courage to bid lower on an item they would have bought for the original price.

• If you don't want to haggle and feel your merchandise is priced fairly, tell buyers who offer less to check back at the end of the sale to see if items didn't sell. Or get the buyer's phone number and call at the end of your sale to see if he or she is still interested.

SECURE IS AS SECURE DOES

Keep your merchandise as well as your other possessions safe.

1. The more people who work at your garage sale, the less likely your chances of being robbed. At least three workers is ideal—one to keep the money, one to help customers and answer questions, and one to watch the sale area for shoplifters. The person watching the sale area can ask people if they'd like to have the merchandise they're carrying around held for them at the cashier's table. If people begin to walk away from the yard with items they haven't paid for, the person monitoring should point out where the cashier's table is and say the person there would be happy to help them. Politeness is important. You don't want to offend people who might have paid and you just missed seeing them check out. You also don't want to get into a nasty confrontation, and sometimes it might be better to just let people go with inexpensive items rather than risking that.

2. Be aware of shoplifter habits. Make special note of people who are constantly handling merchandise and seem to be always looking to see if you're watching them. Sometimes people will pick up merchandise, then if you look away, they'll slip it into their pocket or purse.

3. Keep your doors locked. Burglars are clever and have been known to distract homeowners at a garage sale while an accomplice slips into the house. When he or she walks out with a TV, no one notices because the thief blends in with other shoppers.

4. Whatever you use to keep the money in, empty it regularly by having one person in charge of putting excess amounts inside the house.

5. If you don't have one person to work the checkout and pay station, keep your money on your person.

6. Decide whether you want to accept checks. If you don't accept them, you run the risk of missing sales because many shoppers don't carry a lot of cash. If you do, take preventive measures to lessen your risk of accepting bad checks.

- Take only checks made out to you for the exact amount of purchase.
- Ask for identification—driver's license and credit-card number, and license plate number of his/her car, if possible.
- Don't take out-of-town checks or checks that don't have the name and address of the customer imprinted.

Summer Survival:
Developing the Other Rs

Common Misconception #1: Summer months will take care of themselves.

Common Misconception #2: Summers are fillers between the "real" stuff of school years.

I held both of these misconceptions big-time. But, as often happens in life, my children became my teachers. After only a few days of bored, hot, constantly hungry kids, I realized summer could be more of an endurance test than a picnic in the park. I needed a plan and a purpose to make sure that summer vacation would become a memorable, rewarding adventure. So I began to seek ways to turn tedium into joy without acquiring an advanced degree in childhood development or extraordinary supplies.

Summer is about more than survival. It's not "filler" time. With some planning and thought, it can be a time to help your kids learn the other Rs: responsibility, resourcefulness, and recreational interests. The activities and ideas in this section are all designed to help promote these skills and traits.

They're also designed to help insure that you don't end up at the Home for the Frantically Flustered before Labor Day. I recommend that as you implement ideas you begin your own Summer Survival file. In addition to jotting down what works well from these ideas and your own, clip ideas from magazines and newspapers. Next year you'll have a head start. (Note: Check out 52 Ways to Make Ordinary Days Special, page 231, for more family fun ideas.)

Begin with a declaration of intent: What would you like to see happen in your kids' lives this summer? How do you want to see them develop? Ninety days of progress toward these objectives lie ahead, but only if you have a clear plan. There are four areas every child needs to grow in: intellectual, physical, spiritual, and social-emotional. As you plan summer activities, strive to include a variety of experiences that will enhance growth in each area. If you have trouble motivating yourself to plan summer activities, just remind yourself of the old adage: "If you aim at nothing, you'll very likely hit it."

CONSULT THE EXPERTS

Have a family meeting before the summer begins and list ideas of what goals you want to set for each child. Ask your children for input: What would they enjoy doing the most and what would they like to learn more about? What special abilities or interests would they like to develop? Listen attentively. Even preschoolers will have ideas. Be flexible when they respond negatively to some of your ideas. Then set aside some quiet time when you and your spouse alone can plan summer activities according to the council.

The ideas in this section can help you get started. I'd be surprised if once you put your collective thinking caps on you don't come up with ideas of your own.

In Pursuit of a Plan

This chart with a plethora of ideas will help you get started. When planning your summer, have your child respond to the ideas on the chart. This will help you know what kinds of activities to plan as you consider his or her preferences.

ATHLETIC ACTIVITIES	AWESOME!	OKAY	BORING
Baseball, softball	___	___	___
Baton twirling	___	___	___
Bicycling	___	___	___

ATHLETIC ACTIVITIES	AWESOME!	OKAY	BORING
Boating	___	___	___
Bowling	___	___	___
Croquet	___	___	___
Dancing	___	___	___
Fishing	___	___	___
Gymnastics	___	___	___
Hiking	___	___	___
Horseback riding	___	___	___
In-line skating	___	___	___
Jumping rope	___	___	___
Kite flying	___	___	___
Soccer	___	___	___
Swimming	___	___	___
Tennis	___	___	___
Water games	___	___	___
Waterskiing, water sliding	___	___	___

FUN LEARNING ACTIVITIES	AWESOME!	OKAY	BORING
Animals—adopt and care for one	___	___	___
Building models	___	___	___
Building birdhouses or other simple carpentry projects	___	___	___
Collecting—baseball cards, coins, dolls, shells, or stamps	___	___	___
Computer	___	___	___
Doll and dollhouse making	___	___	___
Drawing and illustrating stories	___	___	___
Film—make home videos	___	___	___
Foreign language—learn one	___	___	___
Humor—write jokes, tell riddles, read and draw comics	___	___	___

FUN LEARNING ACTIVITIES	AWESOME!	OKAY	BORING
Inventions—make new things	____	____	____
Library story hours	____	____	____
Mask making	____	____	____
Musical instrument lessons	____	____	____
Performing magic tricks	____	____	____
Planting a garden—vegetable, flower, or herb	____	____	____
Puppet making	____	____	____
Puzzle making	____	____	____
Research your town and its activities	____	____	____
Sewing	____	____	____
Watercolor painting	____	____	____
Writing	____	____	____

OUTDOOR AND NATURE ACTIVITIES	AWESOME!	OKAY	BORING
Animal farm or shelter—study the animals	____	____	____
Astronomy—learn about the stars	____	____	____
Beach-walking, building sand castles, and studying marine life	____	____	____
Bird feeder—build one and record the types of birds who use it	____	____	____
Forest and wood life—explore it	____	____	____
Geology—collect, identify, and polish rocks	____	____	____
Nature centers—attend a local program and crafts class	____	____	____
Science—attend classes and workshops at museums and planetarium	____	____	____
Zoo—visit and study the animals	____	____	____

FUN PLACES TO GO	AWESOME!	OKAY	BORING
Airport	___	___	___
Aquarium	___	___	___
Bakery	___	___	___
Band concert	___	___	___
Beach	___	___	___
Book publisher	___	___	___
Bottling company	___	___	___
Campsite	___	___	___
Candle factory	___	___	___
Candy factory—watch chocolate being melted, molded, foiled, and packed	___	___	___
Car-manufacturing plant	___	___	___
Circus	___	___	___
Clothing manufacturer	___	___	___
Computer company or store	___	___	___
Country fair	___	___	___
Courthouse or state capitol	___	___	___
Dance recital	___	___	___
Farmers' market	___	___	___
Fireworks display	___	___	___
Fish hatchery	___	___	___
Garage sale or flea market	___	___	___
Greenhouse	___	___	___
Historical site	___	___	___
Hotel	___	___	___
Ice-cream factory	___	___	___
Lake	___	___	___
Library	___	___	___
Local newspaper plant—ask if you and your child can tour the newsroom and layout area, and watch the printing presses	___	___	___

FUN LEARNING ACTIVITIES	AWESOME!	OKAY	BORING
Magic or juggling show	____	____	____
Movies	____	____	____
Museum—bring home souvenir postcards to save the memory	____	____	____
Dairy farm	____	____	____
Music concert	____	____	____
Nature preserve or zoo	____	____	____
Parades	____	____	____
Parents' places of work	____	____	____
Parks—amusement, theme, water, or nature	____	____	____
Place of worship that has a different kind of service from your own	____	____	____
Planetarium	____	____	____
Political rally	____	____	____
Printing company	____	____	____
Puppet show	____	____	____
Radio or TV station—call ahead and ask if you can watch them broadcast	____	____	____
River	____	____	____
Seaport	____	____	____
Sports event	____	____	____
Sugar factory	____	____	____
Telephone company	____	____	____
Theater or summer stock	____	____	____
Top of the highest building near you— see what landmarks you can spot	____	____	____
Toy manufacturer	____	____	____

A Dozen Strategies for a
Super-Duper Summer for Younger Kids

1. Have a summer-launching dinner or event—a time that indicates to your children that a new, fun, and interesting season of life is beginning.

2. Adjust your house rules. If you want to let them stay up later, then you'll want them to rest in the afternoon. Decide how much TV may be watched.

3. Provide a broad mix of activities each week so kids can grow in both character and experience: doing chores, becoming more physically fit, playing well with friends, spending quiet time reading or working on projects.

4. Make a list of ideas you can plug at any point into the schedule. Use this list if an activity has to be changed at the last minute. And stay flexible. What looks good when you plan it on Saturday may not be right when Wednesday arrives.

5. Check which activities need advance planning and make necessary arrangements in plenty of time.

6. On the weekend or the Friday before, make a list of any supplies you will need for the week. Collect or purchase them beforehand.

7. Organize your home so activities and equipment are in easy-to-reach places. Choose a cabinet for art and game supplies. Include drawing supplies, paints, rubber stamps, construction paper, scissors, markers, and glue. Choose another cabinet for plastic eating utensils, paper plates, and snack foods. Set aside a special drawer for paint and craft clothes for kids to wear while doing messy projects.

8. Enlist your friends and neighbors in a series of mothers' and fathers' skills trade-off day. Hold small classes for your child's friends in your home. If your forte is cooking, host a cooking class. If you are a good seamstress, conduct a sewing class. Maybe a neighbor is good with drawing, woodworking, or gardening.

9. Check on summer classes and programs offered through your local library, museum, YMCA, boys' or girls' clubs, community colleges, or parks and recreation departments.

10. Send your children to summer camp. Everybody needs a break—including your kids. There are many excellent camps, some offered by YMCAs and churches, across America. We have found that going away to camp teaches children flexibility, independence, and responsibility. They develop their social skills and observe positive role models, which broaden their understanding of other people from different walks of life.

11. Plan some activities where you and your children will be learning together. A few years ago, James, then age eleven, and I took up in-line skating together.

12. Make sure you schedule time for yourself. Hire a babysitter or barter with other moms. Also plan some activities with other moms and kids so you have adult company while you do "kid stuff."

ADAPTING THESE IDEAS FOR DUAL-CAREER MOMS

As you already know, if you work outside the home, summer can be especially challenging. I was working at other jobs, sometimes full-time, sometimes part-time, when I developed and used the ideas in this section. I encourage you to not be overwhelmed by the number of ideas here and especially to feel free to adapt them to your needs.

For instance, give your babysitter or nanny specific instructions about taking your children on field trips or to classes or programs suggested here. Make sure you get a daily report from both the nanny

A SUMMER TIP FOR KEEPING KIDS RIGHT AS RAIN
With school out, summer is prime time for making doctor and dentist appointments for children. But do you really want to cart them to appointments all summer long? Schedule the visits early in the summer or late in the season to meet school requirements, all during the same week.

and your kids in order to ensure that they aren't "tubing out" in front of the TV and are getting plenty of opportunities to exercise their imaginations and their bodies. If your children will be in day care, choose one that comes closest to meeting your objectives. Discuss with the center what goals you have for your children and see what you can do to help accomplish them.

If your kids are old enough to stay alone, communicate clearly what you expect of them while you are gone. It's crucial that you listen to their goals as well and help them plan to meet them. Assist them in setting goals for each day that contribute to their growth.

BEYOND BABYSITTING: SUPER SUMMER JOBS FOR KIDS

Starting from the time our two oldest boys were nine and five, they had to earn and save money for big purchases and summer camp. In those early days they had flower-bulb-selling and porch-and-driveway-sweeping businesses. As they grew, they worked at odd jobs and ran their own businesses, and

SUMMER SURVIVAL TIPS FOR DUAL-CAREER FAMILY MANAGERS

1. For the summer, minimize cooking and housekeeping chores. If you can afford it, consider hiring a teen to clean your house so you'll have more time free to spend with your children. Serve simple meals. Consider expanding your food budget slightly to buy precooked food, prechopped vegetables, and so on, for the summer months.
2. While you are at work, use your break time to plan how you can maximize the hours you will spend with your family, run errands, and purchase supplies for projects. And spend some quiet time by yourself so you're refreshed for the rest of the day.
3. When you walk through the door at home, your frame of mind is crucial. Take a quick shower before you change into your evening clothes. Or take ten minutes to close your eyes and get your second wind.

> **4.** If at all possible, arrange to take some vacation days for "at home" time. Use those days to do special projects or go on field trips with your children.

they also acquired great experiences. They learned to communicate with adults in a professional manner, realized the importance of being responsible when working for others, and discovered creative ways to advertise. They also learned to delay gratification, found out how to make good financial decisions, and acquired an appreciation for what things cost. Finally, they experienced the satisfaction of knowing what it is to do a job well.

Start by brainstorming about the types of services or products your kids can offer. Check with local government offices to see if a business license or permit is needed. Then create an advertising flyer or a business card to distribute to homes or post on public bulletin boards. Let the following inspire your own ideas:

- Aid the elderly—do their shopping, run errands.
- Babysit.
- Bake and sell homemade bread and cookies.
- Be a birthday clown.
- Caddie for a golfer.
- Clean carpets.
- Clean houses or move furniture.
- Clean swimming pools.
- Clear away old junk and trash.
- Clip and organize coupons in envelopes for Mom. (Let your children keep the refunds.)
- Distribute flyers for local small businesses.
- Groom pets.
- Help people move—pack and clean up.
- Hold a garage sale. (See Garage Sales: Turning Trash into Cash, p. 137.)

- Iron clothes.
- Make and paint signs.
- Mow lawns.
- Offer a messenger service.
- Paint outdoor furniture, fences, doghouses, porches, decks, storage sheds.
- Paint house numbers on curbs with stencils.
- Pet-sit. Many working adults are delighted to pay someone else to give their pet care and affection or to walk their dog while they're at work.
- Plan and host birthday parties. Older kids can help parents give birthday parties for small children. They can dress up like a party-theme character, help with crafts, organize and oversee games, pass out food, pick up trash, and help watch for small guests who might wander off.
- Plant a pumpkin patch. Sell the pumpkins in October.
- Produce a backyard carnival and sell tickets for the games and refreshments.
- Publish a neighborhood newspaper or newsletter. Collect information about opportunities in your community, who has what for sale, services or items that neighbors would like to trade, and other facts of interest to the people in your area. Type out information and make copies to sell to neighbors.
- Pull weeds.
- Put on a backyard day camp.
- Rake leaves.
- Repair bikes.
- Run an errand service, including grocery and dry-cleaning delivery.
- Start an odd-job service. Advertise by passing out flyers in the neighborhood.
- Sweep porches and driveways.
- Tend and entertain younger children.

- Tutor younger children in reading.
- Type, do word processing.
- Wash cars. Try an on-the-spot car wash. Kids can go door-to-door carrying cloths, buckets, window spray, a whisk broom, and a portable minivacuum.
- Wash windows.
- Water plants and yards for vacationing families.

Just for Kids: How to Make Friends and Influence Clients

Be sensitive about what kinds of jobs your kids will feel comfortable performing. An outgoing child won't mind going door-to-door, drumming up business from neighbors. But a shy child may feel threatened at the thought of talking to an adult one-on-one. Teaching your children some simple communication skills can bolster their courage and help them make a good impression on potential customers.

1. Have a neat appearance. An adult is more likely to want to hire a child with clean clothes and combed hair.
2. Make good eye contact and shake hands firmly. Have your child practice looking directly into your eyes while talking. People are more likely to trust someone who will look them in the eye. Practice a firm handshake. This sends the signal that your child has a good self-image and takes his or her business seriously.
3. Give a clear, concise message describing services or products. Help your child write down exact words. Pretend you are the customer and role-play the situation until your child has memorized the lines and feels comfortable saying them.
4. Smile and be courteous—even if you get turned down. A person who says no today may call later.

A BAKER'S DOZEN SUMMER CLASSROOM "LESSON" PLANS

Remember that summer is a time for learning other Rs—responsibility, resourcefulness, and recreational interests. But studies show some kids lose some academic skills over the summer in basics like reading, writing, and arithmetic. What's a concerned Family Manager to do? Should she keep up the drill and have her kids do some worksheets? Or is the summer a time to kick back, roll in the grass, and watch the butterflies flutter by? You can do both by designing activities that use your kids' academic skills and teach some of the other Rs as well.

1. Take Over the Kitchen Night: Let your children use simple cookbooks to create a menu for dinner. With appropriate supervision, they could try a different combination of recipes every week. They'll use reading and math to follow recipes. They can exercise creativity by making a sign, menus, and place mats with the name or logo of their restaurant. They'll also be learning responsibility and how to divide it.

2. Have a toy sale. Ask neighborhood children to look for toys they never use or have outgrown. Children can design posters to advertise the sale, decide on prices, and run the sale. They can then deliver the profits (or a portion thereof) to a shelter for homeless families. They'll learn a lot about relationships and working together, and use their math and planning skills to get everything organized.

3. Help your kids organize a neighborhood Fourth of July parade. Research historical characters and costumes in an encyclopedia, on the Internet, or at your local library. Invite the neighbors to join in. Give small prizes for the most historically accurate costumes, for the funniest, etc. Make sure everybody's efforts get recognized. Or, as an alternative to a Fourth of July parade, have a pageant. Kids can act out scenes from history—Boston Tea Party, Washington crossing the Delaware, the signing of the Declaration of Independence. They can research, write the script (which they could read or memorize), and make costumes.

4. To reinforce writing skills, kids can write their grandparents, aunts and uncles, cousins, even friends. They practice writing—and reading when they receive responses. Plus they're learning about their responsibility in keeping up relationships with family at a distance. If you have a computer, consider getting an e-mail service. Even the most reluctant readers and writers might enjoy e-mail correspondence. Or help your child write a letter to a favorite author. Send the letter to the author's publisher requesting that the letter be forwarded to the author. (Check the copyright page of the author's book for the publisher's address.) Many authors will write back.

5. Experts say kids need to read about twenty minutes a day if they want to maintain their reading skills. Start a summer reading club with some of your children's friends. Charge a small fee to join and use the money to buy a gift certificate at your favorite bookstore for the one who reads the most books. At the end of the summer, have an ice-cream party to announce the winner and award the prize. Present reading certificates to all who participated.

6. Have your child make her own code with numbers representing letters. Send coded messages to friends.

7. Give your child a list of twenty items to find in the newspaper. See how long it takes to find the items on the list.

8. Play the stock market. Give each of your children five hundred dollars' worth of play money and help them "buy" stock listed on the financial page of the newspaper. Keep track of all purchases and sales. Check the financial page each day, comparing the ups and downs of their stocks. Let them buy and sell to try to recoup lost money or make more. Not least among the new skills they'll learn are the benefits and pitfalls of risk taking.

9. Take a challenging trip to the zoo. Before you go, use an encyclopedia to look up animals you will see and make a list of their scientific names. Have your child try to locate each animal by using this list of names and matching them to the scientific names on the cages.

10. Buy a tree-identification book, or check one out at the library. Go on an outing and, together, identify the trees in your region.

11. Take a ride on a bus, train, or subway. Have your child record the experience by writing a travel journal about where you go and what you see and do. Your child will polish observational and writing skills.

12. Take a drive to locate and read historical markers in your area. See what happened in years past right where you are.

13. Visit the statehouse. Watch legislators debate, view the governor's office, and listen to the clerk explain how a bill becomes a law. Call your statehouse beforehand to make sure the congress is in session. Some states allow older children to be pages on the chamber floor. Ask how to sign up your kids if they're interested.

Vacations are a great time to teach your children many different skills. You can start with teaching them how to read a map or atlas. As they begin to get an understanding of the road systems, show them where you live and where your vacation destination is. You can also give them a math lesson by having them add up the miles between certain places. As they progress in their understanding, you could have them figure out the following: Would it be shorter to use another route? How much farther would it be if we were to stop by this certain point of interest? If we average 60 mph, how long will it take to get there? You can also teach them to observe the geographical information on a map and ask: How many rivers will we cross? What is the highest mountain we will cross?

Teach them what a point of interest is and have them observe the points of interest on the map. They could then investigate at the library, look in an encyclopedia, call or visit the chamber of commerce, or look on a Web site to find out more information about points of interest that intrigue them. You could also have them pick out five points of interest they would like to visit on the family vacation.

Start a Summer Growth Spurt

Summer is a perfect time to teach kids important life skills. To make the learning process enjoyable, remember to be patient; be prepared for your children to fail at first, and encourage every step of progress until they learn. To decide what things your kids should know, use the following checklist. Add your own ideas as well.

Children ages five through eight can learn how to:
- React if a fire breaks out.
- Identify poisonous plants.
- Dial 911 for help.
- Answer the telephone politely.
- Wash off a wound and get a Band-Aid.
- Set the table.
- Sweep.
- Make up a bed.
- Help with laundry: fold flat items, match socks, and put things away.
- Pick up clutter.
- Load the dishwasher with unbreakables.
- Respond if confronted by a stranger.
- Cook something simple with supervision, like a grilled cheese sandwich or French toast.

Children ages nine through twelve can learn how to:
- Sew on buttons and do simple mending.
- Use a washer and dryer, and decide which product to use when— stain remover, detergent, bleach, softener.
- Iron simple items with supervision.
- Chop wood and start a fire.
- Operate kitchen appliances.
- Safely use a knife.
- Administer basic first aid.

- Use different kinds of household cleaners.
- Write and follow a simple budget.
- Cope during a power outage.
- Hammer and remove nails.
- Use a screwdriver.
- Read a road map.
- Put air in tires.
- Wash a car.
- Wrap gifts.

Teenagers can learn how to:
- Do business at a bank—open accounts, balance a checkbook, make deposits and withdrawals.
- Set up appointments over the telephone.
- Write a résumé and interview for a job.
- Shut off water in case of a leak.
- Fix a leaky faucet.
- Iron clothes.
- Mow safely.
- Jump-start a car.
- Perform CPR.
- Unstop a toilet.
- Pump gasoline.
- Check the oil level and tire pressure on car.
- Change a flat tire.
- Plan and cook meals.

Under the Stars

There's lots to do outside on a summer's night. Camping out at a state or national park or simply pitching a tent in your own backyard can be a great adventure. Try to pitch your tent on flat ground and facing east so the first rays of sunshine will bring warmth the next morning. It's also fun to hang a flag or pennant at your campsite. (You can make a flag from a rectangular piece of sturdy cloth, tacked to a pole.) Whether you're camping out or just having a late adventure, try some of these activities.

• Create your own constellations. What do you see in the sky in the way of people, animals, common objects? Name them. Some of ours have been The Big Spatula, Nana's Coffee Cup, and Celestial Seesaw.

• Tell a continuing story—an exciting drama or a hilarious comedy. One family member starts the story, and each person adds more to the adventure.

• Make up animal or adventure stories with your children as the main characters.

• Use this opportunity to get to know each other better. Ask questions like: What do you feel you're good at? What do you wish you were better at? What do you wish you could do that you don't know how to do? What's your favorite time of day? Why? What do you like to do with the family? If you could travel anyplace in the world, where would you go?

• Sing songs around a campfire.

• Catch fireflies in a jar and watch them light up. Try to time the intervals between flashes. Notice the variations in color.

• Listen for nocturnal animals; see how many you can identify. You don't need to be near a wild area to hear a number of different animals that hunt for food when the sun goes down. Raccoons, skunks, opossums, and mice are among the mammals that live near people.

• Go on a walk with a flashlight and look for the opening of night-blooming flowers, such as moonflowers, evening primrose, datura, and evening-scented stock.

25 GREAT SUMMER BOREDOM BUSTERS FOR KIDS

Keeping children creatively occupied during summer vacation is a no-brainer for some mothers. They turn ordinary Styrofoam meat trays into multideck bathtub yachts and toilet paper tubes into state-of-the-art binoculars. When their kids cry, "Mom, I'm bored!" they simply pull out their list of 501 things to do with a wooden clothespin.

Other women rank arts and crafts right up there with getting a root canal. As far as they know, plaster of Paris is a fashion designer from France. I fall into the second category.

When our three boys were young, keeping them creatively occupied from Memorial Day until Labor Day was a stretch for a woman who doesn't "do glue." But I'm a pretty quick study. So I didn't have to hear "Mom, I'm bored" more than six thousand times in the first week of summer vacation to decide I needed to find some crafts I could pull together with household items. The key is realizing most kids love to get their hands dirty, especially if it means producing a fun project. Here are some of my kids' favorites.

1. *Textured Paint:* Mix 2 teaspoons salt, 1 teaspoon liquid starch, 1 teaspoon water, and a few drops of tempera paint in a bowl. This paint makes a shiny, grainy picture. Paint with an artist-type brush on heavy paper.

2. *Kid Collage:* Help your kids make collages of their lives with pictures cut from magazines. Include pictures of favorite activities, sports, foods, and animals.

3. *Toothpick Architecture:* Roll modeling clay into tiny beads, about 1/4 inch in diameter. Use the beads as corner joints for holding the toothpicks in place. Build houses, space stations, anything!

4. *Spooky Sponge Creatures:* Cut a 4-inch or larger cellulose sponge (the kind that has large, irregular holes) into an animal-head shape, like a cat, rabbit, or mouse. Cut pieces of black felt to make ears, eyes, nose, and mouth. Use a glue gun to attach the face pieces to the sponge. Draw whiskers on the face with a black marker. Place a flashlight behind your animal's face and it will glow in the dark.

5. *Box Buildings:* Collect empty cereal and cracker boxes, and waxed milk and cream cartons. Turn them into buildings by gluing on construc-

tion paper or brown grocery sacks cut to fit sides. Draw windows, doors, and other features. Budding architects can become city planners by drawing streets and city blocks on a large piece of paper, then placing the food-box buildings on the map. Get out a few toy cars and they can have a fun time out on the town.

6. *Salt Sculptures:* Mix together 4 cups flour, 1½ cups water, and 1 cup salt. Sculpt into shapes of animals, flowers, rockets, whatever. Bake at 350 degrees for one hour. Cool, then paint with acrylic paint if desired.

7. *"Stained Glass":* Cover table or counter area with newspaper. Cut several lengths (12 to 24 inches) of yarn. Mix 2 tablespoons of white glue with 2 tablespoons of water in a bowl. Dip yarn pieces in glue, then squeeze through fingers to remove excess glue. Press yarn pieces onto brightly colored tissue paper, creating a design. Let dry thoroughly, then trim tissue away from outside edge of yarn designs. Hang your "stained glass" designs in a window.

8. *Family Totem Pole:* Cut the tops off of waxed half-gallon milk cartons. Then cut 2-inch slits in the corners so the bottom of one container can be wedged inside the top of the container beneath it. Cover cartons with paper and decorate with designs and faces, or glue on pictures cut from magazines. Or use family photos you have duplicates of and don't mind donating to a creative cause. Put a rock or weight in the bottom carton for stability, then stack others on top.

9. *Twig Architecture:* Have your child collect small twigs and organize them by size. Start a twig house by inserting two upright twigs into the ground diagonally at each corner, then lay horizontal twigs, log-cabin style, to build walls. Place leaves and plant stalks across the top of twig structures to make thatched roofs. Build a fence and even an entire village.

10. *Crazy Caps:* Decorate old baseball caps with beads, ribbons, sequins, feathers, fabric scraps, pipe cleaners, buttons, or artificial flowers. Have a contest to see who can create the craziest cap.

11. *Creative Bubbles:* Mix together equal amounts of dishwashing liquid, water, and glycerin. (You can buy glycerin at any pharmacy. It makes the bubbles last longer.) Put the solution in a wide pan, like a cake pan, and use different things from around the house as wands, like a clean fly-swatter or slotted spatula.

12. *Salt Beads:* Mix 2 cups of salt and 1 cup of flour with enough water to make a doughy mixture. Form bead-size balls from the dough, then make a hole through the center of each bead with a toothpick. Or cover 1-inch pieces of soda straws with dough to make larger beads. Let the beads dry, then paint them with bright-color tempera or acrylic paints. String them into necklaces or bracelets.

13. *Crazy Masks:* Carefully cut empty gallon-size plastic containers in half vertically, then cut out openings for eyes, nose, and mouth. Glue on yarn for hair, and form pipe cleaners into a mustache or eyebrows. Paint, feathers, sequins, and glue can make an exotic look. Use a piece of elastic string to hold the mask in place.

14. *Sponge Garden:* Soak a sponge in water and place it in a shallow dish. Sprinkle with alfalfa or rye grass seeds. Keep it moist and watch the seeds grow.

15. *Tube-it:* Decorate a cardboard paper towel roll using crayons, markers or stickers. Measure and cut a 24-inch piece of string. Securely tape one end of the string about 2 inches down inside the tube. Tape the other end of the string to the center of the bottom of an empty 8-ounce paper cup. Now hold the bottom of the tube and see how many times you can flip the cup and have it land on top of the tube. Score one point each time you are successful.

16. *Festive Flowers:* Stack five paper cupcake liners on top of each other, then feather them out with your fingers. Use a pencil to poke two holes in the center of the stack. Insert one end of a pipe cleaner up through one hole and down the other hole, leaving one end of the cleaner longer than the other. Twist the shorter end around the longer end and extend it down to make the stem of the flower. Cut green leaves from construction paper and glue or staple them to the stem.

17. *Gooey Guck:* This stretches and bounces like Silly Putty. Mix together with a wire whisk 1 cup all-purpose glue, 3/4 cup of water, 1 tablespoon paint (tempera or acrylic). Mix separately 1/3 cup water and 1/2 teaspoon borax. Slowly pour borax mixture into glue mixture and stir. Let stand a few minutes and then knead. Pour off any remaining liquid. Store in a plastic bag.

18. *Stick Puzzle:* Wash and dry some wooden ice-cream sticks; lay them beside each other. Secure a piece of tape across all the sticks. Turn them over and draw a picture with markers. Remove the tape, then mix up the sticks and put the picture together.

19. *Pasta Gems:* Mix 1 tablespoon food coloring with 2 tablespoons rubbing alcohol. Make several different colors. Stir macaroni into the colored solutions and spread on a newspaper to dry. String on a shoelace for bracelets or necklaces.

20. *Sunflower-Seed Necklaces:* Soak seeds in warm water for an hour. Use dental floss and an embroidery needle to string the seeds. Let necklace dry before wearing.

21. *Rice Art:* Draw a simple picture on cardboard. In butter tubs, use food coloring to dye rice different colors. Dip a toothpick in white glue, then pick up one grain of rice. Dip it into the glue again and place the rice grain on the picture. When the picture is completely covered with rice, brush a coat of glue over entire surface. It will dry clear.

22. *Refrigerator Magnets:* Remove the metal lid from frozen juice cans. Cut a round piece of white paper to fit inside the rimmed edge of the lid. Have each family member draw a self-portrait on the paper and glue it to the lid. Glue a magnet to the back of the lid. Everyone will have his or her own magnet to hold messages, papers, or pictures.

23. *Tennis-Ball Puppets:* Cut a slit across an old tennis ball. Outline the slit with a red marker for a mouth. Draw a nose and eyes and glue yarn on for hair. Squeeze the back of the ball to make the puppet talk.

24. *Frisbee Golf:* Make a golf course in your backyard. Draw large numbers on paper plates and nail on trees or tape to shrubs to designate each "hole," which must be hit by the Frisbee.

25. *Shiny Pennies:* Kids love to make pennies look like new. Mix 4 tablespoons vinegar and 1 teaspoon salt in a small bowl. Drop pennies into the solution. If the pennies don't instantly become clean, stir them for a minute with a wooden spoon, then polish them with a soft cloth and a drop of vegetable oil to make them shine.

Big Box Banzai

Fill hours of time with a big box. They're usually free for the asking at furniture or appliance stores.

• Target Practice: Cut a 24-inch hole in a big box. Hang a foil pan with a string from the top of the hole so it swings freely in the center of it. Stand back and throw tennis balls at the target. Balls will collect in the box.

• Construct a castle from an appliance box, cutting the top into notches like a castle wall. Create a door that hinges at the bottom to open like a drawbridge.

• Make a lemonade stand.

• Create a puppet theater. Cut an opening in the front and a door in back. Make a curtain out of an old towel or sheet. On with the show!

• Flatten a big box to make a city or airport for small cars or planes.

• Go sledding without snow. Flatten the box and find a grassy hill to slide down.

Head for the Yard!

These are activities to get young bodies out of the house.

• *Twist Up:* Use chalk to draw a 10-foot square on a driveway or pavement. Draw a lot of footprint-size ovals within the square. Players stand in the square with one foot in an oval. Each player then takes turn telling the player on his or her right which oval to put a foot or hand in without getting out of the original oval. Be ready for a lot of laughs.

• *Batting Practice:* Drill a hole through the center of a baseball. Thread a long piece of rope through the hole in the ball and knot it. Tie the other end of the rope to a tree limb so that the ball hangs down about waist-high to the child. Now the child can practice swinging a bat and hitting the ball, and it will always come back.

• *Tire Fun:* Turn old tires into creative fun. Make a tire swing or a target for a football or Frisbee.

• *Backyard Obstacle Course:* Create an obstacle course where your kids can crawl under lawn chairs or through tunnels made from large boxes, walk or hop along a curvy garden hose, and dodge an oscillating sprinkler. Make it a little more difficult each time they do it by having each child balance a Ping-Pong ball on a paper plate or by trying to get through the course blindfolded.

• *Ring Fling:* Cut out the middle of strong paper plates so the outer circular edge makes a ring. Decorate rings with crayons or markers. Put dowel rods or stakes into the ground and mark off a throwing line. Each player must stay behind the line and toss a ring around a rod or stake to win points or prizes.

• *Backyard Bowling:* Spray-paint ten 2-liter soda bottles to make bowling pins. (Put a little water or sand in each one to weigh it down.) Turn your driveway or patio into a bowling lane.

• *Knock 'em Down:* Cover 16-ounce cans with contact paper. Stack them in pyramid formation and let kids try to knock them down with tennis balls.

• *Balloon Volleyball:* Tie 6 to 10 feet of string between two chairs for a net. Follow regular volleyball rules but use a balloon.

• *Velcro Catch:* Put self-adhesive Velcro dots (available at fabric stores) around a Ping-Pong ball. Cut an 8-inch circle from a piece of cardboard and make a strap for holding it on one side. Glue an 8-inch felt circle on the other side. Let one person toss the ball and the other catch it with the mitt.

• *Gardening Family Style:* Plant and work a garden together. Check with your local seed store for what kind of vegetables, fruits, and flowers grow easily in your area. Or start an herb garden in small pots. Have your children check each day for growth.

• *Water Balloon Toss:* For neighborhood fun, separate the kids into two parallel lines, facing each other. One line will hold the water balloons. Each kid tosses a balloon to his "partner" in the other line. If the partner catches it, he takes one step back and then tosses it back to his partner. If the balloon is dropped and/or breaks, that pair is out. Repeat this process until only one pair remains.

SUMMER IDEAS FOR TEENAGERS

If you have a teenager, keep these ideas handy to alleviate the "We don't know what to do so we're going to hang out at the mall" syndrome. Since going out to eat can get expensive and finding a good movie to watch with a buddy is getting harder, here are some creative ideas to pull out of the hat.

• Write, act out, and videotape your own sitcom. Watch it together and get ready for laughs.

• Have a surprise picnic. Go to a park and eat dinner on quilts.

• Have a "Create a Super Hero" party. Ask friends to come over dressed in a crazy costume depicting a super hero they've made up. (Recently my teenager completely covered his clothes in silver duct tape and a friend covered his clothes in masking tape—"Duct-Tape Man and his sidekick, Masking-Tape Boy.")

• Buy a loaf of day-old bread, find a park or lake where ducks live, and feed them.

• Go to a pet store and have fun looking at the animals.

• Be creative in the kitchen. Create an exotic pizza from scratch or invent a new cookie recipe.

- Spend a morning going to garage sales. Start out with five dollars each and see what you can buy. You may be surprised at some of the great deals you'll find.

- Have "Bad Movie Night." Rent some videos that are so bad they're hilarious—anything with giant insects or primitive rocket ships.

- Puzzle Race. Buy two multipiece jigsaw puzzles. Set up two tables, divide into two teams, and see which team can put their puzzle together first.

- Play a sport—basketball, baseball, miniature golf, bowling. Play guys versus girls or divide up into teams by whose birthdays fall in the same season of the year.

- Have a "Make a Difference" day. Gather clothing and deliver it to a community service organization. Volunteer to work at a food bank, register people to vote, or help out at a Habitat for Humanity project.

- Go on a bike-hike. Take a picnic in a backpack.

- Go in-line skating in a big vacant parking lot. Many places rent skates and equipment if you don't own them.

- Fix dinner together and serve it to your family or your friend's family.

- Buy two kites and fly them in an open field on a windy day.

- Wash and wax your cars together. Have a water fight while you're at it.

- Go to a park at night in a safe part of town and play Sardines. Ask one player to volunteer to be "it." Ask the players except this one to cover their eyes. The person who is it hides. Then everyone hunts for the hidden person. As each player finds the hidden person, that player hides there, too, until all the players are packed into the hiding place—like sardines! The person left becomes it for the next game.

Back to School

MAKE A BIG DEAL

The weekend before school starts for the year, plan a special family dinner. Serve favorite summer foods. Have family members say what they learned this summer, what occasions they most remember. Toast the end of summer and the beginning of the new school year.

Have pencils and paper ready. Spend fifteen minutes having family members write down their goals and hopes for the school year. It might be anything from your daughter learning algebra to your son turning sixteen and getting a driver's license. Maybe Mom or Dad will decide to learn algebra, too. Have each person read his or her slip of paper, then put them in a file folder or a box to bring out at midyear in January and again at the end of the school year.

No More Homework Hassles

As I write this section I realize that our first son started school almost twenty years ago. Our third son has five years to go. I've learned a lot (many times in the school of hard knocks) about enhancing our children's education. I've discovered four simple strategies that have helped make our school year much more peaceful and productive. Try them in your home and see if you don't have fewer hassles. (Also see Evenings: Chaos or Calm? on page 106.)

1. *Have a family meeting and set an evening routine.* When family members know what to expect, chaos evaporates. Our routine involves eating dinner as a family and working together to clean up the kitchen, then the kids do homework. If there's a special program on TV they want to watch before finishing homework, we tape it so they can watch it later.

As a rule, we try to keep afternoons open for playtime, ball practices, and errands. But if their study load is heavy or grades start falling, we start on homework immediately after school.

Whatever routine suits your family, be sure to schedule some time each evening—even if it's just ten minutes—to do something fun as a family. Play a board game or a hand of cards, take the dog for a walk, work on a jigsaw puzzle, or share some ice cream.

2. *Teach your child that school is his or her "career"—equally as important as yours.* When children know that their world is just as valuable as Mom and Dad's, their attitude changes dramatically. Suddenly they see their "work" as significant. A daughter's preparation for a big test is just as important as Dad's preparation for a big department evaluation. Or a son doing research for a term paper is just as significant as Mom's gathering information to make a business proposal.

When you view your children's schooling as their career, you'll see that they are learning much more than math and grammar. They are developing important habits and skills—such as time management, responsibility, and self-discipline—that will help them succeed not only in school, but in their future career as well.

3. *Be sensitive to your child's learning style.* An important element in relieving homework frustration is understanding your child's learning style, which can be auditory, visual, and/or kinesthetic (hands-on). If you've called out spelling words to your daughter five times and she is still struggling to get them right, it's likely she is not an auditory learner. Vocal cues simply don't work. Using letters from a Scrabble game to practice spelling words will work better for her.

Or maybe your son is stumped memorizing the states and their capitals. He may be a kinesthetic learner and can learn better by tracing and color-coding a map, then creating a study sheet from his project.

Each child will transfer from one style to another when the need arises, but one or two learning styles will be predominant throughout life. To determine your children's learning styles, think about whether they talk about what they see (visual) or hear (auditory) or if they say,

"Show me" (kinesthetic). It's also helpful to watch your kids while they play. Do they watch or read to acquire information, listen intently, or want to do it with their hands?

To adapt what you learn about your child's learning style to homework, understand that an auditory learner can learn better in a noisy atmosphere than a visual learner, who prefers a quiet setting. A visual learner needs to write information down and take detailed notes. She also likes colorful illustrations and lots of pictures.

Kinesthetic learners like to feel things and communicate by touching. When they feel confined, they start to move around; when

Each child needs his or her personal work space in order to work efficiently. If your child doesn't have a desk, set aside a specific area for him, even if it's the dining room table. Create the atmosphere of a home office. Be sure your child has all the supplies necessary to do homework, including paper, pens, and construction paper.

Having a designated area and homework "time" gives your child a sense of space and routine. And your preparations will save you from multiple trips to the office-supply store as well as arguing about when and where to do the homework.

they're bored, they usually fiddle with an object. Breaking up their homework into short segments with an activity in between will be effective for this type of learner.

4. *Create a homework-friendly environment.* Since a home is a relatively small space shared by a number of people, it's important that everyone is aware that sound travels—what a person does in one room affects others. This means when a teenager is deciding whether to turn on his CD player, he considers his younger brother, who is next door studying for a geography test. It also means that when Mom and Dad want to turn on the television on a school night, they realize the noise can be distracting to a student trying to work math problems.

> "All television is educational television. The question is: what is it teaching?"
> —Nicholas Johnson

Make the Most of TV

As Family Managers it's important that we help our children turn television into a learning tool instead of an addictive sedative. Educational research suggests that the average child spends thirty to thirty-five hours a week glued to the TV set, and that watching television endlessly at the expense of other worthwhile activities can harm a child's intellectual growth. One study revealed that the more time a child watches television, the lower his or her achievement test scores will be.

This doesn't mean we should ban all television watching in our homes. It does mean that we need to be careful. When viewed in moderation with guidance from discriminating parents, television can become a tool that helps our children become critical thinkers. Let these tips help you make the most of TV in your home.

• Limit how much TV your children view each week; educators suggest a maximum of ten hours a week for elementary school children.

• Help children become aware of misleading audio and visual effects used in television.

• Select specific programs from the television guide. Avoid channel surfing.

• Encourage children to watch programs that teach them to get along with others and appreciate other cultures, and to watch educational programs that stimulate their imagination.

• Help children learn that aggression is not an appropriate way to resolve conflict.

• Turn off the TV during homework time.

• Select programs that offer positive role models.

• Choose programming for younger children that encourages them to be interactive.

• Encourage kids to think about what they're watching rather than being passive viewers.

• Preview programs if possible; then establish your own seal of approval on which programs are okay or off-limits.

• When your child really wants to see a show you're not sure about, watch it with him or her. Then discuss the positives and negatives and what your child learned from the program. Use these questions to guide your discussion:

    a. How would you rate this show on a scale of one to ten?

    b. What was the program's message?

    c. Could you identify with any of the characters?

    d. What would you do to help any of the characters?

    e. Was there anything in the program you did not agree with?

    f. Did you feel this show portrayed life as it really is?

    g. Was this program worth your time to watch it?

    h. What in the program uplifted you or motivated you to be a better person?

OFF TO SCHOOL FOR FIRST-TIMERS
The first day of school is a major transition for young children. Here are some tips to make that first school experience easier for everyone involved.

1. Visit the school beforehand and show your child the different activities he/she will participate in. Go over the names of new people. See if you can get a class list with telephone numbers. Call other parents and try to arrange for your child to play with a few classmates before school starts.

2. Implement schedule changes in household routines a week or two in advance of opening day. Get up, get dressed, and eat breakfast as you will when school starts.

3. Walk with your child to school or the bus stop several times before school starts. Review safety rules about crossing streets and traffic lights. Make sure your child understands any special after-school pickup arrangements. Remind your child not to go home with anyone else or ever, for any reason, to get in a car with strangers. (Never label a child's backpack or school bag with his or her name in large letters. A child might think that if a stranger knows his name, he must be a friend of the family.)

4. Plan a special outing with your child to purchase school supplies and a first-day outfit.

5. Be certain your child is comfortable using a public toilet (including a urinal for boys) so the school rest rooms won't seem strange. Emphasize the need to wash hands even when Mommy or Daddy isn't there to remind them. Make sure school clothes are easy to fasten and unfasten.

6. If your child will be eating lunch in the school cafeteria, have him practice carrying a loaded tray or using a lunch box.

7. Read books to your child designed to help him/her prepare for the first day of school. Ask your local librarian for suggestions.

8. Be sure your child knows his/her full name, address, and your home and work phone numbers. Remind your child never to give this information to strangers.

9. Plan to spend a few extra minutes with your child on the first day. Agree on the amount of time with the teacher in advance. Be patient with and sensitive to your child—even an easygoing child can become distressed in a totally new environment. Accept your child's feelings and help him/her work through them.

10. Take pictures of your child on his or her way to school in the first-day outfit. But avoid taking photographs and videotaping at school. This might single your child out in a way he or she isn't comfortable with and will just add to the first-day chaos at school.

HOME ALONE

Working parents and kids alike struggle with the after-school hours. The child feels her parents' absence and her parents wonder how and what she's doing. You can make the most of these hours with some planning and routine setting.

In general, the less time older children or even preteens spend at home alone, the less bored and less likely to get into trouble they are. You know your own child best. My philosophy is that kids should be trusted. But consider signing them up for sports activities, craft or cooking classes, or other regularly scheduled events. Those hours between school and dinner, five days a week, can seem mighty long to kids.

• Surprise your child with special messages of encouragement or praise. Tack them to the bathroom mirror, TV screen, or refrigerator door.

• Post a list of snack ideas on the fridge.

• Allow your child to make no-bake recipes. Keep appliance use (and therefore, potential burns and other injuries) to a minimum.

• Pack a small emergency kit for your child to keep in her backpack or purse. Put in an extra house key, list of phone numbers, quarters for the phone, and folded money for emergency transportation like cabs.

• Develop a family code word for emergency situations. If you've asked an unfamiliar person to pick up your child at school, give him or her the code word so your child will know the person is safe to leave with. This word can also mean "help" if your child must call you during a frightening situation—assure him or her you will be there as soon as possible.

• Keep your cabinet stocked with medical supplies and teach your child basic first aid. Your local hospital may offer courses for kids.

Ground Rules

You may well need to establish new (and reiterate old) ground rules at the beginning of every school year, even if this isn't the first year your older child or teen has come home from school and been alone until you or your husband get home from work. Here are some issues to consider.

1. Under what circumstances is he or she allowed to use the stove? In my opinion, a child who's not old enough to use the stove is probably not old enough to be home alone on a regular basis.

2. Are friends allowed to visit? When? Under what circumstances? My own rule is if you want to have a friend over when we're not around, then you must ask permission. Other people make a one-friend-at-a-time or friends-of-the-same-gender-only rule. Don't underestimate the power of peer pressure. And talk about your concerns with your stay-at-home kid.

3. As always, establish your expectations about chores, clearly and specifically. Post reminder lists on the refrigerator. Or do a check-in e-mail or phone message to remind them.

4. Set parameters about phone and TV time.

5. Make it clear where your stay-at-homer is allowed to go and that you must be notified where he or she is.

6. Role-play these situations with your children so they'll know what to do:

- answering the phone, taking messages
- going to a friend's house or having friends over
- losing the house key
- missing the bus or car pool
- staying after school
- choking, poisoning, or accidental injury
- fire, storms, weather emergencies, other natural disaster
- a stranger's hassles, threats, or sexual advances
- a stranger on the phone or at the front door

Big Life Changes

Life is change and no one book, or twelve dozen books, can prepare us completely for it. In fact, there's no such thing as being completely prepared for change. If there were, we wouldn't call it change. And we wouldn't anticipate it with the mixed emotions of apprehension and excitement that we do. In my opinion, life would be pretty boring without the dynamics change brings.

But that doesn't mean I don't believe in preparing ourselves and our families for the big changes we encounter as best we can. Preparation is half the battle and half the fun. In this section you'll find some basic tips on preparing for and going through some of life's typical big changes. The list is by no means comprehensive, but it will give you some basic guidelines.

FOR ALL BIG CHANGES:
COMMUNICATE, COMMUNICATE, COMMUNICATE

1. At a family meeting, announce the impending change as soon as it's appropriate. Consider the ages of your children. You might want to tell a teenager about a new baby long before you tell a preschooler. In any event, allow plenty of time for everybody to talk about his or her feelings. Don't get defensive if children raise objections or questions to, say, a proposed move across country for a job. No doubt you and your spouse have mixed feelings as well. Be honest with your kids about your fears and expectations. Don't try to whitewash, but don't paint a gloomy picture.

2. As much as possible, present things in a positive light. A friend whose husband has served in the military for more than twenty years told me that when Mom the Family Manager has a positive attitude about a big move—"It's going to be a little scary living in Japan for a year, but I think it will be an adventure. We'll learn so many new things!" as opposed to "All the government does is move us around. I'm sick of it"—the kids are more likely to adjust well.

3. Repeat your talks about the change frequently, especially as the date for the change, whatever it is, nears. Take little opportunities to bring it up in the course of daily conversation. And take a cue from your kids: pouting or acting out may be their way of letting you know they're feeling insecure and need reassurance or to talk. You might make a countdown calendar especially to prepare for the big change. Include on it certain tasks that need to be done by Big Change Day.

4. Make sure you and your spouse take enough time to talk through your own fears and expectations. Allow each other to voice feelings and hear and acknowledge them without being critical or trying to change them.

5. As a big change approaches, you might consider giving each family member who can write a small, spiral-bound notebook in which to record his or her concerns, fears, and expectations. Invite everybody to read from his or her notebook during a special talking-together session. Young children can draw their ideas.

6. Spend time alone with each of your children so they all have the opportunity to privately share their concerns and be reassured that the change—whether it's an older sibling going off to college or the impending arrival of a new baby—doesn't affect the fact that they're important to you and you care about them.

7. Create opportunities for children to talk about the change with other trusted adults—grandparents, aunts and uncles, friends of the family. Make sure they know that they're free to share their concerns with that adult and those concerns will be kept private—even from you. This may seem counterintuitive, but children sometimes need a safety valve. I know one Family Manager who made sure her daughter had opportunities to talk with her godmother when she and her husband were splitting up. It gave the daughter a chance to vent her angry feelings and opened the way for her to be able to talk with her parents later.

8. If you are having trouble communicating, consider scheduling a few sessions with a trained counselor to teach you some family communication skills.

9. Don't lie to children about your mixed feelings about the change. As much as possible, in age-appropriate ways, tell the truth. Maybe the new baby is a surprise to you, and maybe you weren't so keen on the idea at first either. Let them know that feelings can change. Don't tell them you know exactly what the new change will bring when you don't. (And mostly we don't.)

10. Do reassure children—that you'll still love them when the new baby arrives. That they'll find a scout troop or soccer team or new friends in their new hometown.

PREPARING FOR A NEW BABY

EARLY IN YOUR PREGNANCY

• There are many books available on the subject of preparing your home and family for a new baby. Ask for recommendations from your librarian, your bookseller, or other new moms you might know. Even if you're not a first-time mom, read one or two. There's always something you can learn.

• Talk with older children. Share the good news.

• Enlist them in joining you in an exercise program.

• Enlist them in helping more around the house in exchange for mutually agreed-upon rewards.

• Start more healthy eating routines for the whole family.

• Rely on your spouse, older children, and family and friends to give you a few extra minutes of rest and relaxation in your days. That can make all the difference in how everybody accepts the change.

THREE OR FOUR MONTHS BEFORE YOUR BABY IS DUE

• Start talking with younger children about the baby.

• Get the crib and baby equipment out of storage. Or if you've gotten rid of all of it, shop garage sales, flea markets, and sales for new equipment. Enlist the "help" of young children in buying things for the new baby.

• If you need to move children's rooms around to accommodate the new arrival, do it now. That way your children will be used to it by the time the baby comes home.

• Talk with family members about what you'd like to name the baby.

• Teach toddlers to do things for themselves. Finish toilet training (but don't be alarmed or upset by relapses after the new baby comes). Arrange your toddler's drawers so he or she can reach clothes. Teach him or her to pick out outfits and dress themselves.

• Arrange to spend some extra time with your spouse before you get so far along that you won't enjoy it.

• Over the next weeks, try to have a few special dates alone with each of your children. Choose movies or plays or going out to lunch and to the bookstore to pick out a special book, which could be about welcoming a new brother or sister.

COUNTDOWN: TWO MONTHS BEFORE; THEN BIRTH AND BEYOND

• If you're going to do so, schedule and attend natural childbirth classes. Check to see if there are classes that accommodate siblings in some way.

• Put the finishing touches on the baby's room or space. Again, get children to help—perhaps by folding blankets, attending a shower with you, or arranging the baby clothes in dresser drawers.

• Finalize arrangements for where your children will be while you and your husband are at the hospital. Make sure they know who will be taking care of them and when they'll be able to meet the new baby. Most hospitals now accommodate families so children don't have to wait until you come home.

• Make arrangements to have food ready for those first days at home. Ask a friend or relative to help. Or if you absolutely don't know anybody who lives close enough to you, put food in the freezer.

• In the first few days at home, explain to young children that you need to rest. Let them know in age-appropriate ways that giving birth to a baby means big changes in your body.

> Remember that your role in your child's life is changing. Telling a teenager where he or she should go to college—whether to your alma mater or to the place you always dreamed he or she would go—is a very bad plan. What's not a bad plan is talking realistically with your teen, beginning at least eighteen months in advance, about various colleges.

• Make an effort to spend time, even if it's just ten minutes, alone with each child each and every day. Ask them questions about their school day. Read a favorite book together. Let them talk about their concerns.

• Give siblings time to adjust to a new baby, no matter how many preparations you've made. The real work begins when the baby comes home.

GOING AWAY TO COLLEGE

Choosing a college is probably the first almost-adult choice a teenager makes mostly on his or her own. Research potential schools with your teen and his or her school guidance counselor. Talk realistically about tuition and other costs. Encourage your teen to talk about his or her expectations and goals and fears.

If you can, arrange to visit all the colleges under serious consideration as a family. You might plan a spring vacation around such a tour. Be sure to check in advance whether the college will be in session and make an appointment to meet with someone from the admissions office. If you can't all go, trade off visiting with your spouse.

During your teen's senior year, he or she will need to begin narrowing the field and completing college applications. You may need to fill out financial-aid applications, and having all your information for the past and current tax years at your fingertips will become crucial. (See Quarterly Checklists, page 113.) Work with your college applicant to do a compare-and-contrast worksheet for the various colleges he or she is thinking of applying to. Rank each category listed below for each school visited on a scale of one to five, with five being the highest. This ranking won't make the decision, but it will provide a coherent way of looking at all the factors.

Name of school

Annual tuition

Living costs

Availability of financial aid

Availability of proposed major

Other academic strengths

Other benefits (e.g., strong sports team, good drama department)

Distance from home

Overall rank

Countdown to Departure Day

- Make sure both you and your spouse have a few alone times with your departing teen.
- If he or she wants to have a going-away party, help arrange it.
- Shop for necessities together. (See College Checklist.) Keep new clothing purchases to a minimum so there will be some money left over in your teen's clothing budget to purchase the in things at his or her school.
- Begin packing two weeks in advance. Use the College Checklist. Especially if your departing student is going so far away from home that he or she is traveling by airplane, a week ahead, ship boxes. (Alternatively, if you're traveling with your student, you might want to purchase some items when you get there.)
- Plan a special family dinner in honor of your departee. You might want

to do a photo display on your kitchen or family room wall of pictures taken over the years. Or have a *This Is Your Life* video program if you have videotapes of your son or daughter growing up. Brothers and sisters might be given a chance to toast, or roast, their departing sibling.

- Although you probably will be keeping your teenager's room intact for a while longer, this is a good time to go through files and bookcases, closets and drawers with him or her. Carefully pack away school papers and mementos. Cull clothing and separate it into what will be taken and what will remain behind and what can be given away to charity.
- Obtain a credit card in your name with your teen as an additional cardholder. Carefully go over the ground rules of what the card should and should not be used for. Many credit-card companies offer cards to college students. My personal feeling is that it's better to have a card with a parent for a few years while the student gets used to handling it.
- Make a family notebook and/or photo album. Keep it a secret from the departing student. Slip it in his or her luggage. Or present it when you get to the dorm.
- Tell your college-bound student you love him or her.
- Make plans to keep in touch regularly by phone, e-mail, or mail. (A prepaid phone calling card or 800 number at home is a good investment.)

There's a lot of drinking, drug use, and risky sexual behavior on college campuses. No doubt you've been talking with your teen about these issues for years. But now is a good time to reiterate your values and to ask your child to consider them as he or she faces new challenges and choices.

College Checklist

Room Supplies
Backpack
Travel kit
Tote bag
Lamp
Framed photo of family
Fan
Trash can
Extension cord
Write-on memo board
Bulletin board
Posters
Alarm clock or clock radio
Stereo
Tapes
Tape and CD holder
Over-the-door hooks
Trunk
Hangers
Double-up rod
Stacking baskets
Milk crates
Luggage ID tags
Under-bed storage boxes
Jewelry box
Adhesive hooks
Throw rug
Scrapbook
Reclining pillow
Flashlight

Desk Supplies
Dictionary
Thesaurus
Computer
Printer
Paper
Legal tablets
Sticky-back notes
Letter holder
Paper clips and holder
Correction fluid
Pens and pencils
Stapler
Staples
Ruler
Calculator
Glue
Thumbtacks
Tape dispenser
Tape
Erasers
Rubber bands
Electric pencil sharpener
Desk organizers
Scissors and tape kit
Calendar
Address book
Stamps
Bookends
Stationery
Pencil cup

Bedding and Linens
Pillow
Pillowcases
Sheets
Blankets
Towels
Washcloths
Beach towel
Mattress pad

Laundry Supplies
Iron
Ironing board
Drying rack
Laundry bag
Laundry hamper
Laundry detergent
Fabric softener
Stain remover
Starch

Personal Care Items
Sewing kit
Tool kit
Hair dryer
Curling iron
Electric rollers
Comb
Brush
Shower basket or tote
Shampoo
Conditioner
Toothbrush
Toothpaste
Soap

Soap box
Toothbrush box
Razor
Shaving cream
Cotton balls
Deodorant
Cotton swabs
First-aid kit
Facial tissue
Aspirin or pain reliever
Safety pins
Extra contact lenses or glasses
Prescription for glasses
Cosmetic organizer

Basic Kitchen Supplies
Paper towels
Can opener
Coffee mug
Paper plates
Hot pot
Popcorn popper
Munchies jar or tin
Knives, forks, and spoons
Bathroom cup

Clothing
Undergarments
Socks
Gloves
Scarves
Hats
Winter coat
Raincoat
Lightweight jacket

Jeans	Shirts
Slacks	Sweaters
Shorts	Pajamas or nightgowns
Workout clothes	Shoes
Jogging suits	Boots
Swimsuit	Slippers
Dresses	Shower thongs
Skirts	Umbrella
Blouses	

JOB CHANGE: PUNCHING THE CLOCK, NOT YOURSELF

If you are returning to a job in the workplace, assuming a dual-career role after being a full-time Family Manager . . . Or if you (or your spouse) are changing jobs, either because you've chosen to take on a new opportunity or because circumstances are dictating a choice you might not otherwise make . . . Or if you (or your spouse) are experiencing not-of-your-choosing unemployment through downsizing or some other reason . . . You know the toll in stress any job change—negative or positive—can take on families. The ideas in this section are meant to reduce that stress and help you and your family accentuate the adventurous, positive aspects of such changes.

Whatever the job-change situation is, use For All Big Changes: Communicate, Communicate, Communicate, page 179, to talk with your whole family about what's going on. You need to be honest about the fact that you don't know exactly how this will affect their day-to-day lives *and* reassure children that someone will take care of them, will be there for them, although maybe not immediately after school with home-baked cookies.

Arranging Child Care

Arranging for appropriate child care is probably the single biggest issue you'll face.

1. Research options. Begin as soon as you begin your job search. Ask women you know who work outside the home for references. Check neighborhood newspapers for advertisements. Look in the Yellow Pages under child care, day-care centers, nanny services. Don't narrow the field to one kind of care or the other—in-home or day care—until you've looked at various options.

2. Make a list of your requirements.
   - What hours will you be working? Will you have overtime?
   - Will you or your spouse be traveling, and therefore sometimes unavailable in an emergency or to back the other one up? Who can be your designated backup in such circumstances?
   - What is your budget for child care?
   - What are your children's needs? What special interests do they have and how do the various options meet their needs? I know one Family Manager who returned to work when her daughter was nine. She had two options for day care, within roughly the same distance from her daughter's school. They both provided transportation. One of them offered acting and dancing lessons among the other activity options. That was the one she chose.

3. With your list of requirements and questions in hand, visit day-care centers and interview potential babysitters or nannies. Some questions to consider for day-care centers:
   - What activities do the children regularly participate in?
   - Is homework help available for older children?
   - Do they allow or even encourage drop-in visits during the day?
   - How convenient is the option—is the day-care center close to your home or work?

4. Once you've narrowed the field, take your child or children to visit and see how they react.

Summing up a Sitter

Some questions to consider for babysitters or nannies:
- Can they provide references?
- What will they do with your children during the day? Don't simply ask yes/no questions. Ask them to outline a typical day for you.
- What would they do in an emergency?
- Will they work on a trial basis (with pay) for a few days before you go back to work so you can see how they are with your children?
- When introduced to your child or children, even a baby, how do they get along?

5. Once you've chosen an option, consider starting to use it a week before you begin your job. It will cost some money, but it's probably worth it. And you'll have some time to yourself to prepare for your changes.

6. Be prepared for emergencies. Nannies get sick. Kids get sick. There will be glitches.

(Note: See Home Alone, page 177, for ideas about children who are old enough to come home alone after school and what you can do to make them more comfortable in their more "grown-up" roles.)

Before You Start to Work

If you know ahead of time that you're going to return to a job outside the home, make the time—and again, you might start when you begin your job search rather than when you know you have a job with a start date that's imminent—to get organized at home. (See Clutter Control, page 30, and Sane Storage, page 40.) It's especially important to get your kitchen in prime-efficiency shape because the simple truth is, everybody

---

An Affordable Alternative

My friend Michele Stephens, a dual-career Family Manager, has created an alternative day-care system called "The Affordable Nanny." Here's what she suggests: depending on the number of children involved, band together with two or three like-minded two-career moms and hire one professional nanny. It works best if you live close to each other. Choose the home best equipped to accommodate everyone, or rotate locations. The kids get to be in a home atmosphere and it's just as cheap as day care.

---

needs to eat every day and you won't have as much time to see that your family has nutritious, pleasing meals.

It's also important to go through your closet and prepare your wardrobe. You might consider selling clothes you no longer wear at a used-clothing store, or trading for items more appropriate for your new role. If you haven't been in the workforce for a while, shop for three or four basic mix-and-match pieces that are appropriate to your job. They should get you through the first months.

Your First Week on the Job

• Use foods you've cooked ahead and frozen for the first week to minimize cooking time and get used to the new schedule.

• Review and fine-tune your morning and evening routines. (See page 103 and page 106.)

• Go easy on yourself. Go to bed a bit earlier. Take a minispa break midweek—just half an hour in the bathroom by yourself with fancy bubble bath and candles.

• Talk with each of your children every day to see how their week is going.

> "Life is not always what one wants it to be, but to make the best of it, as it is, is the only way of being happy."
> —Jennie Jerome Churchill

• Change your child-care arrangements to make them more convenient if you need or want to. (A caution: The fewer changes you introduce into young children's lives at a time, the better chance you'll have of a smooth transition.)

• Add to or make changes to your wardrobe if you need to.

Staying Up When You're Downsized

It's never easy when one of the breadwinners of a family is out of work for any reason. The most crucial action is to communicate with your children. Whether they talk about it or not, they will be worried. Reassure them that while money may be tight, they will have what they need—food and clothes and all the basics. Depending on their ages, enlist their help and support in earning money for extras. (See Beyond Babysitting: Super Summer Jobs for Kids, page 153. Many of these jobs can be done on weekends, during school vacations, and after school.)

Refer to Dozens of Ways to Save Money in Every Department, page 93, and institute as many of the ideas as you can as soon as you know of an impending job loss. Don't wait until money gets tight to tighten up your budget.

Make a list of free things to do and take fun breaks as a family even if you're not feeling much like having fun. (See Fun Places to Go, page 149, and 52 Ways to Make Ordinary Days Special, page 231.) Schedule and keep dates with your spouse. Listen to each other's concerns and try to keep accusations out of your discussions. If you or your spouse is going through a job retraining or placement service, check to see if they offer counseling or ideas about family stress during this kind of change.

MOVING HOUSES

For most of our marriage, Bill and I have bought houses, moved in, fixed them up to sell, sold them, and moved on to the next one. We enjoy working together on renovation projects, and living in a fixer-upper has been a way we could afford bigger digs as our kids got bigger. In this section, you'll find important points to consider when buying or selling a house and moving.

Home Buyer Checklist

Make copies of these questions to take with you as you look at prospective homes. Always pick up the description sheet and sketch a floor plan on the back of it as you walk through a house. Keep all the information in one notebook, along with real estate agents' cards and your own agent's office, cell-phone, and pager numbers.

Address:
Asking price:
Availability date:
Size:
Bedrooms:
Bathrooms:
Other rooms:
Dining room:
Family room:
Laundry:
Porch or patio:
Garage:
Plumbing:
Wiring:
Furnace:
Insulation:
Basement/foundation:

Roof:

Driveway:

Paint:

Windows:

Appliances:

First impression:

What would it take to make this house a home for your family?

Marketing a House

As soon as possible before you want your house to go on the market, meet with prospective real estate agents. If you don't know one, ask for references from friends who've recently bought or sold, from your banker, or from other business associates. Have them come to your home to meet them and watch their reactions carefully.

FINISHING TOUCHES

• Repaint any rooms that need it. Note: you may need to do just the walls. Clean the woodwork first to see how it looks.

• Consider hiring a cleaning service that specializes in cleaning for showings.

• Polish wood floors.

• Wash windows inside and out.

• Clear away clutter.

• Make sure all closets and shelving are organized and neat.

• Check with your real estate agent. Some like candles burning, a fire in the fireplace, soft music playing, and the smell of vanilla or cinnamon wafting from the kitchen. Some don't.

When you've eliminated some, meet again with your top two candidates and get down to details.

- Ask them to provide comps of like homes in your area that have recently sold.
- Ask to see a sample of their selling contract. What is their commission? Is there any flexibility in that?
- What do they think needs to be done to your home to maximize its sale potential?

If you're reading in your local newspaper and hearing from everyone you know that you're in a seller's market, beware the agent who says you need to paint every room, redo the driveway, and refinish the wood floors. In any market, if your agent says you need to redo the kitchen and the bathroom, get a second opinion. On the other hand, investments in cosmetic changes can make all the difference in selling price and how fast your home sells.

SURVIVING MOVING DAY

SIX WEEKS IN ADVANCE

1. If you're using professional movers, get competing bids from two or three. Ask if you're getting a guaranteed price. Ask the price differences between their packing some items, especially fragile things like good china, and your doing all the packing.

2. Begin packing, one room at a time, the things that you won't need in the next few weeks. Set aside things to give to charity or sell. (See Clutter Control, page 30, and Garage Sales: Turning Trash into Cash, page 137.)

3. Talk with your children about the reasons for the move, even if you've done so before, and ask them about their fears and expectations. (See For All Big Changes: Communicate, Communicate, Communicate, page 179.)

4. If you haven't done so, arrange for a house- or apartment-hunting trip to the new city or town you'll be living in. If possible, take the whole family.

5. Arrange to transfer funds to a new bank and establish credit in a new city.

6. Arrange for insurance on your new home or apartment.

7. Arrange with schools to transfer your children's school records and credentials.

8. Make arrangements with doctors, dentists, and eye doctors to either have records transferred to your new doctors or to take them with you. Make sure you have current glasses prescriptions and enough prescription medicine for those who need it to see you through a week in the new city.

FOUR WEEKS IN ADVANCE

9. Notify utilities, insurance agencies, and all other businesses you regularly deal with.

10. If you're having a garage sale to dispose of unwanted items, do it now.

11. Begin to use up supplies of canned goods, frozen foods, and other household supplies. Buy small quantities only of things you run out of.

12. If you're flying to your new location, reserve plane tickets. Make hotel or motel reservations.

TWO WEEKS BEFORE MOVING DAY

13. Take time to make farewell visits as a family to parks and other local sites that hold happy memories.

14. Have an informal going-away party—an open house or an informal dinner, maybe a potluck. Keep it simple. The important thing is seeing friends.

15. Offer your children plenty of opportunities to see their friends. I know one Family Manager who arranged a roller-skating party at a local rink for her daughter.

16. If you're driving to your new location, have your car serviced for the trip.

17. Take pets to the veterinarian. See that identification and rabies tags are securely attached to the pets' collars. If your pet is flying with you, you'll need a certificate from your vet for the airlines.

18. Return library books and any items on loan from friends. Collect everything from the dry cleaners, repair shops, and lockers at clubs or gyms.

19. Arrange for a cleaning service to come in and clean your home after your belongings are removed.

THREE DAYS BEFORE THE MOVE

20. Pack suitcases for the trip to the new home. Leave room or designate an extra bag for last-minute items. (For instance, you'll want one phone hooked up right through the time of loading the truck.)

KATHY PEEL ◆ 197

21. Pack activity kits and toys for children, including coloring books, puzzles, things they can play with in the car or on the plane and at their new house. Make sure to include a favorite stuffed animal and/or blanket for younger children. And, as with any other trip, plan for healthy snacks, moist towelettes for cleanup, etc.

22. Arrange for a babysitter for moving day, when all your household items will be loaded onto the moving truck. See if you can find someone—a close family friend or relative—to take smaller children on an outing for at least part of the day.

23. Get traveler's checks and some cash for the trip.

24. Check the contents of drawers and remove all spillables and breakables.

25. Empty the refrigerator and freezer at least twenty-four hours in advance.

26. Make arrangements about where you're going to stay the night before the truck comes—at home with everything packed up, with friends or family, or in a motel.

27. Call to verify when packers or movers are coming. If you're renting a truck, call to verify its availability and the time you can pick it up.

THE DAY BEFORE MOVING

28. Make sure all dishes are washed, dried, and put away for packers. Collect things you definitely want packed together, such as children's toys, and place them in a separate place. Strip beds. Be on hand to answer packers' questions. Put "Do Not Pack and Load" signs on suitcases and other things you're taking with you.

If you're doing your own packing, make sure the packing is done well in advance of the truck's scheduled arrival. Packing dishes and other last-minute packing, even if you've been doing things in advance, will take most of a day. Be sure to check closets, garages, attics, and basements for anything you might have forgotten.

MOVING DAY

29. Be on hand when the movers arrive to answer last-minute questions and sign forms. Check the premises to make sure all goods are loaded. Make sure the van operator has the exact address of your new home.

30. Be sure your family has a healthy, substantial breakfast and is ready to travel.

31. After the movers have left, or your rental truck is loaded, pack last-minute things in your luggage—for example, the telephone.

32. Do a final check around the house. Are windows shut and locked? Have you left anything? Are the furnace and lights turned off? Have you arranged to disconnect or transfer utilities? Leave a note for the new residents, along with any house keys not yet surrendered, with your new address and phone number if you have one, in a prominent location.

FIVE

Special Occasions Throughout the Year

"Memories! We go through life collecting them whether we will or not! . . . Let us make them carefully of all good things."
—Laura Ingalls Wilder

Making Memories Means Making Choices

Making memories is not an option. Our children's minds are like video cameras, constantly recording everything they see, hear, and do. Who's to know which memories will be edited out or recorded over? And which will become part of their permanent archives? We don't choose whether or not our children—and we and our spouses—have memories of our family life. We do get to choose how we live our everyday lives and celebrate our special occasions so the chances are better that some of our memories will be good ones.

Traditions and common experiences cement a family together. Every child's mind is a curator of memories. Fun family times and special traditions go a long way in building a rich museum of positive remembrances for our children. In theory, most of us understand and believe this. But reality is another story. We all have time and money constraints. Just the thought of planning one more thing may send us over the edge without a budgetary safety net.

When I'm tempted to cut family fun from the agenda, I remind myself of the overall goal—creating times we can laugh, love, and enjoy life together. And I remind myself that it's the little things that add up. We can make daily choices that don't cost the contents of Fort Knox or take days of prep time and still add up to good times for all.

TEN TIPS FOR LETTING THE GOOD TIMES ROLL

1. *Guard your time.* Keep family traditions and memory making high on your priority list. Feel free to just say no to people and organizations asking for your time. Remember, life is choices; you're always saying no to something. Don't let it be making memories as a family.

2. *Allocate your resources.* Spending money on making memories is a sound investment. Given a choice between a new sofa and a trip to the Grand Canyon, choose door number two. The sofa, eventually dirty, scratched, and torn, will end up in a garage sale. The family trip will live forever in your children's minds.

3. *Cut yourself some slack.* Take the path of least resistance so you don't drive yourself and everyone else nuts trying to make grandiose memories alone. The goal here is fun—not perfection, and not personal performance. I learned the hard way to let the family help make our memories, to cut back on the have-tos, and to sit back and enjoy the ride.

4. *Learn to laugh.* Expect glitches and plan to roll with them. Don't be afraid to acknowledge the absurd. Trust me, some of your best memories will be of memory-making flops. When calamity comes—and it will—give yourself and your family the gift of humor and lightheartedness. They'll follow your lead and laugh along with you.

5. *Accentuate the positive.* Don't dwell on what you can't afford to do or buy. If you can't take a family trip, take an in-town family vacation. If you can't afford a holiday dinner for everyone you want to invite, host

a cookie party or an afternoon tea. Before any special occasion, talk with your family about your expectations—and one of them might be to accentuate the positive. Then, to reinforce the memory, be sure you take pictures and talk about it afterward.

6. *Keep it simple.* This applies to both time and money. Children aren't likely to know the difference between a supermarket cake and an expensive bakery model. As a general rule, the younger the child, the less elaborate the preparations for a birthday party need to be. Remember, it's your child you're trying to impress, not your friends, family, or the mothers of the other children who will be attending the party. The same goes for holiday gatherings. Would you rather sit down to a simple meal—say, a precooked ham you picked up the day before and your family's favorite side dishes—or spend twelve hours in the kitchen building a five-course dinner your nine-year-old will pick at? It's your choice.

7. *Play to your strengths.* I've said it before and I'll say it again: no Family Manager excels in every department. The same goes for tasks within a department. If you love to cook, then maybe homemade goodies are a part of your family tradition. If you don't, invite Sara Lee. If you're good at making up stories and leading games, then forget about getting a clown or a magician for your children's party and spend money on decorations or food instead. (You might want to find yourself a funny hat and a red nose, though.) If you're good at making centerpieces and decorating a room, spend time and energy doing that, not money at the florist.

8. *Be in the party, not just at it.* People want to see you. This goes for family gatherings as well as parties of all kinds. The point is to enjoy family and friends, not to spend yourself into hock for the next six months or exhaust yourself to the point where you fall asleep in the soup.

9. *Be party-alert.* When you see party items, decorations, or favors on sale anywhere, any time of the year, buy them. Store them in a special drawer or part of your closet. When you see ideas in magazines

Let your child have age-appropriate input about the party theme, guest list, food, decorations, party favors, activities, crafts, and games. Then use our party planner to help you have the best birthday party ever!

for special-occasion foods or theme parties, clip and file them. That way you'll have resources on hand and help at your fingertips when you need to plan a special occasion.

10. *Look for opportunities to make special occasions from ordinary days.* They're abundant: the first snowfall, the first robin sighting in the spring, the day a tooth comes out, the day a child brings home an A on her math quiz. They can also be for no reason at all. Maybe it's just time to take a break from routine. Take the afternoon off, pick the kids up from school, and head to a nearby park for a nature scavenger hunt. (For more ideas, see 52 Ways to Make Ordinary Days Special on page 231.)

Birthday Parties with a Bang

PARTY PLANNING TIPS

• The rule of thumb that the number of guests should equal the child's age doesn't always work. Eight is usually a manageable number, but be sensitive to your child's social comfort level. Two or three friends may be the perfect party. If your child thrives on social activity and wants to invite the whole class, try to create a party where this can happen. If you can't comfortably handle that many at home, go to a park, pizza parlor, or roller-skating rink instead.

• For toddlers, plan a party an hour to ninety minutes long. Children six to nine can handle ninety minutes to two hours if a meal is served. When setting the party time for young kids, consider their nap time. Tired three-year-olds are not fun. For teenagers, on the other hand, the length of the party might depend on parental tolerance for late hours and loud music. Negotiate the length of the party beforehand with your teen.

• Give out or mail invitations about ten days to two weeks before the party. Make sure the guests can find the party location easily. Enclose your phone number and directions. If it's at your house, tie balloons to your mailbox or front stair railing.

• For younger children's parties, have a party assistant—your husband, a friend, an older child. Or hire a responsible teenager to help with the party and take pictures.

• Decorate and do other advance preparations the day before or soon enough in the day so that you and the birthday boy or girl have time to calm down before the party.

• Have an activity ready when guests begin to arrive. Don't wait until everyone is present to begin having fun.

• Be sure the party activities match the guests' age and skill levels. Don't try to teach three-year-olds games with five steps. And don't expect teenagers to be happy blowing bubbles. Here's where it helps to know your children's friends and to involve them in the planning.

• Give away a lot of small prizes for games. Everyone likes to win something.

• Be prepared with more games than you need.

• Don't push food. Many kids are too excited at parties to eat large amounts. Go light on sugar, colas, chocolate, and other foods some children may have trouble handling.

BIRTHDAY THEME PARTIES

1. *Circus Party:* Have guests come dressed as clowns, animal trainers, animals, and gymnasts. Set up a minimidway in your backyard. Create different events for the children to win small prizes.

2. *Fun-at-the-Beach Party:* Ask guests to wear swimsuits and turn your backyard into a pretend beach. Provide squirt guns and water balloons to have water wars. Put lots of pennies at the bottom of a wading pool filled with water. Blindfold participants one at a time and let them see how many pennies they can pick up in thirty seconds.

3. *Artfest Party:* Provide supplies—pipe cleaners, paper, markers, glue, glitter, buttons—for kids to create their own artwork. Hang up for a show and "buy" their artwork with party favors.

4. *Be a Star Party:* Ask guests to come dressed as a famous singer. Borrow or rent a karaoke machine. (Include a song list with the invitation so guests can be ready.) Or play familiar CDs or cassettes and let volunteers take turns doing lip synchs of the songs. Make a video of their performance, then play it back for the "stars" to see themselves on TV.

5. *Let's Get Beautiful Party:* Enlist the help of a local cosmetics salesperson to give facial masks and makeup lessons. Let girls style each other's hair. Take pictures! Give small beauty samples as favors.

6. *Back to the Sixties (or Seventies) Party:* Teenagers love dressing up in "period" costumes, especially if they're from their parents' era. Play the music of the period. If you don't have your old collection of records or tapes, most larger music stores sell best-of-year or -decade CDs—or try the used record store. Search secondhand stores or garage sales for period party favors.

7. *Out on the Town Party:* Parties don't have to be large to be successful. Let your birthday boy or girl choose a play or a concert and invite one or two close friends. Dress can be anything from casual for a concert to very dressed up for the theater. If you can afford it, take the group to dinner before the event or, if it's a matinee, an early dinner or dessert after. Or come back to your house for a special post-event supper.

8. *Your Favorite Historical Character Party:* Ask guests to come dressed as a favorite historical character. Provide them with a list of possibilities. Play charades, acting out famous events in history.

ALTERNATIVES TO STORE-BOUGHT BIRTHDAY INVITES

• Blow up a balloon. Write party information on the balloon with a permanent marker. Deflate the balloon, then put it and some confetti in an envelope.

• Cut out a picture of your child's head from a photograph and tape it over George Washington's head on a dollar bill. Make photocopies of the bill on paper and trim to correct size. On the back of each bill write the information for the party and this message: "This birthday buck is good only at Matt's birthday party!" (Guests can use the buck to "buy" favors at the party.)

• For a pirate-theme party, draw a treasure map that leads to your house or the location of the party. Include pretend coins in the envelope for the guests to trade in at the party for treats.

• Glue small toy mirrors to poster board cut into invitation-size squares. Write "Look who's coming to the party!" under the mirror, along with the party information.

• Tell party details by cutting out words and pictures from magazines and gluing on heavy paper.

• Make a secret-message invitation. Write party information on construction paper. Cut paper into a puzzle and put into an envelope. Receiver must put together the puzzle to find out about the party.

• Write a slumber-party invitation on a colorful tote-style gift bag. Include instructions to bring a toothbrush, night clothes, and other items.

• Write a poem about your party for the invitation. For example:

> *On Friday, March 1, Clint Smith will turn six,*
> *We've invited a clown who performs magic tricks,*
> *We hope you'll come from three until four,*
> *To 515 Fifth Street—just knock on the door.*

MANY FLAVORS OF PARTY FAVORS

I've divided these up into age groups, but be creative. Preschoolers might like shoelaces, too. So pick from any category. Just make sure your prizes are age-appropriate.

FOR PRESCHOOLERS

"Eat proof" washable markers

Drawing pads

Polaroids of themselves at the party

Beach balls

Sand bucket and shovel

Bubbles

Plastic rings, bracelets, necklaces

Books

Coloring books and crayons

Stickers

Colored chalk (for sidewalks)

FOR GRADE-SCHOOLERS

Colored markers

Small notebooks

Paper clips with various shapes on them

Friendship-pin kits—safety pins and beads

Fun shoelaces

Fingernail polish

Marbles

Balsa-wood model planes

FOR TEENS

Small spiral-bound notebooks

Gold ink pens

Calendars

Lipsticks

Perfume/aftershave samplers

Trail mix in plastic bags tied with a fancy bow

Inexpensive T-shirts they can personalize with paint pens at the party

Gift certificates for ice cream or yogurt

SUPER-EASY PARTY IDEAS

My good friend Judie Byrd is a cooking and entertaining expert. She taught me that no matter what the season, with a little planning and organization, anyone can host a successful party. Remember, the idea is not to get a twelve-inch write-up in the society section with elaborate details of the arrangements that cost more time and money than you have. The idea is to have fun being together. Here are some of my favorite easy party ideas.

1. *Pasta Potluck:* Invite five couples to bring their favorite sauces; you supply the pasta. (Allow two ounces dry pasta per person.) Create an antipasto tray and serve with crispy bread sticks. Fix a green salad and garlic bread. Offer Italian fruit ice for dessert. Create atmosphere by setting card tables with red-checked tablecloths and green napkins. Tie raffia around old wine bottles to create candleholders. String tiny white lights in houseplants and play soft background music. That's *amore!*

2. *Family Bowl-Game Party:* Football games are a great excuse to invite other families over for fun and food. Decorate with pennants, banners,

POLAROID ART

Teens and grade-schoolers love this simple project. You need a Polaroid camera, film enough for everyone at the party to do at least one picture, and a coin or an unsharpened pencil to rub on the film. (See if you can buy the film in bulk at a discount store, since it can be expensive.) Shoot a picture and then, as it's developing, rub the solution around with the coin or pencil. You get fun distortions and great color patterns. Experiment before you try it at a party. The only caution is to not rub so much that you blur the whole picture.

If you can't manage a party this year but want to do something special, try this. Send a letter and a self-addressed, stamped envelope to your child's friends, asking that they write a birthday greeting for your child and send it back to you secretly. Present the messages to your child at a special birthday meal.

balloons, and streamers. Create a dining-table centerpiece with cheer-leader pompoms and a basket of mums. Provide plenty of popcorn and peanuts for snacking. At halftime, serve a steaming bowl of chili, jambalaya, or chowder, and French bread. While adults huddle around the TV, let the kids enjoy some craft activities or games planned especially for them.

3. *Dessert Drop-in:* Sampling desserts and visiting with friends is a fun way to spend an evening. Offer guests seven or eight confections. Include an assortment of tastes and textures—crunchy, creamy, rich, and dense. Provide cheese, fruit, and nuts for those who don't eat sugar.

4. *Beat-the-Winter-Blues Beach Party:* Turn the furnace up just a tad higher. Make like it's summer. Tell guests to dress accordingly under their overcoats. Serve summer foods you might take to the beach—cold fried chicken, potato salad, deviled eggs, and fruit punch. Or use recipes from Hawaii or the Caribbean islands. Splurge on plenty of flowers, maybe a gardenia for each of the women to put in their hair. Play music that reminds you of summer.

5. *Special Awards Party:* This party can be adapted for any family member and be as elaborate or as simple as you want to make it. It can be for a "small" achievement, like finishing a history research paper, or a "large" one, like graduation. For larger achievements, plan ahead and begin by consulting the honoree to see what kind of party he or she would like—a smaller dinner on graduation night with extended family and close friends, or a large reception the following day. The focus of the party, of course, is the honoree. For a graduation, make a collage of pictures of your graduate from babyhood on. And/or make a display of trophies and awards. Have siblings make up a song or skit recounting their adventures with their graduating sister or brother.

For a promotion at work or passing a test at school, make a crown for the honoree out of cardboard covered with aluminum foil. Hang large sheets of butcher paper or use a large drawing pad on an easel. Put out plenty of markers. Invite each of the guests to write a message to the honoree.

SHORT-NOTICE PARTY SHORTCUTS

Here are tips to help you be party-ready in minutes:

- Keep paper goods, candles, and decorations on hand at all times.
- Surface-clean only the rooms guests will see. Close the doors to others. (See Emergency Measures: Quick Decluttering Scheme, page 37.)
- Master a quick-fix appetizer and dessert recipe, and keep the ingredients on hand. Here are two I learned from Judie: (1) Keep an 8-ounce package of cream cheese in your refrigerator and a box of interesting crackers hidden. Place the brick of cream cheese on a pretty plate. Then pour a small jar of strawberry jam, jalapeño jelly, or fruit chutney over the top of the cream cheese. Surround with crackers. (2) Keep a frozen pound cake, frozen berries, and paper doilies on hand. Serve a slice of cake with berries on top on a doily. Beautiful and delicious!

BUFFET ENTERTAINING TIPS

Buffets can be a great way to provide a variety of foods with a minimum of fuss. These tips will make the line move more smoothly.

- Lower room temperature before guests arrive.
- Don't put foods on your menu that take a lot of last-minute kitchen preparation.
- Choose foods that will look good after sitting out for over an hour. Buy presliced ham or turkey breasts and serve with tea rolls for sandwiches. Make coleslaw with oil and vinegar instead of mayonnaise. Make quiches ahead and store them, cooked, in the freezer. Thaw them in the oven. Or consider buying premade hors d'oeuvre–sized quiches.

> **If you don't have one, invest in an entertaining cookbook. Ask your friends or your local bookseller to recommend one. They come in a variety of cooking-ability levels and most offer interesting menu-combination ideas.**

• Make arrangements for your pets. Some guests may have allergic reactions to animals.

• Set out platters the day before to plan how traffic flow will work.

• Set up a drinks table in a room away from the food.

• In addition to the main food table in the dining room, place bowls of chips, cheese, and cracker platters in strategic areas in your living room and family room.

• For a large party, assign an outgoing older child to greet guests at the door and take their coats, or direct them to a bedroom where they can leave their coats.

• Use a number of smaller flower arrangements and a low centerpiece on your main table. Even though people won't be sitting across the table from each other, they'll be able to chat with those on the other side of the table as they stand in line. And low centerpieces don't fall over.

• Place lots of votive candles around your dining room and the rest of the party rooms. They won't tip over like tapers might, so they're relatively safe to burn without your constant supervision.

> **When choosing fresh flowers for your party, remember that irises wilt fast. Choose heartier flowers such as daisies, lilies, or alstromeria.**
> **Before the party, line several paper grocery sacks with plastic garbage bags and hide them in your laundry room or pantry. They'll be ready to use for quick cleanup between courses.**

Let Music Set the Mood

Pleasant background music enhances the atmosphere of any party. Keep the volume low so conversations can take place without effort. Introduce guests to your favorite composers. Or ask a local music store to help you find selections by Mozart, Beethoven, or Vivaldi for a formal dinner or buffet. Country-and-western music adds flair to a casual dinner or cookout. And seasonal varieties are appropriate and enjoyable for most any occasion. You can also call your local high school to inquire about band students who play for parties in string quartets or combos. Student groups are usually inexpensive, but be sure to check their fee and repertoire of songs before you book them.

Special Children's Table

If you invite children to your party, create a special table just for them. Cover the table with white craft paper. Use markers to draw place mats at each seat. Put markers on the table for the children to decorate their "tablecloth." Use children's toys for fun serving pieces: for example, fill a small plastic wheelbarrow with chips, or use colorful sand buckets to hold cookies.

> If you're planning a large party or reception, reserve your location, caterer, and entertainment at least three months in advance.

ENTERTAINING AT HOME: WHEN TO DO WHAT

Preplanning is more than half the battle. And it can be fun.

THREE TO FOUR WEEKS BEFORE THE PARTY

- Decide on a theme.
- Make your guest list. If you have a bigger list than your home can comfortably handle for a buffet dinner, consider a Sunday afternoon open house or an evening party with snacks. Or choose a day when you can be out on the patio or in the backyard. For a large, special-occasion party it's best not to rely on the weather. Unless you're very sure it won't rain, consider renting a party tent.
- Send invitations.
- Start polishing silver and brass serving pieces during spare minutes.

TWO WEEKS BEFORE THE PARTY

- Finalize the menu and decorating plans.
- Figure food amounts; plan cooking schedule—when to bake and freeze or meet with caterer. Shop ahead for nonperishables.
- Reserve rental items, if needed. These might include wineglasses, plates, tables and chairs, an outdoor tent top.
- Tape an envelope for receipts to the front of your refrigerator. This will help you keep track of expenses.
- Decide what you'll wear for the party. Mend or take clothes to the dry cleaners if needed, or shop for something new. Be sure to check accessories.
- If you're planning an adult party, make arrangements or plan entertainment for your children.

ONE WEEK BEFORE THE PARTY

- Organize your kitchen for the party.
- Store countertop appliances and other items you won't need.
- Clean your oven to avoid "smoking," rather than baking, your food.
- Begin setting up stations for specifics such as fixing drinks, assembling food platters, and stacking dishes between courses.
- Clean out your refrigerator to create more space.
- Stockpile bags of ice or make ice cubes every day, and store them in plastic bags.
- Get party linens ready. Press tablecloths and napkins. Store carefully so they won't wrinkle.

TWO TO THREE DAYS BEFORE THE PARTY

- Wash plates, glasses, and serving dishes. File down chipped glasses with a damp emery board.
- Shop for everything except last-minute perishables.
- Wash lettuce and produce; store in plastic bags.
- Prepare wood in fireplace.

RENTAL KNOW-HOW

1. Obtain price lists from local rental companies for items they rent.
2. Before choosing a company, ask these questions:
   - Does the cost include same-day or next-day return?
   - Are the quantities and styles you need available on your party date?
   - Are delivery and setup charges included in the price?
   - Is there an extra fee for returning dirty dishes, linens, or cutlery?
   - What is the charge for broken items?
3. Place your order early to assure a wide choice of colors and styles. Have the items delivered as early before your party as possible.
4. When items are delivered, check off each item and make sure it works before the driver leaves.
5. Schedule the pickup time after the party.

ONE DAY BEFORE THE PARTY

- Set table and label serving pieces with what they will hold. (This will help you remember the vegetable salad that's marinating at the back of the refrigerator.)
- Chill wine.
- Set up music.
- Do last-minute housecleaning.
- Buy ice, if needed, and fresh flowers. Arrange flowers in containers.
- Prepare foods that can or need to be stored before serving.

DAY OF THE PARTY

- Buy any last-minute perishables.
- Fix remaining foods as early as possible.
- Freshen bathroom towels.
- Go outside and walk through your front door as if you were the first guest. Are there any last-minute things you need to do?
- Light fire in fireplace.
- Get dressed one hour before guests arrive, but put on an apron.

THE FINAL THIRTY MINUTES

- Turn on music.
- Light candles.
- Set out food and beverages.
- Enjoy greeting your guests at the door.

AFTER THE PARTY

- Depending on your style, do only the cleanup necessary to prevent food spoiling or being eaten by pets during the night.
- Consider hiring a teenager to help during the party and with cleanup afterward.
- Don't forget to note details in your special occasions notebook for next time.

EMERGENCY MEASURES:
ENTERTAINING DISASTERS

Disasters can be big or small, depending on how they're handled. Some of them can be avoided altogether.

1. *Your electrical system blows a fuse, causing a blackout during your party.* A few days before the party, have a trial run to test your home's electrical capacity. Turn on all lights, ceiling fans, music source, and any extra appliances you'll be using. If you blow a fuse or flip a breaker, decide what can be turned off without disrupting the party. You may need to use appliances at differing times, or use candles as an alternative light source.

Send guests home with a small remembrance of the evening. You can wrap cookies in cellophane and tie with a bow; give a clove-studded orange to simmer in their kitchen; share a small jar of special sauce you made for the dinner; or give parsley you planted in a small clay pot for snipping during long winter months.

2. *More guests show up than anticipated.* Make the most of the situation without making your guests feel awkward. Cut food into smaller servings and fill glasses less full. Stretch iced tea by adding orange juice or lemonade. Always keep ingredients on hand to fix an extra spur-of-the-moment hors d'oeuvre or side dish. Enlist an older child or teenager to run the dishwasher midparty so you don't run out of glasses and plates. Or use your stashed paper plates if you have to. If you can't squeeze extra place settings on your table, use inexpensive bamboo lap trays for creating an additional conversational dining group. Note: Your guests will feel more comfortable and welcome if a host or hostess sits at each location.

3. *Fewer guests show up than anticipated.* Avoid this problem by sending out invitations early—at least three weeks in advance. People are more likely to respond to an invitation that says RSVP rather than Regrets Only. Also be sure to mail an invitation back to yourself. If you don't receive it, you'll know to check with the post office to see if a bag of mail

was misdirected. If bad weather or unforeseen circumstances arise and guests cannot come, be sure to make those who do come feel welcome. Keep the party on a positive note by not drawing attention to the missing guests.

4. *A guest spills something and stains your carpet.* Clean up the spill with as little fuss as possible. Let the guest help if this eases the embarrassment. If the carpet is treated with stain repellent, most spills will blot up. Use a little Club Soda to clean the spot if necessary.

5. *A casserole bubbles over and smokes up your kitchen thirty minutes before the party.* Cover the smoldering drips with baking soda immediately. Open windows and doors and use a portable electric fan to disperse smoke.

6. *Your guests are strangers and conversation is slow.* Get things moving by asking each guest to tell where he or she was when a significant event occurred. For example: Where were you when men first landed on the moon? For humor, have each person at the table, one at a time, make three statements about him- or herself, two of which are true. Other guests try to guess which one is false. Introduce one of the guests to the group and say how you know him or her. Ask the rest to introduce themselves and tell how they know you.

CUT COSTS WITHOUT CUTTING STYLE:
ENTERTAINING ON A BUDGET

If you wait until you can afford to have a party, chances are you never will have one. It's common to think you need a fat bank account to throw a great party. But entertaining can be surprisingly inexpensive. Try these tips and see how.

- Decide how much money you can spend. This will help you determine the number of guests, your menu, and decorations.
- Consider an open house instead of a sit-down dinner party. Have a dessert and finger-food buffet.

• Base your guest list on how much food you are capable of preparing and serving. If the crowd is bigger than you can handle, you may have to pay for catering, extra help, and rental items.

• Shop for party food at wholesale clubs or restaurant-supply companies where prices are usually cheaper.

• Save on cleaning bills. Spray tablecloths with Scotchgard fabric protector before your party.

• Split costs with a neighbor who also wants to entertain. For example, if you both need wineglasses, choose matching ones, each neighbor buying twelve to share.

TIPS FOR TEACHING KIDS COMMON TABLE MANNERS

In our house one of the ways we taught manners when the boys were young was with the Swine Fine bucket. It was a white plastic bucket we kept on the counter in the kitchen. It had a picture of a pig painted on top. Whenever anyone—Mom and Dad included—exhibited bad manners, another family member could call "Swine fine!" and the person had to put money in the bucket.

Teaching children common courtesies and table manners will build their self-image and help them feel confident in new social situations. But it's important to teach manners without turning family dinnertime into a nag session. This means watching for moments when you can praise your children for improving and being patient with them while they learn. Some goals to work on:

• Sit upright with good posture.

• Keep chair legs on the floor.

• Try not to cause unnecessary noise—clanging of silverware against plate or screeching chair along the floor.

• Place your napkin in your lap and use it discreetly to keep your face clean.

• Don't start eating until the blessing has been said. Follow the custom of the house as to whether you stand, bow heads, or hold hands during the blessing.

- Wait until everyone has been served before eating. At a buffet dinner, wait until at least three people have served themselves before you begin eating.
- Pass salt, pepper, and condiments around the table, rather than across it.
- Don't stretch to reach for food. Ask someone closer to "please pass" an item to you. Say "Thank you" when you receive the item.
- Take what is offered to you. If you don't like what is served, take a very small portion or say "No, thank you" graciously.
- Don't take huge portions. Have seconds only after others have been served.
- Eat slowly. Put your fork or spoon down between bites.
- Don't stuff food into your mouth. Take small, manageable bites.
- Keep your mouth closed while chewing.
- Don't talk with food in your mouth.
- Swallow your food completely before you drink.
- Don't pick your teeth at the table. If you have food stuck in your teeth and it is noticeable, discreetly remove it. Otherwise, wait until after the meal to use a toothpick.
- Keep your arms and elbows off the table while you are eating. Rest your arms on the table only after the meal is over, but always keep to your own space.
- Ask to be excused before leaving the table.

A DOZEN WAYS TO MAKE
HOUSEGUESTS FEEL WELCOME

1. Flatter guests by being ready when they arrive. Their visit won't seem like it upset your family routine.

2. Prepare a guest basket for their bedroom or bath. Include toothpaste, toothbrush, small bottles of shampoo and creme rinse, and small, fancy soaps—items they may have forgotten or that will make their stay more pleasant.

3. If your guests are staying in a child's room, make space in the closet for their clothes. Place a small vase of flowers, magazines and books, a scented candle, and a bowl of fruit on the bedside table. They will also appreciate an alarm clock.

4. Keep disposable diapers and a jar or two of baby food on hand for guests who have babies.

5. Have clean sheets and extra pillows on the bed. Check bathroom towels for freshness and put out new soaps.

6. Make sure your houseguests have opportunities for quiet time alone.

7. Post a list of foods and leftovers on the refrigerator door. Leave your guests a note to help themselves.

8. Show them where you store your iron and ironing board. They may need to press clothes after traveling.

9. Give a toast to guests at dinner. Tell them how much it means to you to have them there.

10. Pick up maps and information about local places of interest from your chamber of commerce. Give them to your guests along with directions to your favorite local spots.

11. If you're having other friends over, prepare a list of names and a brief description of your friends for your houseguests to study ahead of time. This way they won't feel overwhelmed when meeting a lot of new people.

I know one Family Manager who keeps a stash of gifts in her closet for guests of all ages. These needn't be big-ticket items. Fancy soaps, pens, stationery, paperback novels, CDs, fancy jars of preserves or sauces, cloth napkins, fancy hand towels, bags of potpourri—the list is endless. Include some children's items as well. Add to your collection as you find things at discount stores or at seasonal sales.

12. Give guests a travel survival box when they leave. Include snacks, small cans of fruit juice, gum, mints, and napkins. You can also stick in a map, and small trinkets if they have children.

How to Take a Four-Star Vacation on a Two-Star Budget

Bill and I have always ranked family vacations high on our list of priorities. We've found that by doing some research before the trip it's possible to save significant travel dollars.

PREPLANNING IS PART OF THE FUN

Long-Range Planning

• Select your mode of transportation. It's almost always cheaper to drive. Make the travel time fun by bringing along music and books on cassette the whole family would enjoy; packing a picnic lunch; avoiding expensive convenience-store treats during stops by stocking a small cooler with travel snacks and drinks; purchasing small, inexpensive toys and prizes for en route games.

• Write to the visitors bureau or chamber of commerce in the state and city of your destination as well as the ones you will pass through; ask for sightseeing brochures and interesting information. Request a map and information about lodging and area activities. The information you receive—up-to-date brochures that include points of interest, discount coupons for local restaurants and amusement parks—is usually free and will be invaluable as you plan adventures.

• Schedule a family meeting to discuss your trip budget and expectations. Give each person a say about what he or she wants to do. Estimate the cost of each idea, then prioritize the list.

• Search for workable, affordable lodging at your destination. Compare accommodations brochures from the chamber of commerce, read travel articles in magazines and newspapers, and ask for tips from friends who have vacationed where you're going. Consult a travel agent about family-friendly hotel and resort packages. For each hotel, compare the number of rooms, beds, and baths (be aware that the "standard" double room can vary—two double beds at one place, one double bed at another); how often maid service is provided; kitchen and laundry facilities; if accommodations are on or off the beach; recreational facilities and programs for children; babysitting services; and sports amenities. Don't pay for services and activities you don't plan to use. If no one in your family plays tennis, don't stay at a resort that offers unlimited free tennis. The cost is usually built into the package. And if you plan to spend most of your vacation outside, maid service is not a big deal. You may find from your research that you could stay as cheaply or more cheaply in a two-bedroom, two-bath condominium with a pullout sofa as you could in two hotel rooms or a suite. A condo may not include maid service but will probably have a dishwasher, vacuum cleaner, washing machine, and dryer—a big help for a big family. A fully equipped kitchen with a microwave allows you to eat breakfast and lunch in, saving big bucks.

• Make sure the restaurants where you're staying have children's menus. (Some even have a kids-eat-free program.) An adult-only menu can run up the bill fast, plus lead to disgruntled kids who can't order foods that appeal to them.

• Be careful when using hotel discount coupons. These discounts are usually off the published (rack) rate, and may not be a good deal. For example, a coupon for 25 percent off on a $200-per-night room doesn't mean much if the hotel is running a special $99-dollar weekend promotion. Be sure to ask about *all* the discounts before booking. If you don't ask, you'll get the regular rate.

• Remember that brochures and photos don't guarantee anything. Read the fine print.

• Beware of travel-package scams that promise a free trip or attractive travel discounts—but require you to call a 900 number for further details. When you call, you'll likely be required to pay a fee to join a travel club to take advantage of specific offers. So you'll wind up paying for the "free" trip or discount through the fees and repeated 900 number phone charges.

• Consider vacationing at a national park. For campground reservations, call (800) 365-2267.

• Take the children to the library and let them choose one or two books for your vacation. Set up a reward system to encourage them to spend thirty minutes a day reading while on the trip. Give them a five- or ten-dollar incentive, which they will receive the last day of the trip if they met their reading quota. They can spend the money on whatever they want.

• Let your children start earning their own spending money. Then when they see something on the trip they can't live without, they can buy it and keep peace in the family!

Short-Term Planning

• Guarantee your room for late arrival—even if you plan to arrive early. Flight delays or car trouble may cause you to arrive later than expected. Most hotels won't hold a room after 6 P.M. unless the reservation is guaranteed with a credit card. And be sure to alert the hotel if your plans change. If you don't and the room was guaranteed with a credit card, the hotel could charge one night's lodging to your card. Beware: many hotels now require cancellation notice by 4 P.M., not 6 P.M.

• Avoid embarrassment. Know the existing balance and credit limit on credit cards you'll be using.

• Put your name and phone number on all your luggage and belongings, and never leave your bags unattended in public places.

• Pack curling irons, hair dryers, or anything else that could be mistaken for a weapon or explosive device in easily accessible areas of your luggage. Security guards won't have to mess up your bags to inspect these items.

• To escape lodging costs en route, plan to begin your journey early in the morning and drive all day. On longer trips, make a confirmed reservation for an overnight stop at a motel with suite-type rooms. Many offer free continental breakfast. Use national-motel 800 numbers to compare room prices and amenities.

• Before the trip, write simple meal plans and make a grocery list so you can shop quickly when you arrive. Bring small items like spices from home. Bake and freeze casseroles and transport them in coolers to pop in the oven on nights you eat in.

• Cut out the portion of a map with the highways you'll be traveling, then highlight the route with a yellow marker. Glue your map to a piece of cardboard and laminate it with clear contact paper. Your kids will like tracking your progress.

• Get the car tuned up and check the air pressure in the tires for safety and better gas mileage.

• Be sure to take along a book that you can read aloud to the family. Read a little each night before bed. Choose a book you can begin the first night of your trip and finish before you return home.

• Planning the end of the trip is important, too. Leave a casserole in the freezer at home so you won't have to spend extra money eating out when you return. Plan to do your dirty laundry at a Laundromat where you can do it all at once. Go through your mail while you're waiting. And no matter the length of your vacation or the size of your budget, allow a one-day buffer between the end of your vacation and returning to work. This allows everyone time to readjust, ending the trip on a positive note.

Last-Minute Checklist
- Make sure all bags and gear are in the car.
- Secure items you can't pack until the last moment (child's security blanket, favorite stuffed animal, pillows, toiletry items).
- Confirm that newspaper and mail have been stopped or will be picked up.
- Unplug coffeemaker, small appliances, TV, electronic equipment, and computers to protect from power surges while you're gone.
- Check to see if stove and oven are turned off.
- Remove milk and other perishables from refrigerator.
- Check refrigerator and freezer doors to see that they are securely shut.
- Wash dirty dishes and run disposal.
- Take out garbage.
- Turn off water supply to washing machine and ice maker.
- Set sprinkler system.
- Activate answering machine.
- Adjust thermostat and water heater for vacation setting.
- Set automatic light timers.
- Check to see that all windows and doors are secure.
- Make sure no valuables are visible from the windows.
- Arm security system.
- Exit and lock the door.

ON THE ROAD
- Agree to some simple money-saving techniques. Drinking water with meals when eating out can save ten to fifteen dollars a day for a family of four. Use the public telephone in the lobby of your accommodations instead of the one in your room, since some hotels add surcharges for each connection, which mount up fast. Buy snack foods and soft drinks to have in your room rather than reaching into the in-room re-

frigerator for soft drinks, peanuts, and candy—which usually cost several times the supermarket price. Avoid room service, since prices are usually 10 to 20 percent higher than in hotel restaurants, and there's a 15 to 17 percent delivery charge tacked on.

• Whenever possible buy gasoline at stations that give a discount for paying cash. Check your oil and tire pressure occasionally.

• Have your kids keep a scrapbook of your trip. Help them collect things during the day to put in the scrapbook each night. Include travel brochures, postcards, a free kid's menu or interesting place mat from a restaurant, or a pretty leaf from a tree where you stopped to picnic. Have each child write a note about what the family did that day and what he or she especially enjoyed. Include humorous and unusual incidents like geese crossing the highway and stopping traffic.

• Carry a small notebook to keep pertinent trip information. For future reference, take notes along the way about the places you enjoyed or that gave you good service such as gas stations, motels, picnic spots, and restaurants. Write down what you especially enjoyed and might like doing again.

• Many hotels have VCR service available. This can be a surprise cash-saver. Each day you could use your video camera to make home movies of the children. At night enjoy watching yourselves star in the movies and relive the fun you had that day. And renting movies from a local outlet is probably cheaper than watching those offered on pay-per-view.

• Take advantage of free local entertainment, such as community concerts, museums, and interesting tours. The newspaper, as well as the brochures you can pick up from the tourist bureau at the state line, are valuable sources of information about events and opportunities.

RAISE YOUR FUN QUOTIENT

• Pick a vacation destination that has a range of recreational options for everyone in the family.

• Decide how much your family can do on vacation in the time you have—then plan to do less. Don't come home exhausted.

• Be sure to schedule some time alone for family members who need it.

• Respect the wishes and schedules of children. Don't expect them to enjoy the same things Mom and Dad do. Family vacations work best when planned around the interests and developmental levels of the children.

• Try something different this summer. Take an organized bicycle tour, stay at a working guest ranch, camp out at a national park, or book a cruise on a family-oriented cruise ship.

• Give yourself the freedom to have fun and enjoy your family. Forget about the office and responsibilities back home.

AIRPLANE TRAVEL SAVVY

For making the skies as friendly as possible:

• Sign up for the airline's frequent-flier program. Most offer tangible benefits even to occasional fliers, such as advance boarding and priority waiting lists, which help when traveling with young children.

• Check advertisements in your Sunday newspaper travel section for airline ticket consolidators. These are companies that take blocks of tickets airlines don't think they can sell and offer them at greatly reduced prices. But there are risks. Although tickets can be discounted up to 50 percent or more, you can't change your ticket once you've bought it, and the price can't be refunded.

> Get your office clothes dry-cleaned while you're on vacation. That may be the one time you don't need them.

• On some airlines, families flying together can save substantial dollars over regular coach fare. Airlines define families as husband, wife, and children, ages two through seventeen. (Infants under two years fly free.) Stepparents and stepchildren will need proof of relationship. Sometimes grandparents qualify for family fare. Contact airlines or a travel agent for specifics.

• Ask if land-air packages are available to your destination. These may be less expensive than buying your trip in components (airline, hotel, rental car, etc.).

• Consider taking flights with connections through a hub city. Many times these are more affordable than a nonstop flight. Departure times may not be as convenient, and your flight time may be longer, but it may be worth the dollars you save.

• Take several individually wrapped little toys for your child to make the flight go faster.

• Try to choose flights that have movies. This helps pass the time for kids.

• When flying to a city with several airports, arrive at the one most convenient to your final destination.

• Reserve bulkhead or emergency-exit seats for more leg room. If you have children who nap, sit as far forward as possible for silence, and avoid sitting near the galley or rest rooms.

• Call the airline to order kid-pleasing meals at least twenty-four hours before departure time.

• Take chewing gum on the plane to help unblock ears during takeoff and landing.

• When traveling with a baby, pack enough formula, diapers, and other supplies to more than cover the estimated time spent in transit. Be prepared for delays.

• Wear loose, comfortable clothing and shoes. Make sure kids' clothes are easy to get in and out of during rest-room visits.

• Have children wear a backpack with an assortment of small toys

LUGGAGE LOOPHOLES

If you're flying to your destination, don't arrive at the airport at the last minute. Even if you make the flight, your luggage may not. Watch the agent who checks your bags to make sure the correct destination tags are attached to each one. Confirm by asking the agent to which destination your bags have been checked. Always remove any old airline tags from bags.

Better safe than sorry: be sure to pack all prescription medications and a change of underwear and toothbrush for each family member in your carry-on luggage just in case it takes a day for your luggage to catch up with you. Also pack irreplaceable things like jewelry in carry-ons and have an inventory of what's in each checked bag for claims purposes in the unlikely event that your luggage goes permanently AWOL.

and games to play during the flight and while waiting in airports.

• Tie a bright-colored ribbon around the handle of carry-on hanging bags. Bags look alike, and it's easy for someone else to take yours by mistake from a front closet before you exit the plane. The ribbon will prevent this or call attention to the error.

• Don't fly within twelve hours after dental work. The change in atmospheric pressure can cause severe pain.

• Ask a flight attendant for a blanket and pillow as soon as you are seated. If you wait, they may all be taken.

AVOID CAR RENTAL CASH TRAPS

• Check to see if your auto insurance policy covers car rentals. Buying insurance when renting a car is always expensive and often not necessary. Some credit cards offer automatic coverage when you charge a car rental.

• The convenience of dropping a car off at a site other than where you rented it usually comes at a cost—sometimes a big one. Shop around and know the costs before taking this option.

• For best rental car rates, book advertised specials as soon as you see them, since rental companies change their rates quickly. Consider using smaller rental companies with off-site lots. Many charge up to 20 percent less than the bigger companies.

• Plan flight arrivals and departures for the same time of day to avoid being charged an extra day's rate for just a couple of hours' use of a car.

• Look into taking a shuttle or public transportation to your lodging destination, then rent a car the next day—saving one day's rental cost.

• Many rental companies add as much as three dollars a day or ten dollars a rental for each additional driver. Shop around for competitive rates. Don't try to save money by not adding additional drivers to the contract. If you have an accident, the company may withhold insurance benefits. This can cost you big money.

• Always inspect a rental car before driving. Report anything missing or broken immediately. Make sure the damage is noted on your contract so you won't get charged.

• Remember, all fifty states require child safety seats. Bring your own child seat from home. Or when reserving your car, tell the agent you'll need a child safety seat, too. They are available for a nominal daily or weekly rate.

TWO-FAMILY VACATIONS:
SPLIT THE COST AND DOUBLE YOUR FUN

This summer, why not try vacationing with a family you enjoy with children close to the same ages as yours? Let these ideas simplify the planning.

1. Find a family who wants to vacation in the same place you do and plan a meeting to discuss the details: your vacation budget, possible lodging options and prices, and available activities in the area. Be truthful on the front end about your family's likes and dislikes.

2. Choose accommodations big enough for both families. Ask the rental agent about the square footage and the number of bathrooms and bedrooms of the houses or condominiums you're considering. Ask for a floor plan if it's available—then you can decide who sleeps where before you arrive. Make sure the kitchen is stocked with enough dishes for both families.

3. Agree to divide the rental cost, and appoint one person to take care of administrative details such as filling out rental papers, sending in a deposit, or confirming your stay by credit card.

4. Talk about which outings and activities you want to do together and which alone. Above all, remember that things change, so be ready to be flexible. Everyone will enjoy the trip more.

5. Decide who will be in charge of cooking which meals and divide cleanup responsibilities.

6. Make a list of supplies you'll need and divide the list. You'll save luggage space.

7. Be sure to pack board games, cards, and a big jigsaw puzzle for rainy-day or nightly entertainment.

8. Decide on a meeting place for the day of your departure. If you travel caravan-style, the kids can take turns riding in different cars and can trade card games and cassette tapes, which makes the trip less monotonous for them. And if one family has car trouble, the other is there to help out.

9. If you'll be traveling all day, let each family pack one picnic meal for both families. This way you don't have to bring so many items, plus you cut the cost by eating less in restaurants.

10. When you arrive at your vacation spot, unpack and talk to the kids about any house rules you mutually decide upon. Make sure they understand that the family room and kitchen are community territory, but each family needs privacy in their bedrooms and baths.

11. Let the parents take a turn entertaining all the kids for one day or night of the trip. This way, each set of parents gets a break.

12. Because even the best of friends sometimes see too much of each other on a trip, plan at least two or three half-day sojourns that are single-family only.

52 Ways to Make Ordinary Days Special

Coming full circle in this section, I'll say it again. Devoting time and energy to making sure your family has shared fun to remember is one of the most important parts of the Family Manager's job description. My rule of thumb is that we should try for some fun at least one day a week. Ergo, here are fifty-two ideas to get you started. (See also 25 Great Summer Boredom Busters for Kids, page 146, for ideas.)

1. Plan a Friday night at home. Rent one or two videos, maybe one for the whole family to watch early in the evening and one for Mom and Dad to watch with or without older kids after the little ones are in bed. For supper, have popcorn, apples, cheese sticks, vegetable sticks, and maybe some cookies. (You cover all the basic food groups, but have a meal that feels like it's treats only.) Eat in the family room while you watch the movie.

2. Play hooky from work and/or school for half a day. Take a field trip to see a museum exhibit you've been anticipating or go to the beach. Once or twice a year, this can be an incredibly spirit-lifting experience for the whole family.

3. Celebrate small accomplishments at a dinner with the honoree's favorite menu. You might have a crown or a wide-ribbon banner that you can pin different sorts of paper medallions on, things like: "A on a test"; "Finished a project"; "Half-year birthday"; "Learned something new." Enlist your chil-

> "Happiness is produced not so much by great pieces of good fortune that seldom happen, as by little advantages that occur every day."
> —Benjamin Franklin

dren and spouse to be on the lookout for things to celebrate about each family member.

4. Have a Family Appreciation Night. Fix your favorite foods. Turn on the answering machine and settle down for a confab. Have each family member say what he or she appreciates about other family members. Look at vacation pictures or family videos. Tell stories about when the kids or Mom and Dad were little.

5. Celebrate your ethnic heritage. This could be at a time of year that's a holiday for your ethnic group: Cinco de Mayo or St. Patrick's Day. Or it can be any time of the year. Fix foods that reflect your heritage. Have older children research information about the country and culture of your origin and give an informal presentation. Rent a video that takes place in the country your forebears came from and has a story that tells something of its history. Check out picture books from the library. Tell stories your parents or grandparents told you about the "old country."

6. Buy each family member his or her own bouquet of flowers for no special reason at all.

7. Start keeping a spare change jar or basket in your kitchen and/or the master bedroom. When it's full, roll the coins into tubes and trade them in for dollars. Use the money to go out to dinner or on a special family outing. One outing might be to a bookstore or music store where each family member gets to buy a book, tape, or CD of his or her choosing.

8. Have a family read-aloud evening. Each family member who can read should come prepared with a short story or poem. It might be something he or she has written or an old favorite.

9. If your children are older, stage a reading of a play together. Ask your librarian for recommendations. Choose old favorites like *I Remember Mama* or *Our Town*, or classics like *Romeo and Juliet* or *A Midsummer Night's Dream*.

10. Have a family sing-along. If you have a guitar player or a pianist in the family, use him or her. If not, just sing your favorite songs a cappella one night after dinner. Or sing along to recorded music.

11. Have a family music recital. All members prepare a piano piece or a piece on some other instrument they play. Or they get to play favorite classical or contemporary music on the stereo and tell something about the composer or performer and why they like the music. Serve a fancy dessert and herbal tea or other favorite refreshment during intermission. Dress up as you would to go to a recital or concert.

12. Have a dress-up dinner for no special reason. Set the table with your best china, silver, crystal, and linens. Serve your favorite foods in three or four courses.

13. Create your own special family recipe for homemade ice cream. Make a batch of plain vanilla and provide various ingredients and toppings to stir in.

14. On a Saturday afternoon, instead of supper, have a late-afternoon high tea. (You can serve snacks later before bedtime if you think your children won't get enough to eat.) Make several kinds of fancy sandwiches by trimming off the crusts, filling them with your favorite sandwich spreads, and cutting them into triangles, squares, or fancier shapes with cookie cutters. Pick up a variety of tea cakes and cookies from a bakery where you can buy just a few of each kind and arrange them on a doily on a silver tray. Serve seasonal or frozen berries and crème fraiche. Use your best china—small plates and teacups. For young children, serve juice or fruit tea. Dress up in high-tea finery.

15. Once a year, make a family collage. Gather old magazines and maybe "outtake" snapshots that aren't going into family albums. Everybody cuts out things that appeal to them. Then work together to glue them onto a large poster board. Each person can tell the family story the picture reminded them of, or simply why they chose the picture. Use markers to write favorite family sayings or decorate around the pictures. Hang your collage in the family room.

16. On a day when your schedule has some flexibility, wake up everybody half an hour early. Kidnap them and take them out for breakfast at a favorite pancake house.

17. If you've been stuck inside for a few days because of inclement weather, arrange for a spur-of-the-moment outing. Go swimming at your club or YMCA. Go roller-skating or bowling.

18. Declare a chore-free weekend. It's hard to do. It will require some advance planning. But it can be done. Eat off paper plates, or eat simple preprepared foods so all you have to do is load the dishwasher. Lay in a supply of books and games. Take long walks. Go see a matinee movie.

19. Take a spontaneous evening field trip. Drive out in the country to buy apples. Or take a picnic to a park with a view and watch the sunset.

20. Start a family gratitude book. Pick an attractive blank book and a place to keep it—perhaps on a table in the living room or family room. At a family dinner one night, explain what the gratitude book is for: recording anything each member is grateful for that involves the family. They can be simple things: "I'm grateful that Tommy remembered to take out the garbage"; "I'm grateful that Mom baked a cake for the rest of the family for no special reason"; "I'm grateful for Spot and Bunny" or "for our house." Or they can be for broader or more amorphous things: "I'm grateful for the family's support while I've started my new job" or "I'm grateful for your love." Make sure that family members who can't write yet get a chance to say what they want written in the book and maybe to draw a picture. Periodically have a dinner at which you add to the gratitude book and take time to read aloud and reminisce about what you've written there.

> "Write in your heart that every day is the best day of the year."
> —Ralph Waldo Emerson

21. Start a list of things that make your family members happy. It can be in a simple notebook or on a piece of paper that you mount on the refrigerator or in some other place where you'll all see it frequently. Caution: These lists tend to grow like Topsy once you start them. One woman started a list of things that made her happy and ended up with a published book of them. So you may soon need more than one sheet of paper.

22. Congratulate yourselves for finishing a monumental task—such as putting up a basketball goal, building a tree house, cleaning the house from top to bottom, painting the kids' rooms. Make homemade ice cream and enjoy it together.

23. Honor a family member who's had a hard week. Kidnap your victim and take him or her to a favorite restaurant. Use a bandanna as a blindfold and travel in a roundabout way to your destination.

24. Welcome a neighborhood family to their new home. Take over a sack of soft drinks, sandwich supplies, chips, dessert, paper plates, and cups. Put together a "Welcome to the Neighborhood" booklet that lists the best of the area: best grocery store, cheapest gas station, best bookstore, best ice-cream shop, etc.

25. Turn an ordinary weekend into a mini-vacation at home. Choose a weekend and put it on the family calendar. Stock up on groceries and snacks. Get out board games and check for missing pieces. Rent a few family movies and pop some popcorn. Turn on your answering machine and put a sign on your front door that says your children can play *after* your mini-vacation. Keep chores and cooking to a minimum. Plan some fun Saturday outings everyone will enjoy.

26. Plan a surprise weekend for your family and enjoy the pool, health club, and maid service at a nearby hotel. Many have inexpensive weekend package deals that include breakfast. Play tourist in your own hometown. Take advantage of local attractions and current events you normally might not take the time to enjoy.

27. Have a family game night. Turn off the TV and turn on the answering machine. Lay in your favorite snacks. Set up your favorite board or card games. You might want to have small prizes for first place, second place, most creative move, most interesting attempt at getting around the rules—in enough different categories so everybody gets a prize. Or give out chits for various good moves, etc. They can be worth differing amounts of points. At the end of the evening everybody can turn in their chits for prizes, which can then be slightly bigger. Note: If family members are agreeable, prizes can also be things like certificates for one night of not having to cook dinner or do dishes, or a free babysitting night that an older child would give you, or other fun things the family member likes to do.

28. Throw caution and nutrition to the wind. Have a weekend family meal that includes everybody's favorite food. This might make for some hilarious combinations. Spaghetti and BLTs? It also might make for a meal made up mostly of desserts—if that's the case, try to make sure one of them has some fruit in it.

29. Designate one evening a month family fun time. Use some of the suggestions in this section. Or make up your own ideas. Anybody for a water-balloon fight? Or a build-your-own-pizza feast?

30. Take a walk in a park or nature preserve near you. Give each child a notebook and ask them to record different animals and flowers they see. How many different bird calls do they hear?

31. Even if you've lived in your area for a long time, research new places to go on family field trips. Museums are obvious choices. Also look into historical sites and businesses that might conduct tours.

32. Do something different. Look for a farm or ranch near you that rents horses for riding by the hour. (It's best to go on a trail ride conducted by an expert.) Or rent in-line skates. Or rent a rowboat or sailboat for an afternoon. If you're a nature-loving family, go on a weekend hike. Many different organizations run inexpensive day trips. Look in the Yellow Pages or ask a friend. Whatever you choose should be something that at least some of your family members aren't expert at. If others are expert, they can act as guides or tutors. Then find another time to do some activity that's new to different members of the family so the experts have a chance to be beginners as well.

33. Decorate your dining room with streamers and balloons for a special dinner on an ordinary day.

34. Put little presents under everybody's pillow one night. This could be new toothbrushes, wild socks, or a small book.

35. Dedicate a day in praise of each family member's favorite color. Everyone can dress in his or her favorite color. Make bookmarks or buy markers or pens for family members with ink in their favorite color. Cook a dinner that includes at least one thing in everybody's favorite color. It may take some planning ahead to find food in odd colors, so poll everybody in advance about what they're choosing for their favorite color. For pink, there's grapefruit or juice. For purple, try eggplant or icing on cupcakes. For black, what about blackened grilled fish?

36. For the next time grandparents come to town or perhaps for an extended family party, turn stories Mom or Dad tell about when they were growing up into a short play to perform.

37. Make appointments for mother/daughter or father/son haircuts.

38. Build self-esteem and celebrate each other by having everyone in the family make a wall hanging from poster board or construction paper that celebrates his or her ten favorite things about him- or herself. Mom and Dad should participate in this exercise as well. You can hang them in bedrooms when you've finished them, perhaps on the inside of a closet door for shyer people.

39. When happy times are scarce—and it happens to all of us—spend time together remembering happy times. This can be an especially good thing to do when a beloved grandparent or older relative is ill or dies.

40. Some cold or snowy Saturday, work together cooking a comfort food you have never made together. Bread is ideal. There are a number of different ingredients to measure and assemble. Everybody can take a turn kneading. And while you're waiting for it to rise, you can do more mundane weekend chores and still have something to look forward to. When it comes out of the oven, let it cool for a bit. Serve warm with butter and jam, tea or coffee, and milk.

41. Spend part of a weekend being someone else. Be a pirate or a princess or a superhero. Each family member should pick a character. Then carry on your day, but in the role of your character.

42. In weeks when you're all simply too busy to do anything special outside your ordinary routines, make up family IOUs: "We owe ourselves one special break from the week of May 2." Post on the refrigerator or someplace where you'll see them and remember to treat yourselves to something special twice some week soon.

43. Volunteer to cook or serve food as a family at a homeless shelter or soup kitchen. Or visit a person who lives in a nursing home and doesn't have family nearby. So many times we wait for the holidays to do this. Do it now.

44. See if you can find a farmers' market in your area. Everybody gets to pick out one thing. Then go home and make a meal of your fresh produce.

45. Start a book of family quotations. Keep a notebook in a handy place, maybe in your Control Central. When Mom or Dad or older kids come across quotes they like and think the rest of the family will enjoy, too, they should write them down. You might also include "family" quotes. Then periodically read your quotes out loud after dinner one night.

46. Have a "Stealthy Benefactor" day or week. There are several ways to do this, depending on the ages and number of people in your family. With children old enough to deliver good deeds on their own, you can simply draw family names out of a hat. The idea is to leave little hidden gifts for your "benefactee," do his or her chores or something nice—but don't get caught. At the end of the day or week, everyone should try to guess who his or her benefactor was. Younger children can pair up with a parent or older sibling to become benefactors. If there are only two children too young to participate on their own, each parent can take one and do nice things for the other team. Of course that way it's not anonymous, but it's still fun.

47. Have a family costume party. Have family members come as each other and do imitations of them. Or come as your favorite character from a book or artist or musician. Rules are: You need to ask to borrow another person's clothing or accessories. You need to use props and costumes you can find in your home. And no hurtful humor.

48. Make silly faces at each other. Try it at the dinner table one night. Try not to laugh. See who can make others laugh fastest or longest. Caution: Wait until you're finished eating.

49. Have a family treasure hunt. Make up written clues. Pair younger nonreaders with a reading partner. Each person follows the clues to his or her own special prize. Or have the clues lead to the makings for a special family dessert—for example, a jar of chocolate sauce in the fireplace, strawberries in the meat compartment of the refrigerator, and bananas in the bathroom sink, spoons and bowls in out-of-the-way places all over the house, and ice cream "disguised" inside a large pan in the freezer. Or have the clues lead to parts of a new game.

50. Play flashlight hide-and-seek after dinner on a warm summer night. Just like regular hide-and-seek, the player who is "it" counts to twenty (or whatever number you choose) while the other players hide. Then "it" tries to shine his or her light on the players to catch them. It's fun to play a variation of this game indoors if you have small children. First, turn out the lights in your house. One parent hides stuffed animals all over the house while the other parent and children close their eyes and count to twenty. Then they try to find the stuffed animals with flashlights.

51. Have a family joke night. Announce it in advance. Everybody

> Invest in a good camera and take a lot of family photos. You'll be glad you did.

should come prepared with a funny story or joke(s) to share.

52. Have a sock hop. Roll up the rug, put on some dancing music, kick off your shoes, and dance, dance, dance. Teach each other new steps. Make up routines to teach each other.

53. Begin your own list of things you can do to make special occasions out of ordinary days. Don't stop at fifty-two.

Tips for Taking Great Pictures

• Use high-speed film to make lighting less critical.

• Move in tight on people. Make "more face, less feet" your picture-taking motto.

• Don't shoot down at your subjects. Most kids open their presents sitting on the floor, so get down on their level.

• Capture spontaneous expressions rather than posed smiles.

• Move people away from walls to avoid harsh shadows.

• When photographing a cluster of people, stagger the back row so heads are not stacked.

• Wrap toilet paper or tissue around your flash to create a picture with a softer effect.

> "Don't put off for tomorrow what you can do today, because if you enjoy it today you can do it again tomorrow."
> —James A. Michener

- To photograph still objects, place dark objects in front of a light background and light objects in front of a dark background.
- Press the shutter button gently to prevent jerking.
- Ask your subjects to wear bright-colored clothes.
- Keep extra film and camera batteries on hand.

SIX

Holiday Bonus Section

"For somehow, not only at Christmas, but all the long year through,
The joy that you give to others is the joy that comes back to you."
—John Greenleaf Whittier

Extra, extra, read all about it! This is your one-stop guide to planning special holiday celebrations throughout the year, with a super-big section for Christmas.

Holidays provide opportunities for creating special traditions and family bonding. There's something about being able to say, "This is the way we always do it" that fuses a family in heart and memory.

There are more holidays than one family can possibly celebrate. Your family's heritage may guide you to which holidays you choose to highlight and how you decide to celebrate them. Or you can learn about other holidays at your library or bookstore, on the Internet, and from older people in your community, church, or synagogue.

Tips for Happy Holidays—Throughout the Year

• Plan ahead as much as possible. Use a colored marker to highlight holidays on your Control Central calendar.

• Prepare as a family. For children, anticipation of the holiday is almost as much fun as the holiday itself. Let them be involved as much as possible with all the preparations: putting up decorations, making special foods, selecting music.

• Don't feel guilty if you can't put on a big production. If you're caught off guard when a holiday rolls around, it's still worth celebrating. There are plenty of things you can do spur-of-the-moment. Keep various colors of balloons, candles, and crepe paper streamers on hand. A festive dining-table centerpiece can come from your own yard. Just try to do a few of the same things year after year. Add and subtract as your schedule and situation change.

Fourteen Holidays at a Glance

Use the ideas here for holiday fun, or let them spur ideas of your own. Feel free to mix and match. For instance, homemade cards are a good idea for almost any holiday.

Feel free to celebrate holidays outside your personal faith or ethnic traditions. Hanukkah, for example, celebrates the ever-present reality of miracles. Scandinavian communities often celebrate the feast of Saint Lucy. In the dead of winter, it's a festival of lights, in which the oldest girl in the family or community wears a wreath of candles and delivers special breakfast rolls to the whole family. Attending ethnic celebrations in your town or nearby city can be another way of celebrating. In some larger cities, the variety is astounding—from Greek Independence Day to Japanese cherry blossom festivals. By reaching outside your own traditions you teach your children appreciation for other people and ways of life and prepare them to be better global citizens.

1. Valentine's Day

• Use today as an opportunity to say "I love you" in a special way to those you care about. Tuck a note with a Valentine's Day message in a

ALL-PURPOSE HOLIDAY CENTERPIECE

Buy a large glass hurricane candle shade, at least twelve inches tall. Use a clear glass plate or a tray for a base. Fill the shade with various seasonal items. For example, use alternating layers of pastel eggs and Spanish moss for Easter. In the fall, fill it with tiny pumpkins, acorns, and pecans. At Christmas fill it with crabapples or colorful glass balls.

• Start a collection of cookie cutters in shapes such as hearts, shamrocks, pumpkins, or bells. Bake a batch of sugar cookies with your child for various holidays. Keep different colors of store-bought frosting in tubes, candy sprinkles, and colored sugar on hand to decorate.

• Let your children decorate their own rooms for holidays.

• Buy a big stuffed bear to keep on display in your home. Dress him for each holiday you celebrate.

• Pay as little attention as possible to the commercialization of holidays. Focus on what you want the holiday to mean to your family.

lunch sack, backpack, or briefcase. Or send an e-mail or pager message.

• Homemade cards are still the best, and young children love to make them. Gather arts and crafts materials and spend time together making special cards for loved ones.

• Have a Valentine's Day scavenger hunt. Starting at the bathroom mirror, give your children the first clue, which leads to another clue somewhere in your house. Make up seven or eight clues, with the last one leading to a gift. (This has been a tradition at our house for years, and even when the boys became teenagers, they still loved waking up to this game every Valentine's Day.)

• At the dinner table have family members state reasons why they love each other. Get ready for silly as well as serious.

• Here is an easy centerpiece: wedding pictures surrounded by confetti, Valentine's cards, and candles.

2. Passover

Passover, the Jewish feast of freedom, is celebrated on the fourteenth of the Jewish month of Nisan (March or April). It's a celebration and memorial of God's deliverance of the Jews from slavery in Egypt. The name Passover also recalls God's sparing (passing over) the Jewish firstborn sons during the plagues Moses pronounced on Egypt. The holiday is marked by eating only unleavened foods and participating in a Seder, a carefully orchestrated meal full of stories, rituals, and symbols. Each food item on the Seder plate is symbolic of the time the Israelites left Egypt and went into the desert on their way to the Promised Land.

- Take pictures. Be camera-ready. (See Tips for Taking Great Pictures on Page 240.)
- After the holiday, get out your special-projects notebook and file notes about what worked or didn't, and ideas for next year.
- After each holiday, buy half-price decorations for next year.

Unleavened bread called matzoh is eaten during Passover as a reminder of the long trip from Egypt. The Jews did not have time to let dough rise before they fled, so they had to bake their bread, skipping this part of the process. They rolled it into thin wafers, put it on flat boards, and baked it in the desert sun.

You can help children better understand the purpose of yeast in bread by filling two glasses half full with warm water. Dissolve a little yeast in one of the glasses, then add the same amount of flour to both glasses. Put both glasses in a warm place for about an hour and see what happens.

Passover is a good time to talk as a family about what freedom—or the lack of it—means to individuals, and how freedom on any level carries with it certain responsibilities.

3. Easter

For Christians, Easter commemorates the resurrection of Jesus Christ from death to life. It falls on the first Sunday after the first full moon following the vernal equinox sometime between March 22 and April 25.

The tradition of wearing new clothes for Easter evolved from celebrating the earth dressed in a fresh cloak of greenery and flowers. The custom of the Easter rabbit and eggs came from ancient Egypt and Persia. The eggs are a symbol of life.

Below are some fun ways you and your family can celebrate Easter.

• Kids love the tradition of dyeing eggs, and it's something the whole family can have fun doing. Family members can personalize eggs by using a needle to scratch their names in the shell before dyeing. The letters will show through.

• Make your eggs shine by wiping a lightly greased cloth over them.

• Make your eggs look marbled by wrapping each egg in fabric and securing it at the ends. Soak the egg in dye and let it dry overnight. Remove the cloth.

About Eggs

Hard-boiled eggs will keep up to ten days when refrigerated, 3–4 days at room temperature.

Before dyeing eggs, wash them in mild soapy water and pat dry. The dye will adhere better to the eggs.

• Even when kids get older, they still enjoy getting an Easter basket of treats on Easter morning. I learned this the hard way when a college-age son came home for Easter weekend and wanted to know if he was getting an Easter basket. I didn't have one for him.

- Check your local newspaper for Easter-egg hunts. Or start the tradition of having an egg hunt for the kids in your neighborhood.
- Early on Easter morning, deliver treats such as chocolate eggs, hot-cross buns, or decorated cookies to your neighbors' front doors. Keep them guessing about the identity of the Easter bunny.

4. Mother's Day

- Set a good example for your own kids: let them see you remembering your mother on Mother's Day. Make your mom a homemade card telling her why you're glad she is your mom, listing things you appreciate about her.
- If your mom is in a nursing home, ask two or three of her friends to join you there for tea. Take pieces of her china and silver to use.
- Give your mom a scrapbook that includes photos and memorabilia of each of her children.
- Enlarge an old photo of the two of you together—one she has forgotten about—and have it framed.
- Give a gift certificate for a day of beauty—manicure, pedicure, facial.
- Have dinner at a special restaurant.
- Give tickets to a play or concert.
- Find a new tool or book for her hobby; give her plants and seeds and help her plant a garden—include new garden gloves, a kneeling pad, a spade.
- Whatever gift you give, remember the inestimable value of time and attention. Parents never want to stop feeling needed and loved by us.

As for being the recipient of honor this day, don't expect your husband and kids to read your mind about what you'd like—that's both unfair and a guarantee for disappointment. Give them some advance ideas of what might make the day special for you—breakfast in bed, the "day off," a certificate for things you want done around the house.

5. Memorial Day

It's important that our children understand and appreciate those people who have gone before us. Since the Civil War, this day has been set aside to pray for peace and honor soldiers who have lost their lives in service to our country. Although it has turned into a day when we think about presummer sales at stores and auto racing, let's not forget its significance. This is a good time to talk to our children about the privilege of living in a free country and the blessings we enjoy because of it.

On any patriotic holiday it's fun to pull out the red, white, and blue decorations and fly the flag. I have a special wreath for our front door for these days. Keep tiny American flags on hand to decorate foods. Your kids can make festive place mats for these holidays: cut white poster board into 18-by-13-inch rectangles. Let them decorate the mats by drawing stars, flags, etc. Cover the mats with clear contact paper or take them to an office-supply store and have them laminated.

6. Child Appreciation Day

One family I know started this tradition on the first day of summer vacation every year. They show appreciation to their children by talking about their positive qualities, giving them small gifts, and saying a prayer of thanksgiving for their children's lives. The parents also use this day to talk about summer plans, goals, and procedures.

7. Father's Day

• It's never too late to say a special thank-you to your own dad. Send him a special card.

• Have his old home movies transferred onto videotape.

• Give him something pertaining to a hobby, such as a gift basket filled with fishing lures, extra line, hooks.

• Plant a tree in his honor.

• Help your kids make coupons for Dad that promise to shine his shoes, clean his car, do his least-favorite chores in the yard or garage or his laundry, give a fifteen-minute back or foot massage.

8. Fourth of July

Talk with your children about the birthday of the United States. Explain what the Declaration of Independence proclaims: that every person has a right to life, liberty, and the pursuit of happiness. It's a good time to talk about what these words mean. Other ideas:

- Coordinate a neighborhood effort to display flags big and small in every front yard.
- If they don't already know it, teach your children the words of "The Star-Spangled Banner."
- Organize a neighborhood parade. Help children decorate their tricycles, bicycles, and wagons with red, white, and blue crepe paper streamers. Or organize a block party/picnic. Keep it simple: Each family brings their own meat and/or vegetables to grill. Divide up side dishes, drinks, and desserts by assigning them to people whose names begin with specific letters of the alphabet—for example, A to Fs bring drinks.
- At dusk gather a few quilts and go watch your local fireworks display. Also, many community orchestras will have a concert that features the War of 1812 Overture, sure to stir the patriot in all of you.

9. Labor Day

This is the day we honor the labor force in America. It's a good time to talk to your children about the importance of various occupations and careers. Ask them to think about what would happen if some of the important behind-the-scenes jobs went undone. Encourage them to talk about what they would like to do when they grow up.

Today is a great day for a picnic.

Picnic Checklist

Use this list to make sure you're ready for food and fun in the outdoors.
- Food and condiments
- Beverages
- Water
- Ice
- Paper plates
- Paper cups
- Eating utensils
- Serving utensils
- Napkins
- Tablecloth or old quilt to cover a table or spread on the ground
- Packaged premoistened towels to clean hands
- Paper towels for cleanup
- Garbage bag to take care of litter
- Bug spray
- First-aid kit
- Toilet paper if you're in a remote location
- Flashlights if you'll be out after dark
- Camera

10. Halloween

Children can dress up and enjoy this holiday in many positive, nonviolent ways—ways that focus on the fun of creative costumes, the beauties of fall, and jack-o'-lantern carving.

One Family Manager told me her family started a different kind of Halloween tradition. Instead of trick-or-treating, the kids go out in costume and collect canned goods for a local shelter. She provides special treats for the family when they get home. Here are some other ideas:

- Organize a neighborhood scarecrow contest. Appoint judges, and ask each neighbor to contribute a small entry fee toward a prize. Have families make and display creative scarecrows in their front yards.
- A few days before Halloween take a drive to a pumpkin patch and buy pumpkins in several sizes. Older children and teens might like to invite a few friends over for a pumpkin-carving party. Spread newspapers thickly on the basement or garage floor or in the kitchen. Provide knives, sturdy spoons for scooping out the insides, big bowls for pumpkin "innards," and candles to put in the finished product. Have enough pumpkins available so everybody gets to take one home and you have enough left over to decorate your front steps for the big event.
- Roast pumpkin seeds saved from carving pumpkins.

11. Thanksgiving

Whatever our circumstances, we all need to take time out to enjoy our family and reflect on our many blessings. Whether you enjoy a simple meal with your immediate family or pull out all the stops and spread your table elaborately for many, Thanksgiving can be about more than food. Free yourself to enjoy the meaning of the day by sharing the load. Some Family Managers find it helpful to assign parts of the meal to extended family members and friends. To make your preparation as painless as possible, do as much as you can ahead of time so you can enjoy the day. If you like company in the kitchen, make your preparation a family affair. If you feel the need for uninterrupted kitchen time, suggest that Dad take the kids on an overnight campout the night before.

Most family members expect the "usuals" for Thanksgiving dinner. So don't knock yourself out fixing winter-squash-and-kumquat pie when plain old pumpkin is what everyone's expecting. Do follow the instructions in your cookbook or that come with your turkey for safe storage, handling, and cooking. Going to the emergency room on a holiday is no fun.

• Have everyone take a turn at the table saying what he or she is thankful for. I started this tradition more than fifteen years ago. One person acted as the recorder and I've saved the lists from year to year. Now we not only say what we're thankful for this year, but we read from prior years' lists as well. As the boys have grown up, it's rewarding for all of us to remember who they were "back then."

• Consider inviting a college student or single person over for Thanksgiving—many can't afford to travel long distances to go home. A new family in town or a single-parent family might also appreciate invitations.

• Fix a takeout plate of your dinner goodies to deliver to a homebound neighbor or friend.

• Start a Thanksgiving tradition or two that doesn't have to do with food. Before dinner organize friends or neighbors in a touch-football game. Bundle up and take a long walk in a nearby park or at the beach.

• Organize an after-dinner game of charades. Make all the titles and words you act out have something to do with Thanksgiving.

• Plan activities for the long Thanksgiving weekend that do not have to do with shopping. The "biggest shopping day of the year" can happen without you and your family. (See 52 Ways to Make Ordinary Days Special, page 231, for specific ideas.)

12. Hanukkah

On the twenty-fifth of Kislev on the Jewish calendar, Jewish families all over the world gather with loved ones to celebrate Hanukkah. The holiday commemorates the victory of the Maccabees over the Syrians. When the Temple was cleansed and rededicated after the Syrian desecration, the lamp in the Temple miraculously burned for eight days even though there was oil for only one day. Families celebrate by giving gifts, eating traditional foods, and playing games.

Dreidels are four-sided toys that are spun like tops in Hanukkah games. Kids can create a dreidel from a half-pint milk carton or small, square box. Simply staple the spout shut and paint the carton with tempera paints. When dry, turn it upside down and write a different Hebrew letter on each side. The letters look like this:

בגהש

The letters begin the Hebrew words that translate, "A great miracle happened here."

Decorate the carton and poke a pencil through the bottom to use as a spinner. If you are using a square box, poke the pencil all the way through and out the opposite end.

Kids will also enjoy making edible dreidels. Insert a toothpick through a regular-size marshmallow and then into the flat side of a chocolate kiss–shaped candy. Use the candy dreidels to decorate the tops of cupcakes or eat them as treats.

13. Kwanzaa

Kwanzaa, a weeklong African-American celebration, begins December 26. The word Kwanzaa means first fruits and was created as a unique tradition that focuses on family and culture. Each of the seven days of the celebration is devoted to one principle: unity, self-determination, collective work and responsibility, cooperative economics, purpose, creativity, and faith.

The intent of gift giving during Kwanzaa is to give something personally made or crafted so the gift bears your "spirit." The colors green and black are significant, so gifts of these colors are appropriate.

Kwanzaa is celebrated around the country with storytelling, poetry, readings, dances and music, art exhibits, plays, and lectures.

No matter what traditions you celebrate, don't bypass the Christmas section of this chapter. You'll find many special project-management strategies there that apply to any holiday celebration.

Share background about this holiday with your family. Stop by the library for some children's books about Kwanzaa and read these together. Check your local newspaper for a listing of Kwanzaa events.

14. New Year's Day

By the time this holiday rolls around, many of us don't have a lot of energy or discretionary income left for elaborate celebrations. Like many other "problems," this is an opportunity in disguise because there are lots of meaningful activities you can do to celebrate new beginnings.

Make New Year's Eve a stay-at-home-and-celebrate-as-a-family event. Or even consider asking another family to join you, maybe spending the night, if the weather is inclement and you'll be up late.

• Participate as a family in fixing simple foods that you can snack on all during the evening. Solicit everyone for their favorites. Splurge on some out-of-season fruit.

• Mark the stroke of midnight in some way that doesn't necessarily have to do with watching television. (If you don't want your children to try to stay awake that late, do it earlier. It's always midnight somewhere.) Put your favorite peppy music on the stereo and dance in the new year.

• Collect and put all the candles in the house on a card or coffee table covered with butcher paper for easier cleanup. A few minutes before midnight, light them all. Then on the stroke of midnight, everybody makes a wish and blows the candles out together.

• If you have a fireplace, have everybody gathered write things they'd like to leave behind in the old year—overeating, fear of the water, snapping at each other—on small pieces of paper. These can remain private or they can be shared, but it should be everyone's choice whether or not they share what they've written. Then, at the stroke of midnight, throw the slips of paper into the fire and welcome the new year and your new selves.

• At the Peel house we take some time individually to write down how we want to grow intellectually, physically, emotionally, and spiritually over the coming year. Then we get together and share with each other our goals. If you have young children, you will need to help them think of ways they would like to grow in these areas, using terms they will understand. For example, you might ask your five-year-old if he would like to become a better reader this year and practice reading favorite books to Mom or Dad for a few minutes each day.

• Start a scrapbook for the new year. Your children can decorate an inexpensive notebook or album and use this book throughout the year to collect and save mementos from school and special events, letters from friends and relatives, and other treasures.

If You're Going Out

• Make sure to book a babysitter three to four weeks in advance. Many parents will be going out tonight and sitters will be in demand.
• Have special treats and snacks for your children. Even if they're not old enough to stay up until midnight, you might provide party hats and noisemakers for their own celebration earlier in the evening.
• Don't overdo with food or alcohol. The cost of overindulgence is high.
• Consider going in a cab rather than driving your own car.
• Pamper yourself with a long bath. Give yourself a manicure. Take some time to relax before you leave home.

• New Year's Day can be a good time to have an open house, which is traditional in many cultures. Some say cooking and eating black-eyed peas, beans, or lentils on the first day of the year brings good luck year-round. I don't know about that, but simple dishes seem like a good thing after all the holiday goodies.

If you don't have an open house or attend one, do an outdoor activity as a family. Or go to a movie. If you are a football family, see Family Bowl-Game Party, page 207. Over the years, I've learned from Family Managers who are married to football fanatics that this might be the one holiday of the year that doesn't have to be, at least when the games are on, a family-togetherness experience. If you have a large enough house, have a multi-purpose party. Set up activities and games for kids in one of your children's bedrooms, the kitchen, or the basement. Ask teens from among the families attending to rotate shifts entertaining younger children or hire one or two babysitters. Serious football watching happens wherever the television is. (You could even ask friends to bring a portable set or two so the real fanatics can watch more than one game.) For the nonfootball fans, organize an adult board game marathon in another room in the house. Ask everybody to bring food to share, and come together during halftime or between games for a simple lunch or supper. If your house is not big enough, ask a neighbor or two to cohost this event with you.

Extra Days to Celebrate

Use this list to remember upcoming holidays or to pick ones that sound interesting to celebrate. Once you and your family agree on which days to highlight, research what each is all about and apply some of the general ideas from this section (or specific ones, as appropriate from other holidays). My feeling is you can't have too many options when thinking of days to celebrate.

New Year's Day	January 1
Feast of the Magi	January 6
Martin Luther King Day	Third Monday in January
Inauguration Day	January 20
Chinese New Year	January 21–February 19
National Freedom Day	February 1
Groundhog Day	February 2

Lincoln's Birthday	February 12
Valentine's Day	February 14
Washington's Birthday	February 22
Ash Wednesday	February 25
President's Day	Third Monday in February
St. Patrick's Day	March 17
First Day of Spring	March 21
Passover	March or April (fourteenth of Nisan)
Palm Sunday	Sunday before Easter
Good Friday	Friday before Easter
Easter	March or April
Easter Monday	Monday after Easter
April Fool's Day	April 1
Pan-American Day	April 14
Earth Day	Third Sunday in April
Arbor Day	Last Friday in April
Professional Secretaries Week	Fourth week in April
May Day	May 1
National Day of Prayer	First Thursday in May
National Teacher Day	Tuesday of the first full week of May
Cinco de Mayo	May 5
Mother's Day	Second Sunday in May
Armed Forces Day	Third Saturday in May
Victoria Day	First Monday preceding May 25
Memorial Day (observed)	Last Monday in May
Memorial Day	May 30
Flag Day	June 14
Father's Day	Third Sunday in June
First Day of Summer	June 21
Canada Day	July 1
Fourth of July	July 4
Bastille Day	July 14
Labor Day	First Monday in September
Grandparents' Day	First Sunday after Labor Day

Citizenship Day	September 17
First Day of Autumn	September 21
Succos	September/October
Rosh Hashanah	September or October
Yom Kippur	September or October
Columbus Day	Second Monday in October
National Boss Day	October 16
Thanksgiving in Canada	Second Monday in October
United Nations Day	October 24
Halloween	October 31
All Saints' Day	November 1
All Souls' Day	November 2
Election Day	First Tuesday after the first Monday in November
Veterans' Day	November 11
Thanksgiving	Fourth Thursday in November
Hanukkah	November or December
First Day of Advent	December 1
First Day of Winter	December 21
Christmas	December 25
Boxing Day	December 26
Kwanzaa	December 26–January 1
New Year's Eve	December 31

'Tis the Season to Be Jolly: How to Reduce Holiday Hassle

For years I tried to be Super Mom, Santa Claus, and Julia Child all rolled into one. Just browsing through the December issue of my favorite home magazine made me reach for an antacid. Compared to the lavishly decorated trees in the photos, my tree always looks like the runt of a particularly scruffy litter. In fact, it looked best when tied to the top of our car.

And I figured out why department stores defer payments until March

1: that's when you finally get waited on. In search of the perfect gift, I've traipsed from store to store, risked my life in mall parking lots, and stood in lines that span two zip codes only to watch my gifts go back to the store on December 26.

I finally realized I was making myself and everyone else in a five-mile radius miserable when I tried to create my notion of a perfect holiday based on a magazine-worthy Christmas. In fact, it never worked. I finally decided I was trying to do too much, I was doing things my family didn't necessarily like, and I couldn't do it all myself. After all, even Santa needs helpers. Now, I've cut back on my holiday have-tos and our family works together to make Christmas more enjoyable for everyone.

MAKE A HOLIDAY HIT LIST

Start the first week of December by creating a master list of everything—every single thing—you need to do, buy, and cook this holiday season. Don't try to organize this list into departments yet; just list everything that comes to mind.

Now take that list, which is probably longer than the string of lights on the White House Christmas tree, and prepare to see it shrink to doable proportions.

Step 1. Classify and cut.

Divide a piece of paper into five sections labeled To Buy, To Cook, To Attend, and To Do. Leave the fifth section blank for now. Now transfer each item on your long to-do list to the appropriate category on your Holiday Hit List. Be as specific and as thorough as you can. When you're finished, star the most important things—traditions, foods, and activities—you and your family think Christmas wouldn't be Christmas without.

Now apply the principle of selective neglect. Are there things on your list you can do without? Things you just don't think you'll get to? Cross them off.

You'll use the remaining list for Steps 2 and 3.

> **Make sure all family members have a say about their holiday expectations.**

Step 2. Share the joy . . . and the work.

Make Christmas a family affair. Give everyone a copy of your Holiday Hit List. Or, if you're used to having family meetings and collaborating, work together to generate the list. Study the list of everything that needs to be done and delegate skill- and age-appropriate jobs to family members—even young children. Put an approximate date, the initials of the person responsible, and when the task should be completed beside each item. Post it on the refrigerator or keep it in an accessible place at Control Central. Cross each item off your Holiday Hit List as it's finished.

Step 3. Take a joy break every day.

In the fifth section of your Holiday Hit List write down things that bring you joy. At least once a day, stop and do one of those things. It may be doing something for yourself. It may be doing something for someone else so he or she can experience joy, which will bring you joy as well.

Joy Breaks

(See also 52 Ways to Make Ordinary Days Special, page 231.)
Here are some ideas to get you started:

- Replace your shoelaces with a red one and a green one. Tie on some jingle bells.
- Turn off all the lights and eat dinner in a room illuminated only by the Christmas tree.
- Read an article in a favorite magazine.
- Listen to a recording of Bing Crosby singing "White Christmas" while you're baking or wrapping gifts.
- Relax and watch a cup of tea cool down. Let the rising steam carry off your worries.

- Take a walk around the block. Breathe deeply, swing your arms, lift your feet. Feel like skipping? Do it!
- Treat yourself to a decadent dessert without saying, "I shouldn't be doing this."
- Trade rubs for sore feet, backs, or necks with family members.
- Reread your kids' letters to Santa from years past.
- Go to a church and sit in the chapel. Reflect on the real meaning of Christmas.
- Take yourself or a friend or your spouse out for lunch in the middle of a hectic shopping day.
- Treat yourself to a manicure, pedicure, facial, or haircut.
- Walk to a close-by café and enjoy a cup of cappuccino.
- Take some time out to sit in the mall and watch children sit on Santa's knee.
- Buy a new Christmas cassette or CD for your music collection.
- Fix a cup of hot cocoa, curl up in your favorite chair, and read "The Gift of the Magi" by O. Henry.
- Write a letter to someone who has had a positive influence in your life. Thank him or her for this special gift he or she gave to you.
- Invite a child to join you in roasting miniature marshmallows over a candle.
- Attend a children's Christmas pageant.
- Attend a *Messiah* concert or a *Nutcracker* performance.
- Once all your neighbors have their decorations up, take a walk around the block and enjoy the scenery.
- Take a different route home from work and enjoy the decorations in another neighborhood.
- Take time to tour a historic home or hotel in your area that has been decorated for the holidays and is open to the public.
- Throw orange peels in your fire and fill the room with a spicy aroma.
- Put on a pair of outrageous Christmas socks.
- Write down all your blessings. Chances are, you'll be uplifted.
- Take a few minutes to work part of a jigsaw puzzle.
- Get out old photo albums and enjoy memories of past Christmases.

- Call a church, synagogue, or community service organization and ask what you can do to help someone in need.
- Bake your favorite Christmas treat, doubling the recipe so you can share some with a friend.
- Recall your biggest Christmas goof-up. Laugh at yourself.
- Stop and smell the evergreens.

CHRISTMAS-DAY COUNTDOWN

Recovering holiday sanity for me meant putting into practice one of my best skills: I'm an inveterate list-maker and -keeper. Here are the tips that have helped me simplify the season. May they help you and inspire you to find your own. Hint: Don't try to do *everything* on this list. The idea is to simplify. And involve your family—the celebration is theirs, too!

WEEK FOUR

- After Thanksgiving, have family members write all of their holiday activities, as soon as they know about them, on your Control Central calendar.
- Set a goal to do something joyous every day—attend a Christmas concert, run errands for a homebound neighbor, have lunch with a friend you haven't seen in a while, go ice-skating. (See Daily Joy Breaks, page 100.)
- Check your Holiday Hit List every morning to see what needs to be done that day. Add any new things that have come up unexpectedly.
- Secure babysitters for social outings.
- Add Christmas wrap/decor to your Gift/Wrapping Center. (See User-Friendly Work Centers Make Work Easier, page 74.)
- Pick a night for the entire family to work on Christmas cards.
- Get your whole family involved in decorating your house.

- Make appointments with your hairdresser or manicurist for holiday events.
- Decide what you'll wear to holiday parties. Take care of cleaning or mending now.
- Finish catalog shopping. Have gifts wrapped and mailed directly to the recipient whenever possible.
- Stockpile holiday staples and nonperishables before the stores get crowded.
- Serve easy meals to your family. A big pot of chili or stew can last a few days.

WEEK TWO

- Have a baking day. Get all your supplies ready the night before. Measure out dry ingredients.
- Schedule shopping times—not during peak hours. Mornings and evenings are best. Avoid the noon hour and Saturdays if possible.
- Buy a few extra generic gifts—picture frames, pretty writing pens, bottles of gourmet hot sauce or salad dressing—for last-minute guests or people who surprise you with gifts.

Shopping Simplified

The key to stress-less holiday shopping is good planning. Tackle the mall with a well-thought-out list and a goal to get it all done in a couple of days. You can spend the rest of the month doing fun holiday things with your family. (See Daily Joy Breaks, page 100.)

- Schedule two full days on your calendar for shopping.
- Decide on a gift theme and get everybody on your list similar gifts—books, sporting equipment, kitchen gadgets, wardrobe accessories, etc.
- Recheck clothing sizes before you go.

- Buy children's items first since popular toys sometimes sell out quickly.
- Shop with a list.
- Categorize ideas. List stores where you can buy several items in one visit.
- Map out your route so you don't backtrack. Shop in one area until you're sure you've finished.
- Shop with a backpack to leave your hands free.
- Take your checkbook, credit cards, cash, calculator, *and* address book—so you can mail gifts from the store.
- Save all sales slips and price tags. Write the item and the recipient on the back of your receipt. Keep them in an envelope in your backpack.
- Double-check your receipts before you leave a checkout desk.
- Request a box for each item you purchase.
- Divide shopping duties with your husband, according to items you're each comfortable buying.
- To avoid futile shopping trips and frustration, call stores ahead to check on prices and availability of items.
- If a large chain store is out of a popular toy or game, ask whether the item is available at another of its stores. Many times they can have the item delivered to the store in your area.
- Do two things at once. While you're waiting for packages to be wrapped, visit other shops. Go over your to-do list when standing in checkout lines.
- Take breaks while you're shopping. Sitting down to rest and think about what you're going to do next will save time and reduce your stress level.
- Don't waste time searching for the perfect gift for someone on your list who's hard to please. Give a magazine subscription or a gift certificate.
- If you find a gift you like in a catalog, order a few to give to several people.
- Use your local department store's personal shopping service. This service is usually free.

- So you don't waste time worrying if you've given someone a certain item before, make a list of what gifts you buy for whom each year. Keep the lists in a file for easy referral.
- Buy yourself a special soap or bath salts and soak in a hot tub when you get home.

WEEK THREE

- Schedule your child's visit to Santa for a time when there won't be long lines or crowds.
- Stock up on batteries, film, and videotape for Christmas morning.
- Watch local newspapers for special Christmas plays, musicals, and library events. Attend one as a family.
- Have a potluck dinner with two or three other families, then go caroling.
- Set up a card table in an out-of-the-way place for kids to create Christmas arts and crafts.

WEEK FOUR

- Finish wrapping gifts.
- Deliver presents to friends and neighbors.
- Volunteer your time or resources as a family. Call community service organizations or a local church or synagogue and ask how you can help.
- Cook and freeze whatever you can for Christmas dinner.
- Trade off babysitting with a friend—to give each of you some time to run last-minute errands.
- Watch a favorite Christmas video as a family.
- Start a holiday-memories scrapbook. Include notes about family events, favorite cards, photos, and letters to Santa. Add to it each year.
- Rekindle a relationship with a friend or relative.
- Attend a Christmas Eve candlelight service with your family.
- Relax and enjoy Christmas Day.

Cards: Make a Mountain into a Molehill

Sending heartfelt greetings doesn't have to be a tedious chore. Slenderize the procedure into something orderly and doable.

- Address envelopes first, then write the cards to go in them. Work straight through your address book at one time. It's quicker than looking up each address separately.
- Put a few cards in your purse and write notes while waiting at appointments.
- Buy self-sticking stamps and keep them near the phone with some envelopes. Affix stamps while you're on the phone.
- Instead of sending Christmas or Hanukkah cards, consider waiting until after the holiday rush and sending New Year's greetings.

How Kids Can Help

It's a win-win scenario: not only do kids want to participate, they can really make a dent in holiday chores.

Younger Kids
- Seal holiday card envelopes and affix stamps.
- Display cards on a door, wall, or banister.
- Help decorate the tree.
- Decorate their own rooms.
- Tape tags to packages.
- Help bake cookies.
- Set the table.
- Clean up fallen Christmas-tree needles with a lightweight, handheld vacuum.

Older Kids
- Address Christmas cards.

- Help compose a Christmas letter.
- Fix dinner a couple of nights. You may get tomato soup and grilled-cheese sandwiches, but that's okay.
- Wrap packages.
- Help make and put up decorations.
- Bake cookies and simple sweet breads.
- Deliver baked goods to neighbors.
- Help shop, unload and put away groceries.
- Write down return addresses of all holiday cards you receive. Compare your card list to these addresses and make necessary changes.
- Help younger siblings get ready for holiday outings.

MAKING GIFTS EASY TO GIVE

Gifts tend to be the center of the holiday season. Here are ways to enjoy them without being exasperated by them.

- Overspending causes stress. Discuss gift expectations with your spouse and children. Set a budget and stick to it.
- Mail gifts early to avoid long lines. Or consider using a private shipping company. Some will pick up your packages at your home for a nominal charge.
- Many companies now offer packing services. You give them the presents, and they wrap and pack and send them for a fee.
- Hire responsible teenagers to run some of your holiday errands. This saves you time and provides a way for them to earn extra money.
- As you buy stocking stuffers, keep them organized in paper bags labeled for each person.
- Save time and confusion by separating gifts for drop-by friends and relatives from gifts to be given out Christmas Day.

Caution! Don't overdo gift certificates for your time and energy. Even though in December it appears you'll have a lot of time later to fulfill these, remember that you haven't transferred activities to your new calendar yet.

Get Creative about Gift Ideas

Maybe Great-aunt Mary, who has everything she possibly could want, would like a gift certificate to a local spa or hairdresser, a day out on the town with you—lunch and the museum—in February, or a donation in her name to her favorite charity. There are three good reasons to get creative with gifts:

1. You've got people who already have every material thing they need.

2. Your budget is limited—whose isn't?

3. You want to add a personal touch, reminding your loved ones that you thought of them, not a generic aunt, uncle, cousin, coworker, or friend.

So here are some ideas for you to adapt and personalize:

• Gift certificates don't have to be from a store. Give gifts of your time and energy: a certificate for babysitting, yard work, or a meal delivered. Your whole family can be involved in thinking up the certificates and share in the work and fun when the recipients redeem them.

• Outings with you. Aunt Mary may not be the only one who'd like to spend some quality time with you sharing a favorite activity.

• Create a gift basket. Line a basket with green and red tissue paper, then fill it with items that have a specific theme—kitchen gadgets, fishing paraphernalia, makeup and beauty items—the recipient would enjoy.

• For grandparents and other older relatives: a photo album of you and your family. Or videotapes from your family's year. (See also A Dozen Ways to Close the Gap and Share Christmas Cheer with Long-Distance Family and Friends, page 281.)

• Match the gift to the recipient. During the year, make notes to yourself about things people say they wish they had, or contribute to a hobby. If you aren't sure about a particular hobby item, a gift certificate to a specialty store or mail-order catalog might be just the thing. A subscription to a magazine is a good gift, too. For example, Uncle Dan, the garden enthusiast, might appreciate getting a gardening magazine in his mailbox every month.

• When giving homemade or store-bought food gifts, consider giving things that are canned or frozen and aren't necessarily "holiday" foods. For example: a collection of gourmet barbecue sauces for the backyard chef; a bag of coffee beans and a mug for the coffee connoisseur. For an elderly relative, check into giving a gift certificate that covers the delivery cost of his or her grocery orders. Fruit preserves can be decorated with red bows and bells. Holiday food gifts don't have to be "sweets." Consider homemade stock or stew frozen in mason jars. Home-baked goods or casseroles should be wrapped and frozen.

• Special finds in secondhand stores aren't just for decorating your home. Young couples just starting out can almost always use more serving dishes and utensils. Consider something like a cake server from an antique store. Other used items that are often "better" than new: glassware, teapots, table linens. I know one Family Manager who's made a habit of buying her nieces inexpensive antique costume jewelry. For a really special present, you might find and refinish a stool, a wooden chair, or a small storage box. The total cost, depending on where you find it, could easily be less than fifty dollars plus several hours of your time.

Help Your Kids Focus on *Giving* Instead of *Getting*
Holidays are a prime teaching time. Use these guidelines to help your kids see money's meaning (to supply needs) and the season's opportunities to use it in a way that benefits others.

• Take your children with you when you make a donation to a charity. Talk to them about what the money will be used for.

• Ask children, "What are you *giving* for Christmas?" instead of "What are you *getting* for Christmas?"

• Read *The Littlest Angel* by Charles Tazewell or *The Little Drummer*

Four Keys to Buying Good Gifts for Your Kids

1. *Look beyond their wish list.* You may not be doing your kids a favor by purchasing gifts on their list if they've only seen the items on TV commercials. Ask yourself, What are my children's needs? At their current state of development—physical, emotional, intellectual—what else should be on their list? Incorporate some of these items along with your children's desires.

2. *Look for toys that stimulate rather than entertain.* Beware of toys that tranquilize kids with mindless entertainment. Instead, choose gifts that encourage creativity and stimulate the intellect or senses. Good choices are books, sports equipment, art supplies, or musical instruments.

3. *Look for ways to provide experiences.* Consider giving lessons for special interests, such as arts and crafts, computers, music, or sports. Or give tickets to concerts, or travel money to visit family or friends.

4. *Look for ways to emphasize the uniqueness of the child.* Celebrate your child's individuality by giving presents that correspond to his or her special gifts or talents.

Boy by Ezra Jack Keats aloud to your child. These books are traditional tales that illustrate the true meaning of giving.

• Help your young child make note cards on which you write a thank-you message. They can sign the cards by tracing around their hands, leaving the outlines as their signatures.

• Host a Junior Santa party for your children and their friends. Ask the children to bring toys they've outgrown but are still in good condition. At the party, clean up the toys and provide supplies for the kids to wrap and label them. Donate the toys to a children's hospital, orphanage, or a group collecting gifts for needy children.

- Volunteer as a family to help out at a food bank or shelter.
- Pack up some goodies and take them to the firefighters and police officers who are on duty Christmas Eve.
- Take your children to the grocery store and let them help you pick out foods for an extra sack of groceries to donate to a citywide food pantry.
- Have a family brainstorming session and write down ways you can give others joy this season—decorate the rooms of nursing-home residents, give blood, buy a book and donate it to a local library, buy a menorah and candles or a Christmas tree and some decorations for a family who can't afford them.

TEN WAYS TO ENHANCE FAMILY CLOSENESS DURING THE HOLIDAYS

1. Set aside one weekend in December to be a "family-bound" weekend. Spend time together visiting holiday exhibits, working a giant puzzle, wrapping packages, and baking treats. At night, sip hot chocolate and watch favorite Christmas videos.

2. Get out holiday photographs and videos of your children from years past. Praise them about how much they've grown and learned each year.

3. Start a special project early in the month and work on it together a little each night. You might build a doghouse for a new puppy, create a table to display a model train, or sew a holiday wardrobe for a favorite doll.

4. Open holiday cards as a family at the dinner table. Take turns reading the messages.

5. Have an annual family holiday program. Ask each family member to perform a song, read a poem or scripture passage, draw a picture, or express the meaning of Christmas in a personal way. Keep content of performances secret until called upon.

6. Start a special collection of things like angels, unique ornaments, Nativity sets, Christmas bells, or nutcrackers for each child. Display the collection prominently, and add one item each year.

7. Write your own lyrics to the tune of a well-known carol. Memorize

and sing it each year. (When our kids were small, we made up our own silly version of "The Twelve Days of Christmas." Fifteen years later, we still sing it.)

8. Each year, buy one new ornament for your child. When the child marries or sets up his or her first apartment, give the collection of ornaments as a wedding present to decorate that first tree.

9. Have a New Year's Family Awards Night. Invent crazy awards and present fun prizes to each person: Possible categories might be Best Sport When Kidded, Messiest Closet, Best Plate Cleaner, or Quickest to Answer the Phone.

10. Attend a religious service together as a family.

HOLIDAY FOODS

Do you know anyone who doesn't complain about eating too much during the holiday season? Try to alleviate the problem at your house by serving simple foods that are or will become family tradition, by not putting out all the goodies at once, and by varying elaborate Christmas dinner and party menus with simple suppers of soup or stews.

• Cook casseroles and soups for December in November. Label them clearly and store them near the front of your freezer. Beans are a great alternative. Not every meal has to have meat.

• Include as many do-ahead dishes as you can in your Christmas dinner preparations. In general, the rule for holiday dinners, especially where children are involved, is that the simple, traditional foods are best. If you're not a gourmet cook with gourmet traditions, don't try to wrap your turkey in homemade puff pastry like I once did, unless you want to end up eating underdone turkey in a crisp black dress, or worse yet, visit the emergency room. Cranberry sauce doesn't need seventeen ingredients to be festive. Your supermarket probably makes dried bread cubes for stuffing. It's a lot easier than cutting bread into cubes and drying it yourself. Include at least one or two low-fat, sugar-free alternatives for family members and friends with special dietary needs.

• If you're hosting your extended family, or even if you're not, you might broach the subject of potluck. Maybe your mother or sister is tired of cooking all the food, baking all the desserts, and getting all the side dishes together as well. Approach this from a positive note. Play to people's strengths. Don't ask your sister to bake the desserts if she hasn't seen her electric mixer in a decade.

• It's not a sin to buy things that the bakery or deli can make better than you can.

ENTERTAINING MADE EASIER

Here are ways to host a party and enjoy it, too.

• Instead of hosting a holiday party by yourself, organize a progressive dinner party with a few friends. Have appetizers at one home, the first course at another, the main course at another, and dessert at the last.

• If you're having two holiday parties, hold them back-to-back and serve similar foods. It takes the same amount of time to make a double batch. All your serving pieces will be out, and your house will be fresh.

• Turn the lights down low and light candles at parties. Nobody will notice you didn't have time to dust.

• Put mats inside and outside of doors to catch dirt from extra holiday traffic.

• Before adult holiday parties, ask sitters to arrive early enough to give you plenty of time to dress at leisure.

• Don't prepare a recipe for a holiday party unless you've tried it out at least once beforehand.

• Consider holding a holiday party *after* Christmas when the house still looks great and you're not as rushed.

When purchasing a live tree, find out if the climate and soil conditions in your area are conducive to its growth. Visit your nursery or garden center early so you'll have a good selection. Look for a tree with a straight trunk, a full, symmetrical body, and a sturdy root ball. When you take it home, leave it on a porch or in a garage for one to two days and water it thoroughly before bringing inside. Place the root ball in a leakproof container so you can keep it watered. Don't keep a live tree inside a heated house for more than ten days. After Christmas, return it to the porch for one to two days to allow it to acclimate before planting.

• If young children will attend your party, set up a separate area for them with simple games and crafts.

• Avoid serving red punch. It leaves the worst stains.

(See also Entertaining at Home: When to Do What, page 212)

Christmas Tree Guidelines

1. When choosing a tree, pick it up, bounce it on its trunk, then run your hand along a branch. A fresh tree shouldn't drop more than a few green needles. Put your tree in an ample container—one that holds about a gallon of water is a good size. If you use a tree stand with a water pan, place a long funnel (the kind used for a car transmission, sold at auto-parts stores) in the water pan. You won't have to crawl under the tree to water it. Keep the tree fresher longer by cutting an inch off the trunk to allow for maximum absorption of water.

2. Fireproof your tree by treating it with this fire retardant: 2 gallons hot water, 2 cups Karo syrup, 2 ounces liquid bleach, 2 pinches Epsom salts, and 1/2 teaspoon Boraxo. Keep this solution in your tree-stand bowl during the holidays. It will also keep the needles green.

3. For a longer-lasting tree, have it sprayed with a wilt-proofing agent at the dealer. Flocking your tree—spraying it with white snowlike topping—is not only decorative, but it preserves moisture and reduces shedding needles. Make sure the flocking is fireproof.

SEASONAL STRESS-SAVERS

Holidays are major stress material—the kind that ruins not only your personal pleasure but the moods of everyone around you. Use these tips to keep your cool.

• Look at unexpected delays as opportunities to slow down and regroup.

• Give up trying to do twenty things when you have time for only ten.

• Plan at least one evening alone with your husband. Go out to dinner or send the kids to a friend or relative.

• One day this month, don't schedule anything.

SAFETY REMINDERS
• Make sure your tree is fresh when you buy it. Dried-out needles are a big fire hazard.
• Decorate your tree with small twinkle lights. They generate very little heat and won't dry out the needles.
• Throw away frayed extension cords and ones that feel hot when plugged in or that have broken sockets.
• Always unplug lights before leaving home or going to bed.

If you have a cut tree, mulch it when you take it down. (Your local or county recycling office should have information about mulching locations.)

• Don't feel guilty because you can't do everything. Just say, "No, we need this time together as a family," or "No, I can't make a side dish for the office party, but I can buy one at the deli."

• Don't fill up your calendar with appointments that can wait until after the holiday season.

• Hang mistletoe and encourage your family to use it frequently.

• Check for loose or burned-out bulbs *before* you put the lights on the tree.

• Give up making your own elaborate bows, baking difficult recipes you don't like anyway—anything that makes you nuts.

- Feel free to not attend some functions. You really don't have to accept every invitation.

- As much as possible, see that young children follow their normal routine.

- If your office is at home, be realistic about how much you'll be able to accomplish during the holidays when the children are out of school.

- If you have a blended family, avoid misunderstandings during the holidays by settling schedules and other controversial matters beforehand.

- Don't let a grumpy person spoil your holiday spirit.

- Avoid being frustrated by snooping kids. Wrap gifts before you hide them, then put a color-coded dot on each one so only you'll know whose it is.

- Don't wait until one-thirty Christmas morning to put together "Some Assembly Required" toys.

- Save confusion Christmas Day. Write each family member's name on the top of a separate page and note the giver and the gift as each is opened. Each person will have his or her own list of people to thank.

- If you feel stressed over some holiday jobs but don't mind others, trade with a friend—she bakes your breads, you wrap her gifts.

- Keep to your exercise routine as much as possible. Exercise relieves stress. Park far enough away to give yourself a brisk walk to and from the office or the mall. Take the stairs whenever possible.

- December is not the time to start a diet, but be sure you eat some fruits and vegetables every day.

- Give yourself a tea break late in the afternoon, or whenever your energy flags. Taking time for yourself allows you to finish chores with renewed vigor.

- Keep inspiring holiday books around your home or office for some quick positive thoughts.

- Be flexible when things don't go as you expected. Remember that the only thing predictable about life is that it's unpredictable.

SIMPLE CASH-SAVING TIPS

We've all felt the Christmas crunch, and exploding checkbooks do nothing to brighten holiday spirit. These ideas can help keep your Yule low-cost but high-fun.

1. Send postcards instead of traditional Christmas cards.

2. Buy an imperfect Christmas tree. Small defects can mean big savings. Place it in a corner or with the bad side against the wall. After it's decorated, you'll forget it's not perfect.

3. Instead of buying new decorations, enlist your kids' help and be creative with ones you already have. Refurbish old ornaments with glitter. Give life to an old wreath with fresh ribbon. And rely on old standards like popcorn and cranberry strings, construction-paper chains, or use your imagination.

4. Turn plain socks into festive footwear by sewing on fringe, rickrack, jingle bells, and bows.

5. Rejuvenate last year's potpourri. Spray on a little gold paint for highlights, and add some fragrance oil.

6. Don't wait for last-minute price cuts. You may end up impulse shopping.

7. Buy some of your gifts at charity bazaars. Many times lovely handmade gifts are less expensive.

8. Save money on wrapping paper by purchasing a large roll of white butcher paper and a large bolt of red plaid ribbon from a florist-supply store.

9. Before you buy any item, check into the store or mail-order catalog's return or refund policy.

10. Return unwanted or mistaken mail-order gifts promptly to ensure proper credit.

11. Do your shopping at stores that wrap gifts at no charge.

12. Beware of 900 numbers touting "free" holiday gift offers. Many times the phone call costs more than the gift is worth.

13. Never give your credit-card number over the phone unless you initiated the call.

14. If you have a large family or extended circle of friends with whom you exchange gifts, consider drawing names or buying presents for only the children.

15. Make simple gifts—baked goods, homemade jam or jelly in pretty jars, embroidered towels. Or write poems or make note cards. Whatever your special talent is, share it.

16. Create your own holiday linens from pretty fabric. For napkins, cut 22-inch squares of fabric. For a tablecloth, cut the fabric 10 inches longer and wider than the table. Hem by machine or with stitchless glue.

17. If you work full-time and won't be able to spend the entire vacation at home with your children, evaluate exactly when you and your spouse will be off and determine the extra child-care coverage you'll need. Between the two of you, you may be able to cover the home front more than you expect.

NO-FUSS HOLIDAY TRADITIONS

Want to start memorable, yet easy-to-coordinate holiday traditions? Try one or more of these.

• Host a yearly holiday work party for a few friends. Get together and work on whatever—baking (they bring the dough), decorations, greeting cards, gift wrapping. Chores are more fun when you do them with friends.

• Form a cookie exchange with neighbors or coworkers. If you have eight people and each one bakes a batch of cookies to share, you'll all have eight different kinds.

• Make Christmas last a little longer by letting children open a series of smaller presents on each of the twelve days before Christmas, then a big present on Christmas Day.

• Draw names to designate Secret Santas in your family so each person is responsible for filling the stocking of another family member.

• Keep a Christmas guest book each year for family members and friends to write holiday messages in. Get out the old books every year and reminisce about Christmases past.

• Have a special Christmas gift box that is passed between family members from year to year to hold a gift. Each time a gift is given in it, record the date and the names of the giver and the receiver on the side of the box.

• Get out your old model train and set it up under the tree every year.

• Study the Christmas traditions of a different country each year. Incorporate one foreign tradition into your own. Follow an old Scandinavian custom and hide an almond in one bowl of rice pudding on Christmas Day. Have a special treat ready for the person who finds the nut. Or try this holiday custom from Northern Germany: A family member receives a large wrapped package. Inside is a smaller package for someone else; inside that one, yet another for someone else. The fun continues until the true recipient discovers a small gift.

• When relatives gather, ask everyone to describe a memorable Christmas.

• Buy a Santa hat for Mom or Dad to wear when handing out gifts on Christmas morning.

• As you decorate your tree, tell where each ornament came from and when you got it.

WAYS TO CATCH THE SPIRIT OF CHRISTMAS

Maybe you can pull off a festive celebration, but your heart's not in it. Here are ways to ignite your expectation and draw you into the soul of the season.

• Try one new holiday recipe and one new decorating idea this year.
• Bring your lunch to work every day in a red paper bag.

- Attach a wreath to the front grille of your car.
- Encourage the editor of your local paper to run an essay contest for kids: "What Christmas Means to Me."
- Play holiday music while cleaning your house.
- Take time to help an elderly neighbor with holiday chores.
- Offer to hide your neighbors' Christmas gifts for their children.
- Celebrate St. Nicholas Day, December 6, by making an anonymous donation to a cause in honor of Bishop Nicholas of Myra, who helped children and families during the fourth century.
- Write a season's greetings message at the top of your business faxes.
- Throw a party and ask guests to bring food or gifts for families who can't afford to celebrate Christmas.
- Donate leftover party food to a shelter in your community.
- If you know someone who has lost a family member since last Christmas, make a special effort to call and cheer him or her during the holidays.
- Invite a shut-in on a driving tour through town to see the Christmas lights and store windows decorated for the holidays.
- Visit a disabled person and offer to help him or her send Christmas cards.
- Read the Gospel story of Christmas. Make this a family affair by reading it aloud.
- Sing Christmas carols to yourself in the shower.
- Put a special holiday message on your answering machine.
- Smile at people in shopping centers. Wish harried clerks a happy holiday season.
- Let someone who looks more tired or hurried than you have your place in a long line.
- Give a bag of toys and goodies anonymously to a family who's hurting financially.

• Help elderly neighbors decorate their home. After Christmas, help them take down and store decorations.

• Invite a foreign student or single person without family close by to share Christmas dinner with you.

• Give your church or a community agency the gift of your time.

• Shovel snow or do something totally unexpected for a neighbor.

• Bring a special lunch from home for a friend at the office who could use a lift.

• Instead of giving gifts at the office, take up a collection to give to a designated charity.

• Organize a group from your office or neighborhood to give something back to your community—such as serving dinner one night at a homeless shelter.

• Celebrate Boxing Day—the first weekday after Christmas. Give gifts to those who serve you throughout the year, such as newspaper or mail carriers, police officers, or firefighters.

A DOZEN WAYS TO CLOSE THE GAP AND SHARE CHRISTMAS CHEER WITH LONG-DISTANCE FAMILY AND FRIENDS

1. If one family member lives far away and can't afford to fly home, suggest that other family members chip in and buy him a ticket in lieu of buying a present.

2. Record your tree trimming and other holiday preparations on video to send as an extra present to grandparents at a distance.

3. Send a special personalized ornament from your family to theirs. Include a warm message, your name, and the date.

4. Mail a Christmas survival kit to a loved one who's extra-busy and can't be with you for the holidays. Include wrapping supplies, small decorations, and festive paper plates and cups.

5. Write a family newsletter. Include photos and details of family hap-

penings from the past year. Make photocopies and send it to friends and loved ones.

6. Wire a Christmas floral arrangement across the country.

7. Bake and mail your favorite goodies with copies of the recipes.

8. Create and send a homemade calendar to extended family members. Write in important holidays, anniversaries, and birthdays. Add favorite family photos and have color photocopies made of each calendar page to make several calendars. Punch two holes in the top and secure pages together with ribbon.

9. Photograph the family gathering for loved ones who are unable to attend. Make signs such as "We miss you, Susie" to hold up in the pictures.

10. When you write a thank-you note for a present from someone far away, enclose a snapshot of yourself enjoying the gift.

11. Enclose a tea bag with a letter to a dear friend. It's the next best thing to being there and having a chat over a warm cup of tea.

12. Set a time to have a conference call with relatives or friends in different states. Check with your long-distance provider ahead of time for instructions.

AFTER THE HOLIDAY

In light of all the gift giving you've just enjoyed, here's a strategy for tossing the tinsel when the new year beckons.

• Have family closet-cleanout day to make room for new gifts. Have boxes ready for clothing and toys that are in good condition for passing on to others.

• Designate a place in the garage, attic, or basement for Christmas items.

• Store large ornaments in wooden fruit crates. (These are usually free at grocery stores.) Layer newspaper or tissue between ornaments to prevent breakage.

• Pack small ornaments in egg cartons.

- Wrap lights around paper-towel tubes, and store extension cords inside tubes.
- Put wads of tissue between the loops of big bows to help maintain their shape.
- Label all boxes.

YEARLONG CHRISTMAS PLAN

I was getting tired of Christmas being a joyful time of the year for everyone but me, the Family Manager. So I began a search for better ways to manage this huge project. That's when it came to me: Divide and conquer—work on Christmas a little each month, all year long. In other words, start a yearlong Christmas plan. It's really very simple, and you can start any month of the year and still reap benefits. Here's how.

JANUARY

- After Christmas, take some time to write down what would make things go smoother next year. Incorporate those ideas into your next year's yearlong Christmas plan. Avoid gift duplications next December by writing down who received what this past season. Also make a note of which gifts were a hit and which ones weren't.
- Hit the half-price holiday trimmings sales.
- Go through holiday-card envelopes and make necessary corrections on your card list.

FEBRUARY

- Before throwing out holiday issues of your favorite magazines, cut out ideas and recipes you want to keep. Start a file box for holiday ideas—decorations, crafts, gift ideas, foods.
- Begin jotting down family news every month for your Christmas newsletter.

MARCH

• Start a special Christmas savings account so you won't have to charge your Christmas gifts and end up paying a high interest rate. (One way to do this is to take the money you get back from coupons each week and deposit it directly into a savings account at a nearby bank.)

APRIL

• Start looking for gifts in mail-order catalogs. When you find a gift, mark the page so you can locate it easily when you're ready to buy. If it's on sale now, go ahead and order it.

MAY

• Get the whole family involved in having a garage sale. Save some of the proceeds for Christmas presents or a special family trip during the holidays.

JUNE

• When your kids say, "Mom, I'm bored!" get them involved in home-made Christmas present projects.

• Schedule a day to take photos of your kids outside. Have one of the photos enlarged to give to Grandma and Grandpa for Christmas.

JULY

• While you're on vacation, look for unusual gifts for those hard-to-buy-for people on your list. If you find one great gift, buy several to give to different friends or relatives.

• Want to start the tradition with extended family members of drawing names for gift giving? Suggest this change now so family members can plan and budget accordingly. Set a time to draw names.

AUGUST

• Go berry-picking and make jams for holiday giving.

• Start talking about holiday travel plans. His family or yours? Christmas Eve or Christmas Day? Drive or fly? Buy plane tickets now if possible. Pencil in travel days on your calendar.

• Stock up on transparent tape now while school and office supplies are on sale.

SEPTEMBER

• Plan your Christmas budget. Realistically estimate how much you can afford to spend. Make a list of gifts to buy and the approximate price of each item. When writing your budget, don't forget to add items such as the tree, decorations, gift wrap, Christmas cards and postage, and entertaining. A quick total may show that you need to scale back—better now than later.

• Have a family photo taken if you plan to include one in your cards or give as a present to Grandma and Grandpa.

OCTOBER

• Purchase Christmas cards if you didn't get them on sale after Christmas last year.

• Get serious about catalog shopping. Make copies of orders before you call or mail them in. Have gifts wrapped and mailed directly to recipients at the appropriate date whenever possible.

• Prepare pots of flower bulbs now so they'll bloom in early December for gift giving.

NOVEMBER

• Start your Holiday Hit List. Write down everything you need to do, cook, give, and attend during December. Study your list to see what you can cross off and what you can delegate.

• Stock up on the staples and nonperishable foods you'll need for the holidays before the crowds get heavy at the supermarket. Start baking and freezing Christmas goodies.

• Schedule a night after Thanksgiving for family members to help sign, address, seal, and stamp Christmas cards.

DECEMBER

• Congratulations! You will now have time on your hands and can feel justifiably pleased with yourself because your list will be shorter and you'll have more time for fun. Proceed directly to the Christmas Day Countdown on page 262.

NOTE FROM THE AUTHOR

I said at the beginning that I developed the ideas in this book in the laboratory of everyday experience and that I didn't develop them alone. I've learned a lot from others, and I've shared a lot of what I've learned in this book in hopes that the ideas will help you as they have helped me.

I'd like to invite you to jot me a note or send me an e-mail to share with me what you've learned. We are each other's best teachers and can gain from each other's successes and failures.

Also, if you'd like to schedule or inquire about a Family Manager Seminar in your area, receive the Family Manager newsletter, or find out how to become a Family Manager consultant, please contact the Family Manager office:

Kathy Peel
c/o Family Manager
P.O. Box 50577
Nashville, TN 37205
TheFamMgr@aol.com
(615) 376-5619

Visit the Family Manager Web site at www.familymanager.com

ABOUT THE AUTHOR

Kathy Peel is the bestselling author of fourteen books, which have sold over 1.6 million copies. She is the founder and president of Family Manager, Inc., a company committed to providing helpful resources to strengthen busy families and enhance the home.

She is the founder and editor-in-chief of *Family Manager* magazine and serves on the staff of *Family Circle* magazine. She speaks frequently at conferences and conventions and is a popular guest on television and radio programs. She has been featured in numerous newspapers and magazines.

Kathy Peel has been married for twenty-seven years and is the mother of three boys, ages twenty-four, twenty, and thirteen.

Delegation, 80–81
  gender issues in, 81
  and Hit List, 260
  and skills training, 16, 81
  and team building, 15–16
Den. *See* Living area
Desk decluttering, 37
Documents, filing, 72–73
Dry cleanables, 18, 62, 226
Dual-career moms
  after school, 177–78
  cleaning routine for, 137
  and job change, 188–92
  summer ideas for, 152–53
  vacation days, 154, 278

Easter, 246–47
E-mail, uses of, 87, 113, 158,
    178, 185, 244
Emergency measures
  and child care, 190
  home system breakdowns,
    122–23
  for kids, 177, 178
  preparedness, 117
  while entertaining, 215–16
Entertaining
  easy ideas for, 207–11
  holiday, 273–74, 280
  large gatherings, 212–14
  low-budget, 216–17
  See also Birthday parties; Parties

Errands
  consolidation of, 87
  co-op for, 98
  preparation for, 105
Exercise
  and family fitness, 116–17, 121
  for Family Manager, 27
  and pregnancy, 181
Expectations, 18, 21, 178, 201

Family Manager, 77–78
  daily private time, 27, 153
  education/classes, 116
  as knowledge worker, 9–12
  and long-term plans, 112
  management style, 11–12
  motivation for, 1 5, 7
  and organization, 6–7, 8, 78
  personal files, 74
  Top Ten Want-Tos, 12–13
  See also Control Center
Family meetings
  and Control Center, 71
  goal setting in, 146
  for life changes, 179
  to set routines, 171
  ten tips for, 23–25
  for vacation plans, 25, 220
Family reunions, 93, 113
Family room. *See* Living area
Family workdays, 45, 113
Father's Day, 248–49